Political
Philosophy

Dimensions of Philosophy Series
Norman Daniels and Keith Lehrer, Editors

Political Philosophy, Jean Hampton

Philosophy of Mind, Jaegwon Kim

Philosophy of Social Science, Second Edition,
Alexander Rosenberg

Philosophy of Education, Nel Noddings

Philosophy of Biology, Elliott Sober

Metaphysics, Peter van Inwagen

Philosophy of Physics, Lawrence Sklar

Theory of Knowledge, Keith Lehrer

Philosophy of Law: An Introduction to Jurisprudence, Revised Edition,
Jeffrie G. Murphy and Jules L. Coleman

Introduction to Marx and Engels: A Critical Reconstruction,
Richard Schmitt

FORTHCOMING

Philosophical Ethics, Stephen L. Darwall

Philosophy of Science, Clark Glymour

Philosophy of Language, Stephen Neale

Philosophy of Cognitive Science, edited by Barbara Von Eckardt

Contemporary Continental Philosophy, Bernd Magnus

Normative Ethics, Shelly Kagan

Political
Philosophy

Jean Hampton
UNIVERSITY OF ARIZONA

Westview Press
A Subsidiary of Perseus Books, L.L.C.

Dimensions of Philosophy Series

Copyright © 1998 by Westview Press, Inc., A subsidiary of Perseus Books, L.L.C.

Published in 1997 in the United States of America by Westview Press, 5500 Central Avenue, Boulder, Colorado 80301-2877, and in the United Kingdom by Westview Press, 12 Hid's Copse Road, Cumnor Hill, Oxford OX2 9JJ

Library of Congress Cataloging-in-Publication Data
Hampton, Jean.
   Political philosophy / Jean Hampton.
      p.   cm— (Dimensions of philosophy series)
   Includes bibliographical references (p.   ) and index.
   ISBN 0-8133-0857-7 (hc.).—ISBN 0-8133-0858-5 (pbk.)
   1. Political science—Philosophy.   I. Title.   II. Series.
JA71.H275   1997
320´.01—dc20   96-33006
                                                                          CIP

The paper used in this publication meets the requirements of the American National Standard for Permanence of Paper for Printed Library Materials Z39.48-1984.

10   9   8   7   6   5   4   3

To Bradley, Gracie,
Rosie, Samantha, and Ashley—
FRIENDS ON THE TRAIL

Contents

Foreword

Jean Hampton died suddenly and unexpectedly on April 2, 1996. The manuscript of this book was complete and undergoing copyediting at the time of her death. The final stages of copyediting were completed later. This work involved only minor corrections and stylistic modifications, which in no way affected either the arguments or the conclusions of the book. And so, tragically, this volume represents the author's own last words on its topics. If these should both prepare and inspire her readers to enter into the debate to which she refers in her epilogue, they will not have been written in vain.

Richard Healey
Tucson, Arizona

Acknowledgments

Books are sufficiently difficult to write that their authors succeed only when they get help, and I have a number of people to whom I owe thanks for their help.

For his patience, support, and insightful comments during the (overly long) period in which this book was being written, I am grateful to Westview's philosophy editor, Spencer Carr, who refused to despair of the book's completion and who has been unfailingly encouraging.

For their superb work in helping me to research various issues explored in this book, and for their excellent comments, criticisms, and discussions of many of the issues I raise in this book, I wish to thank Ken O'Day and Cindy Holder. I am also indebted to Sarah Harding for her work in researching citizenship and immigration policy, discussed in Chapter 6.

For their comments, criticisms, and reactions to the book's arguments, I thank Julia Annas, Jules Coleman, Linda Hirshman, Christopher Morris, and an anonymous reader of Westview Press. I am also indebted to audiences at Pomona College, Occidental College, and the University of Notre Dame, where I presented portions of this book for discussions of some of its arguments. Finally, I am grateful to the students in my political theory and feminist theory classes at the University of Arizona, who provided "test markets" for parts of the book (and whose complaints were often heeded, albeit perhaps not as often as they would have liked).

This book has been written during the tenure of a number of fellowships; I wish to thank the American Council of Learned Societies, the Pew Foundation (and in particular their Evangelical Scholars Program), and the National Endowment for the Humanities for grants I received while I worked on this book, which enabled me to secure the research time necessary for its completion. I also wish to thank the Social Philosophy and Policy Center at Bowling Green State University for generously supporting my research during the summer of 1993.

As always, I owe a great debt of gratitude to my husband, Richard Healey, and my son, Andrew Hampton-Healey, not only for their love and forbearance as the book was being written but also for their interesting discussions with me about many of the book's issues and for the many times they successfully and pleasantly distracted me from my labors on it in order to keep me from working too hard.

Finally, my thanks to Bradley, Gracie, Rosie, Samantha, and Ashley. This book is for them—just for the fun of it.

Jean Hampton
Tucson, Arizona

Introduction

Political philosophy is about political societies—what they are, which forms can be justified, and what they should do. Political philosophers don't focus on the day-to-day politics of a state, nor are they primarily interested in understanding any particular institution in existing states: The task of political philosophy is not any surface description of particular political societies. Instead, the political philosopher wants to understand at the deepest level the foundations of states and their ethical justification. What does a society have to be like in order to be a political society? How do political societies arise? Why should they be considered morally legitimate? How do you tell a good political society from a bad one? How are people in these societies bound together? These questions are the business of political philosophers, and answers to them cannot be found simply by examining the day-to-day operations of existing societies. The political philosopher must go beyond mere description and engage in both conceptual analysis and moral theorizing to formulate possible answers. And thus far, many (but not all) of the answers proposed remain contested.

The purpose of this book is to acquaint the student of political philosophy both with these questions and with the various answers to them proposed by philosophers since the ancient Greeks. It is intended to be a kind of map of the philosophical terrain in this area, as well as a guide to the writings and ideas of the major political philosophers whose work has created the conceptual contours of this map. It does so by pursuing two overarching issues: first, the nature of political authority, which is the subject of Part 1 of the book and is pursued in Chapters 1, 2, and 3; and second, the scope or extent of political authority when it is justly exercised, which is the subject of Part 2 of the book and is pursued in Chapters 4, 5, and 6.

Because I survey so much, I must necessarily refrain from going into great detail about many of the ideas and philosophical works I discuss. Indeed, writing a book of this sort presents two related and difficult problems: figuring out what to put in it and figuring out how to organize the topics one has decided to put in it. The authors of books in the Westview

Press Dimensions of Philosophy Series are like painters told to represent a highly complicated landscape. The limitations of time and space require that only some parts of the landscape be rendered in detail or rendered at all, meaning that there will be people who are puzzled about why their favorite parts of the landscape were left out or only sketched in and why other parts appear in great detail. I can only say that in choosing what to present I have tried to select those elements of the tradition of political philosophy that have proved enduringly important, and to choose those issues animating contemporary philosophy that are most likely to be important to the next generation of philosophers in their own political theorizing. But in a book of this sort, no matter how much one tries, there will always be many interesting issues in political theory that are not sufficiently explored, so I have attempted to design the book using endnotes and parenthetical remarks to note such issues and to give the reader references for exploring them further. I have also tried to construct this book so that it can be usefully accompanied by primary texts, many of which I discuss, although the use of those texts is certainly not necessary to understand anything I have written. Finally, the book tends to focus on issues that relate to the political experiences of North America, but I have tried to make the book as international as possible (particularly in Chapter 6, which looks at citizenship, immigration policy, nationalism, and secession), and, once again, I have indicated in endnotes places where students interested in certain international political issues can pursue them in more depth.

Writers in political theory have varied enormously in the past twenty-five years in what they have thought appropriate to include in their texts. In the late 1960s and early 1970s, a book of this sort would have been designed to focus almost exclusively on the topic of distributive justice, an issue that political philosophers of that time took to be not only the most important but almost the only issue in political philosophy. The importance of this issue has persisted into our time; for example, in Will Kymlicka's excellent *Contemporary Political Philosophy: An Introduction* that issue figures far more prominently than any other. However, although I certainly discuss the issue of distributive justice (in Chapter 4), I present other issues that have been important historically and that are becoming important again as our political world changes. For example, the rise of the civil rights movement, feminist political theorizing, and communitarian concerns have led people to think about justice in ways that transcend distributive concerns, and I spend a great deal of time (in Chapter 5) discussing theories of justice that attempt to go beyond a mere theory of the distribution of resources. Moreover, with the growth of secessionist movements, renewed interest in nationalism, and concern about the stability (and not merely the distributive justice) of political communities over the past few years, what I call "structural issues" have become an increasingly significant part of political philosophizing. These issues were always important in traditional political theory, and those who thought about them from ancient Greece through the early modern period bequeathed to us theories of sovereignty, of desirable forms of political society, of boundary determinations, and of secession rights. This book will include substantial discussions (particularly in Chapters 1, 2, and 3) of many of these "old-fashioned" issues, which are again becoming important to a world that is rethinking old political units and attempting to devise and justify new ones. Nonetheless, I will be relating these issues to contemporary theorizing about distributive justice, because issues of justice are clearly relevant to defining and justifying political societies.

Deemphasis on the issue of distributive justice also reflects my sympathy with the Marxist view that distributions of resources in any society are fundamentally connected with its political and social "deep structure," which generates not only forms of interaction that make certain kinds of distributions inevitable but also moral theories that justify those distributions. Hence what kinds of distributions count as fair can, in my view, be assessed only by looking at the structural conditions of society, by which I do not mean merely the economic modes of production but also legal structures establishing the government's role and jurisdiction, forms of family life, and social practices defining the life prospects of different sorts of people depending upon their gender or race or religion. As I seek to show, particularly in Chapter 5, the way in which social structures affect the operation of any political society critically determines the way in which resources in that society are allocated.

In constructing this book, I have not simply reviewed extant political theories but also attempted to provide original theorizing of my own about some of the central issues I discuss. This is, in part, to prevent the book from being boring: There is no joy in reading mere summaries of existing literature. (Why not read the literature itself?) But it is also an attempt to show readers that these issues are still "live," open to new reflection and new solutions, issues that they should not be afraid to tackle with their own original reflections.

I cannot overestimate the importance of feminism to the development of this project. Although I do not provide a separate chapter on feminist political theory, feminist ideas and perspectives pervade every chapter of the book, insofar as I believe they provide a way of looking at past and present political theorizing that generates original criticisms and perspectives that will be illuminating and intriguing to the reader.

This book also includes a study of the history of political theorizing. We contemporary political theorists have been on the scene only a little while, and a great deal of important and influential political theorizing has occurred prior to the twentieth century. I present political theories of ancient Greece, the medieval period, the early modern period, and the nineteenth century not only because they are interesting and important in their own right but also because these theories have generated many of the ideas that contemporary philosophers use in their own theories (ideas such as "rights," "consent," "social contract," "utility," "perfectionism," "equality"), along with many of the arguments (e.g., social contract arguments, utilitarian arguments) that are the stock-in-trade of contemporary political theory. Unless the reader understands how and why these ideas and arguments were constructed, he or she will not be able to understand their strengths and weaknesses and hence will be at a disadvantage in assessing their use in contemporary political argumentation. Moreover, those political theorists who came before us, particularly in the early modern period, forged political theories that have greatly influenced existing political structures: Our democracies, our constitutions, our "bills of rights," our court systems and laws, and our economic systems all reflect the views, arguments, and theories of past political theorists. If we are to know where to go next, we must know from where we have come. Sometimes historical material will also raise interesting issues for the reader contemplating certain contemporary theories: For example, when one appreciates the context in which certain ideas have emerged, modern philosophers' use of those ideas in very different contexts may seem (rightly) puzzling and inappropriate.

Finally, my intentions in this book are not merely to tell you, the reader, about how "the professionals" in philosophy have thought about issues in political theory, but to convince you that these are *your* issues, too, and that your own reflection on them not only can help you better understand the political world in which you live but also enable you to contribute to ongoing discussions in your culture about the nature and purpose of the state, whether you become a professional philosopher or not. Philosophy belongs to no particular elite but rather to all human beings.

PART ONE

The Nature of
Political Authority

1

The Problem of Political Authority

There is the question what renders it just to exercise force in, say, requiring what is just. The parent may in effect say, "Don't hit your little brother, or I will hit you." What is the difference—*is* there a difference—between his threat and the threat of the child he so threatens? After all, the little brother may have been doing something quite unfair. The same question arises about the violence of the state. I judge that this is the fundamental question of political theory.

—G.E.M. Anscombe, "On the Source of the Authority of the State"[1]

Think for a minute about your own political subjugation. You are continually subject to rules not directly of your own making, called laws, governing not only you but others, mandating, for example, how fast you can drive on a highway, what kind of behavior you can exhibit in public, what kinds of treatment of other human beings are permissible, what objects count as "yours" or "theirs," and so forth. These rules are enforced by certain people following the directives of those who create the rules and who set the penalties for breaking them. Thus you know that if you don't obey the rules, you are likely to suffer undesirable consequences, which can range from small fines to incarceration and even (in some societies) to death.

But on the surface this seems to mean that when you are ruled you are not only subjugated but coerced. We don't approve of a gunman's pointing a gun at your head and demanding that you give him your money, so why should we approve of *any* group's using threats of fines, jail, or death to demand that you behave in a certain way or that you pay them money (which they call "taxes") or that you fight in wars of their making? Is this subjugation really permissible from a moral point of view, especially given that human beings require freedom in order to flourish?[2]

In order to answer this question, we need to think about the difference between what intuitively strikes us as "good" and "bad" kinds of control. The control of a parent over a two-year-old is normally thought to be not only permissible but morally required. The control of a gunman over a victim he has kidnapped at gunpoint is normally thought to be highly impermissible. The second kind of control is condemned as morally unjustified—a violation of the coerced person's "rights." The first kind of control is thought to be morally justified and consistent with, and even supportive of, the child's rights. But what is the difference between rightful and wrongful kinds of control over human beings? And since political control is importantly different from the control that parents have over children, why should it count as an example of the "good" rather than the "bad" sort of control?

Intuitively, we speak of the good forms of control as arising from some sort of *authority* that the controller rightfully exercises over the person she is controlling. Hence we speak of the authority of the parent over the child or the authority of the teacher over her students in the classroom or the authority of the priest over her religious congregation. Hence a person's rightful control over others in certain areas seems to arise from that person's authority in that area. But from where does such authority come? Do rulers in a political society have it? If so, what kind of authority is it?

Whatever it is, it is not the same as (sheer) power. Authority is about the *entitlement* to rule; mere power isn't enough to supply entitlement. There is an old maxim popular among tyrants that "might makes right." (Joseph Stalin's acceptance of this maxim explains why, on being asked in 1935 to encourage Catholicism in Russia in order to conciliate the pope, he replied, "The Pope! How many divisions has *he* got?")[3] But most people, particularly those who have had the misfortune to be subject to the power of tyrants, have condemned and rejected this maxim, arguing that there is a huge difference between a ruler who has authority to govern and a mighty robber baron who, with his henchmen, controls people using terror and fear in a way that they despise. Rulers are said to have not only the power to make and enforce rules but also the entitlement to do so. And when they do so, they are said to have (political) authority.

Connected to this entitlement is the obligation the subjects have to obey the (authoritative) ruler's commands. If I am a subject of a government I take to be authoritative, then not only do I obey a command of the state because I am fearful of the sanction if I disobey it and I am caught, but also (and more importantly) because I believe I ought to do so: "I have to do this because it's the law," I think to myself. And its being a law puts me under an obligation, independently of the content of its directive. I can hate or like what I am being commanded to do, but as long as that command comes from an authoritative political ruler, I understand that I have an obligation to obey it. That obligation purports to preempt, or "trump," all sorts of reasons I may have against performing as the command directs (although we might not think it trumps *all* reasons—in particular, it might not trump reasons based on certain moral principles that can seem more important than the legal obligation, or so advocates of civil disobedience will argue).

To summarize, we can define political authority along the lines suggested by one recent philosopher as follows:

> Person x has political authority over person y if and only if the fact that x requires y to perform some action p gives y a reason to do p, regardless of what p is, where this reason purports to override all (or almost all) reasons he may have not to do p.[4]

But where does this political authority come from? Answering this question involves understanding the *kind* of authority political rulers have. Clearly, they have authority to make and enforce rules, but into what areas can these rules extend? Does their authority allow them to make rules in any area of human life? Or are there constraints or limits on the scope of their control over us? And does their authority have any moral constraints? That is, must the rules they generate have a certain (moral) content in order to be considered authoritative (or binding) for us? Or are we subject to them no matter what their content simply by virtue of their having been commanded by people who have authority over us? Historically, political theorists have been divided about how to answer these questions: As we discuss in the next chapter, some, such as Thomas Hobbes in *Leviathan* (1651), argue that political authority is unlimited in scope (thus extending to all areas of human life) and substantively unconstrained. Others, such as John Locke in *Two Treatises of Government* (1689), contend that political authority is considerably constrained in both scope and content. However, no matter how this controversy is settled, note that even the most ardent supporter of the idea that political authority is limited must still accept that it is a very substantial kind of authority, involving, among other things, authority over the life and death of those subject to it. This power is most obvious in the context of punishment, but even in a society that eschews capital punishment, the state's control over life exhibits itself in its right to conduct war and its right to use various deadly means to pursue dangerous lawbreakers. If political authority involves this much control, how can it be defended as legitimate?

Some thinkers known as *anarchists* have concluded that it cannot be defended and have criticized philosophical views that take for granted the idea that political domination is a special, morally justified form of domination. These anarchists have insisted that the only morally defensible form of human association is one in which there are no persons or institutions issuing commands that they back up through the use of force. Henry David Thoreau is an example of an anarchist, and this position enjoyed some popularity among intellectuals in nineteenth-century America and Russia.[5] Anarchists such as Thoreau influenced twentieth-century advocates of civil disobedience and peaceful political revolution, such as Mahatma Gandhi and Martin Luther King Jr. But King and Gandhi embraced the idea of peaceful revolution as a tool to combat only *unjust* political rule, not the idea of political rule itself. They, like most political theorists in our time, have believed that some forms of ruling political authority are legitimate. But given the inherently coercive nature of governments and ruling institutions, how can that legitimacy be established?

In this chapter we review four theories that attempt, in different ways, to legitimate and define the extent and nature of political authority. They are the divine authority theory, the natural subordination theory, the perfectionist theory, and the consent-based theory. All of them have their roots in the political theorizing of ancient Greece, and the first three have been largely (but not entirely) rejected in the modern world for reasons that we shall review. The fourth, the consent-based theory, enjoys considerable popularity and has been developed in a number of ways. After introducing this theory in this chapter, we shall explore in subsequent chapters whether it merits its current popularity.

The Divine Authority Theory

The first theory of the source of political authority is what I will call the divine authority theory. On this view, a ruler has legitimate authority to govern people if and only if that authority in some way comes from the authority possessed by God, whose rule over human beings is supposed to be unquestionable. Of course, where God's authority comes from is an interesting question: Does he rule only because he is supremely mighty—so that in God's case, at least, "might makes right" after all? Or does he rule because he is supremely good, in which case his authority comes from his goodness? Or does he have an authority over us that is somehow fundamental and intrinsic to his nature? Whatever the explanation of God's authority, the theorist who advocates this view maintains that

God's authority (whatever its basis) is in some way the source of any authority that a political ruler possesses over his people.

Historically, there were three basic ways in which a ruler's authority was "derived" from God.[6] First, the ruler could turn out to *be* God in human form. It was not uncommon in the ancient world for rulers to proclaim themselves to have divine status.[7] What better way to establish your divine authority to rule than by proclaiming yourself to *be* the divine authority? Call this the "ruler is God" view. Second, if the people to be ruled would take such a proclamation to be dubious (or blasphemous), the rulers often tried arguing that even though they weren't God, they were (in some way) related to God or had (to some degree or other) divine status, and in this way partook of the divine authority to rule. There were a number of ways that rulers made this connection with the divine: For example, in Egypt there are written and pictorial documents declaring that any person who is the legitimate king of the people is someone who is the son of a god by union with the royal mother; in Sumeria some kings claimed divine status by calling themselves "husbands of goddesses"; and in both realms kings often claimed they were nourished with divine milk.[8] Call this the "ruler is related to God" view.

But the third and probably most common way that rulers appealed to the divine as a basis for their own authority was to admit their full humanity but argue that they had been *given* the authority to rule by God. This view is known as the "divine right" view of political authority. Such a view was invoked in biblical times by rulers of the kingdom of Israel (many of whom were priests and ruled as priests) and in medieval times by the popes of the Christian Church, who argued that by virtue of being God's vicar on earth, they should have not only religious authority but also political authority over all of Christendom. In early modern times, the kings and queens of European states maintained that it was not the pope but *they* who had been authorized by God to rule over their particular kingdoms. An especially prominent form of this theory, called the "divine rights" theory, famously advocated by the seventeenth-century writer Robert Filmer in *Patriarcha* (c. 1635),[9] derived the authority of the monarchs of Europe from the (supposed) original granting of political authority by God to Adam in the Garden of Eden. On this view, Adam bequeathed that authority to his descendants, and by tracing that bequeathal down through the ages, one would find that it has descended to the present monarchs of Europe. So Filmer makes God's authorization of any current ruler indirect, since the authorization is understood to be bequeathed to him or her from the previous ruler. On Filmer's view, only God's authorization of Adam was direct. Filmer's theory of political authority is also part of a larger theory that explains all authority as coming from God, including the authority of parents over children and husbands over wives.[10]

There were, however, obvious problems with the idea of divine authorization, the most obvious being that the current monarchs of Europe were all descendants of people who had usurped power from the "rightful" kings of their day. The only way to consider the usurpers and their descendants divinely authorized to rule was to believe that God sometimes withdrew his authority from sitting monarchs and gave it directly to another, better candidate for rule (who could then bequeath that authorization to his descendants). Indeed, contra Filmer, some kings insisted that the authorization of every monarch is always direct: For example, King James (James VI of Scotland and James I of England [1566–1625]) instructed his son, the future Charles I, "God has made you a little god, to sit on your throne and rule men."[11]

An important aspect of any claim to divine entitlement to rule was the *kind* of authority that this entitlement was supposed to give the ruler. If one gets one's power from God, one would seem to be able to claim the right to act like a god on the throne, and so Filmer argued. Of course monarchs were supposed to be concerned with the welfare of their subjects; after all, God is the father of all peoples, and hence many divine rights theorists believed along with Filmer that a godlike king would also use his absolute authority in a fatherly way (although note that female rulers would dislike such a characterization, along with the title of Filmer's book, *Patriarcha*).[12] Nonetheless, this fatherly concern was still thought to rest in the hands of a person vested with absolute authority. In the words of King James: "Kings are justly called Gods, for that they exercise a manner or resemblance of Divine power upon earth. For if you will consider the attributes of God, you shall see how they agree in the person of a King."[13]

Strong words, considering that two such attributes are omniscience and omnipotence! Even more striking, advocates of the divine authority theory were prepared to consider human beings *slaves* to their divinely appointed kings. John Locke paraphrases Filmer's position as follows: "Men are not born free, and therefore could never have the liberty to choose either Governors, or Forms of Government. Princes have their Power Absolute and by Divine Right for slaves could never have a Right to Compact of Consent. Adam was an absolute monarch, and so are all Princes ever since."[14]

So these divine rights theorists insisted that even if kings weren't literally gods, they still had the same kind of authority that God has. Unsurprisingly, these theorists balked at the idea that the enslaved subjects of such a king could ever have the right to rebel against and replace their divinely appointed king: Only God was taken to have the right to review and withdraw authorization from a ruler.

Although there are still parts of the world in which some variant of the divine authority theory survives (e.g., in Morocco),[15] in our time this theory of political authority has been largely rejected (so, for example, in today's Britain, no one considers Queen Elizabeth II or her son Charles "little gods"!). This is, in part, because the beliefs that many modern people hold about religion generally do not support such a theory. But the theory has also been rejected by many devoutly religious people, and many religious people in the seventeenth century were among its most prominent critics. (For example, John Locke, who was an orthodox Christian, became one of Filmer's chief opponents.) Aside from shifts in religious views, there are two reasons why the theory's popularity has plummeted.

First, the claim to divine authority is empty, in the sense that it is easy for anyone to make but impossible for anyone to prove. I can "feel" divinely authorized, but does that mean I am? Someone can proclaim that she has received divine authorization, but does that mean she has? If there are a number of claimants to divine authorization, would we ever be able to tell who really had it? In fact, throughout history such claims have often been contested, with both sitting monarchs and those who have rebelled against them declaring possession of God's right to rule. Since anyone can make such a claim but no one can prove it, how can it be effective in establishing authority? We need proof of such a claim to believe that it establishes political authority, and no such proof seems to exist. Of course successful usurpers to a throne can claim that the very fact that they were victorious over the sitting monarch shows that God has authorized them to rule. On this view, even if might doesn't make right, it does reveal right. Yet because on this position God's authorization exactly tracks political power, skeptics can insist that it is political power and not any supposed (and unheard) directive from God that is the real indication of political authority. Moreover, if we believe that certain successful usurpers may nonetheless *not* be rightful rulers despite their victory over the sitting rulers, then we will reject the identification of God's authorization with such success. And once we do so, then whenever there is a competition among two or more people for political power, we seem to be left with no way of knowing which candidate is God's choice.

The problem of establishing who has God's authorization has never been satisfactorily resolved, with the result that the divine authorization theory is empty: That is, it fails as a theory that would tell us who has political authority. Moreover, since all of us (regardless of our religious beliefs) make judgments about who has political authority and who doesn't, we can't be using the (empty) divine authority theory when we make those judgments. So the theory also fails as an account of the ideas people actually rely upon (regardless of their religious beliefs) when they are determining whether or not someone who exercises political control has the authority to do so.

Second, the idea that political authority is received from God has tended to encourage in some rulers the thought that because their authority comes from a divine source, that authority is absolute, meaning that it is unlimited in scope and content. This conception of the nature of political authority has been (often bitterly and violently) attacked in the modern world, insofar as it is easily used to license the worst abuses by rulers. While many rulers who accepted this view, particularly in the medieval and early modern periods, believed that their divine authorization obligated them to be stewards rather than masters of their subjects, there were also kings, such as King James, who took themselves to be "little gods" with the authority that was godlike in nature. Such rulers accepted a theory of the extent and nature of political authority that recognized few, if any, limits. Hence many political theorists in both the ancient and modern world (including Plato, Aristotle, Locke, and Hobbes—all of whom professed belief in God) disliked the divine authorization approach because it could be dangerous in the hands of unscrupulous or evil rulers. People began to look for a theory of authority that acknowledged what they took to be the very real limits on a ruler's authority— limits that could not be effectively acknowledged in a theory that saw kings as "little gods."[16]

For these reasons, the divine authority theory has few advocates today.[17] We must look elsewhere for a theory of political authority that can meet the anarchists' challenge.

Natural Subordination

Consider the way in which many people see themselves as entitled to control what they regard as "their" animals, such as pets or herds of cattle, horses, and so forth. Animals are generally considered to be creatures that can be owned, or possessed, by human beings. Most people do not attribute to domestic animals any inherent right to independence or any "say" in how a family or a farm operates. Instead, most (albeit not all) people take it for granted that animals are not our equals. There are two types of theory setting out the nature of our unequal moral relationship to animals:[18] One considers human beings keepers or stewards or custodians of animals, the other considers us their masters, entitled by our superiority to dominate them. According to the latter view, animals' inferior reasoning abilities make it both possible and permissible for us human beings to control them and (at least sometimes) use them for our purposes. This view doesn't deny that we have moral obligations to our animals—making it wrong, for example, to gratuitously torture them. But despite disagreements about the nature and extent of our obligations toward animals, people who accept this "domination" view believe that by virtue of the fact that animals are our "inferiors," we have a right to dominate over them, own them, and use them for morally permissible ends (e.g., for companionship or food).

This is an instance of the belief in what I call "natural subordination," which I define as the theory that some beings' natures are such that they instinctively do, and ought to, submit to and take direction from other beings whose natures fit them for dominance, rulership, and power. It is a very ancient view: In Psalm 8 God is lauded for allowing the human being, by virtue of his superior nature, to "have dominion over the works of thy hands; thou hast put all *things* under his feet/ All sheep and oxen, yea, and all the beasts of the field;/ the fowl of the air, and the fish of the sea, and whatsoever passeth through the path of the seas" (Psalm 8:6–8).

But can there be natural dominance *within* the human species? That is, can human beings be sufficiently unequal in capacities and talents such that the better-endowed human beings naturally (and inevitably) have dominion over these lesser-endowed human beings in the way that human beings have dominion over an ox or a sheep? The psalm-writer suggests no such thing, but it has been commonplace throughout history to assume that the answer to this last question is yes. And those who do so accept an instance of what I call the *natural subordination theory of political authority.* In this view:

> A person type x has authority over a person type y if and only if ys have a nature that makes them fitted to take direction from xs, and xs have a nature that makes them fitted to give direction to ys, such that we can say the nature of xs fits them for rulership and dominance over ys, and the nature of ys fits them for governance and domination by xs.

Institutions such as slavery, racism, and the subordination of women have all been justified on the basis that those being ruled are inferiors who are naturally—and rightfully—dominated by their betters. Conceptions of how that domination should be construed have varied: Sometimes the inferior has actually been allowed to be owned (as property) by the superior (e.g., in systems of slavery, which can vary in how much control the master has over the slave by virtue of owning him); other times the inferior is merely controlled by the superior, who is taken to be more like a guardian or a trustee than a master (for example, in nineteenth-century Britain married women were not allowed to have property in their own name, so that any property left to them would have to be administered for them by a male trustee).

There are two questions this theory raises. First, is there really the kind of substantive inequality among human beings that consistently results in the superiors' dominating inferiors? This view assumes that the biology of the human species is such that each of us is born with traits that, when developed, determine in any relationship with another human being whether we are dominant over the other or else dominated by the other. (For example, a male slave may have traits such that he is viewed as naturally dominated by his master but naturally dominant over his wife.) Nonetheless, as I shall explore later in this and the next chapter, there are many theorists, particularly in modern times, who have attacked the factual assumption that there is substantial inequality among human beings. If that assumption is wrong, this theory of authority collapses.

Aside from this issue, the second question this theory must address is *why* natural superiority entitles someone to dominate over an inferior, and what sort of natural superiority does so. Even if there is substantial inequality among people that results in the inferiors' being dominated by the superiors, that alone is *not* sufficient to explain why the superiors are supposed to be *entitled* to dominate over the inferiors. Just because they will dominate (unless stopped from doing so) doesn't mean that they may, or ought to, do so. So we must understand the difference between a (mere) *descriptive* account of the origination of power relationships among human beings and a *normative* account of these relationships that establishes their legitimacy. Descriptions merely tell us what these relations are and where they come from: That is, *descriptive accounts* tell us what is. Normative accounts tell us why these relationships are justified and hence ought to prevail: That is, *normative accounts* tell us what ought to be. So to be effective as a theory of political authority, the natural subordination theory must add to its description of some people as the "natural" rulers of others a normative argument to the effect that this rule is somehow good or right. It is only when a rightful entitlement to rule is established that this theory can genuinely be said to offer a theory of authority: Without establishing it, the most it offers us is an explanation of the generation of power relationships, not an account of their legitimacy.

There are two ways of developing such an account. The first involves arguing that nature itself provides the entitlement. On this view, insofar as such dominance will occur in nature, it is therefore justifiable: There is no more reason to object to the dominance of superior human beings over their inferiors than there is to object to the dominance of a queen bee over her worker bees. The idea is that all of us, given our (biological) natures, will tend to accept certain roles in our dealings with other members of our species, meaning that power relationships in a political society are simply the expression of these roles, in just the way that hierarchies within certain animal species are expressions of the natures of these animals. Thus to say that among human beings it is "natural" that some of them dominate others is to advocate the acceptance of a principle of governance provided by nature itself. Stating this principle of governance is tricky: Consider that those who take this view cannot maintain that inferiors are *unable* to dominate their betters, because rebellion of people taken to be "inferiors" against those taken to be their "betters" happens all the time (e.g., when women ascend to the throne or blacks seize power from whites or peasants wrest political control from the nobility). Since this view cannot deny the reality of such events, it has to regard them as aberrant, abhorred by nature, and doomed not to succeed for very long given natural features predisposing the inferior group to behave in ways ultimately incompatible with dominion.

The idea that built into nature are laws or rules about who should rule is very old—evident, for example, in Shakespeare's play *Macbeth*, in which the natural principles of rulership are flouted and an offended nature takes revenge on those who tried to defy it. Thus after the main character, Macbeth, who seeks the throne of Scotland, kills the ruling king in the middle of the night (stabbing him while he sleeps), nature itself is affected; two characters in the play who do not yet know about the murder comment the following morning on how strange the night had been:

> *The night has been unruly: where we lay,*
> *Our chimneys were blown down; and, as they say,*
> *Lamentings heard i' th' air: strange screams of death,*
> *And prophesying with accents terrible*
> *Of dire combustion and confused events*
> *New hatch'd to the woeful time: the obscure bird*
> *Clamour'd the livelong night: some say, the earth*
> *Was feverous and did shake.*[19]

This way of thinking about the world mixes facts with norms: The world is a place where the relationship of objects, living and nonliving, is fixed by rules about what "ought to be"—rules that nature is prepared to enforce in its own way. So on this view, those who fail to respect the natural rules of domination will, like Macbeth, be thwarted and punished by the world they seek to defy. The idea is that just as there are physical laws of nature, there are political laws of nature that invariably determine political hierarchies in human communities.

This view of nature is antithetical to the view of the world taken by modern science. Biologists today, for example, do not think that within any species nature provides its members with a "right" way to behave or operate, and they certainly deny that the world contains any normative principles about who "ought" to rule over whom. And when biologists' studies of various species frequently involve statements concerning which gender of the species is dominant, they do not purport to establish the dominance as "right" or "justifiable" by virtue of some fundamental natural order. So, for example, even if in the hyena species females tend to dominate over males, that fact does not mean, for the biologists who study them, that they *ought* to do so or that nature has ordained (and will also enforce) that dominance. Still, even if the idea that entitlements to rule are carried *within* the natural order is unbelievable to many people who live in the age of science, this way of responding to the world has currency among some people in our world, for example, those who have objected to certain forms of procreation (e.g., artificial insemination) or certain kinds of sexual practices as "unnatural"—that is, in violation of "nature's laws." Consider also those who defend certain sexist practices as arising from the "natural" domination of men over women; such views assume that nature has within it certain rules that should govern our behavior and institutions.[20] (Indeed, even the common idea that we are all "naturally equal" is a violation of a scientific conception of the world, if this is taken to mean that nature has within it some kind of moral principle that makes us all equal.)

However, the natural subordination theory can also explain the authority of the superior over the inferior in a second way, such that it is consistent with a more scientific view of nature. On this view, an inferior ought to be subordinated to a superior if and only if the nature of the inferiority is such that the inferior and/or the community of which he is a part would, on the whole, be *better off* if his actions were subject to the control of the superior. Thus, for example, if the inferior were unable to reason well, one might argue that both he and the community of which he is a part would be better off if he were subject to the control of someone who was able to reason well; such a rational superior could direct him to behave in ways that would ensure his safety and the safety of others and help him to satisfy his desires and achieve his plans better than he would be able to do on his own. In view of the fact that this argument derives the naturally superior person's authority to rule from the good consequences that he takes to follow from such rule, I call it a "consequentialist" argument for natural subordination.

This second explanation is suggested in the work of Aristotle, whose *Politics* is one of the great classics of Western political philosophy. Although Aristotle was not mainly interested in developing a natural subordination theory of political authority in that book—and actually suggests a quite different, consent-based justification of authority in most of it (which I discuss later in this chapter)—he does believe that natural subordination exists and suggests that such subordination is justified by virtue of its good consequences for all concerned. Aristotle recognizes two forms of natural domination: the domination of the (natural) master over the (natural) slave and the domination of men over women. Both forms of domination presuppose the idea that some human beings, in particular those with "slavish" natures and those who are female, are unable to reason effectively about the world, and it is in virtue of that deficiency that they must be subordinated to the control of others, both for their own good and the good of the community.

Natural slaves, according to Aristotle, are those whose reasoning is quite radically deficient. Although they partake of reason sufficiently to qualify as human, they do not partake of it sufficiently to make it desirable that they rule their own lives: "Whenever there is the same wide discrepancy between human beings as there is between soul and body or between man and beast, then those whose condition is such that their function is the use of their bodies and nothing better can be expected of them, those, I say, are slaves by nature."[21]

A natural slave "participates in reason so far as to recognize it but not so far as to possess it,"[22] by which Aristotle seems to mean they have sufficient reasoning ability to obey commands issued to them but not sufficient reason to formulate rational imperatives on which they can act. Aristotle also speaks of these slaves as lacking "deliberative capacity."[23] Such people are natural order-takers; that is, they do not have the rational capacity to give orders about what to do either to themselves or others. Hence they naturally gravitate to and even welcome (i.e., accept as an appropriate and good thing) the control of those "higher" human beings whose reason is sufficiently developed to enable them to construct and follow rational plans for living.[24]

But Aristotle wants to claim that this dominance is not merely inevitable but a *good thing*, for both master and slave. It is easy to see why it is a good thing for the master: He gains a kind of "living tool" that he can use to achieve his ends. Some apologists for slavery subsequent to Aristotle also thought it was a role that morally improved the one who played it: Said one nineteenth-century American southerner, "It has been frequently remarked that slavery tends to exalt and refine the character, and that the class of our people referred to are generally more elevated in their sense of duty, more polished, than any other portion of our population."[25] In light of the kind of abusive treatment that many slaves received at the hands of their masters, such an assertion seems morally absurd, even sickening, to us today. But it is certainly an assertion that supporters of slavery *wanted* to believe in order to reconcile themselves and others to the institution.

How is slavery good for the slave? Aristotle explains that the slave needs the master because his own reason is insufficient to develop a life plan. By participating in the life plans of the master, he is enabled to pursue projects he could not pursue using his own reason, in a way that will be safe and effective. As a result, the slave comes to see himself as an extension of the master who benefits when the master's plans are pursued well. He therefore has every reason to follow the master's plans conscientiously: "The slave is in a sense a part of his master, a living but separate part of his body. For this reason there is an interest in common and a feeling of friendship between master and slave, wherever they are by nature fitted for this relationship."[26]

In other words, the slave *needs* the master to direct him because he can't do it himself. And he will welcome the direction when he gets it because he will see how it provides him with a rational control that he is unable to provide to himself, thereby enabling him to secure his own well-being, which he could not do alone. So the superior rational master, on this view, is entitled to rule substantially deficient reasoners because of the way in which such rule is likely to produce good consequences. Indeed, Aristotle suggests that natural slaves will actively seek subordination in virtue of its good consequences unless they are in some way prevented from doing so. This thesis was elaborated upon by American supporters of slavery in the nineteenth century, who maintained that the American institution of slavery also improved the moral character of the slave by "civilizing" him, converting him to Christianity, and providing him with constraints that kept him on a moral path: "The moral influence of slavery upon those subject to its obligation, may be perhaps ascribed to the fact, that the slave has, in that condition, nothing to tempt or urge him into immorality, and every thing both in hope and fear, to restrain him from it."[27]

Again, such sentiments strike modern readers as fantastic and offensive. But notice that neither Aristotle nor the American apologists for slavery ever suggest that if in a particular case these good consequences don't occur, the slave is entitled to "rebel" against the inadequate rule of his master. It is the entire practice of mastery that is legitimated by the good consequences produced by that practice on the whole, so that even if some masters do not rule their slaves well, nonetheless they still have the right to dominate them because the system of natural slavery is legitimated by its *overall* good consequences for both master and slave. That it was also a social system vital to the functioning of economies like that of Athens or the American South is surely a major reason why the institution was supported in these places, but the argument that Aristotle and American advocates of slavery make is that the institution is also on the whole *just* by virtue of the fact that (usually, albeit not always) it effectively responds to and meets the needs of very different kinds of human beings.[28]

Finally, Aristotle insists that the system of natural subordination is good for the community, as well as for the individual masters and slaves. For if the slaves are prevented from assuming their subordinate role and unnaturally thrust into the role of master, Aristotle says that calamity will follow. In book 2 of *The Politics*, Aristotle discusses those states which have encouraged inferiors to rule and reviews (what he takes to be) all the bad consequences that have followed from such rule. A social system that encourages the wrong people to take control will, he implies, be disastrous economically, militarily, culturally, and legally for everyone, especially for those who have been wrongly encouraged to think that they are able to reason well enough to govern themselves and others.

Aside from slavery, Aristotle recognizes another category of dominated persons—women. According to Aristotle, those women who do not already qualify as natural slaves have full rationality, the same as their non-slavish male counterparts, so that he says the "deliberative faculty" is present in women, but not in slaves. However, although it is present it is not, he says, "effective."[29] Aristotle says little about what he means by this word, but scholars have generally interpreted him to mean that women's reasoning is constantly "overruled" by passions or emotions, making it unable to govern. So whereas slaves are missing the capacity to rationally direct their lives, on this view women have that capacity but (given their natures) continually find it disrupted and thus ineffective. Assuming that only reason and not passion can direct people toward the good, Aristotle concludes that by virtue of being unable to rely consistently on their reason, women need (and are supposed to welcome) rule by those whose nature is such that reason continually dominates. For just as it is good for domesticated animals to be ruled by men "because it secures their safety,"[30] so, too, it is good for women to be guided and protected by men to ensure their safety: "Again, as between male and female, the former is by nature superior and ruler, the latter inferior and subject."[31]

In a sense, Aristotle's argument portrays women as permanent children. It has been relatively uncontroversial in all times and places that parents have authority over children insofar as the latter are deficient in ruling themselves through reason because they lack the experience necessary to draw rational inferences or because they lack the intellectual development necessary to perform various sorts of reasoning or because they are easily swayed by emotions or passions. Aristotle is in effect saying that female children never actually rid themselves of these immaturities, necessitating their subordination to free male adults who do achieve rational maturation.

Down through the ages the supposedly bad consequences that would follow from allowing women to rule have often been cited as a reason for their subordination, although often those constructing it have emphasized other supposed weaknesses of females besides the ineffectiveness of their reasoning ability (e.g., their supposed timidity, tendency to panic, dislike of public participation, or lack of aggressiveness). This is true, for example, of John Knox, whose (remarkably titled) "First Blast of the Trumpet Against the Monstrous Regiment of Women" (1558) argues that:

"To promote a Woman to beare rule, superioritie, dominion, or empire above any Realme, Nation or Citie, is repugnant to Nature, contumelie to God, a thing most contrarious to his revealed will and approved ordinance; and finallie, it is the subversion of good Order, of all equitie and justice."[32] Knox insists that "nature" (as ordained by God) has disabled women from having ruling authority not so much by disabling their rational abilities but by depriving them of virtues that are essential to good rule: "Nature, I say, doth paynt them further to be weake, fraile, impacient, feble, and foolishe; and experience hath declared them to be unconstant, variable, cruell, and lacking the spirit of counsel and regiment."[33] Similar sentiments were expressed in the eighteenth century by the French philosopher Jean-Jacques Rousseau, who argues that the ideal education of females should make them cheerfully and readily accept their subordinate role to men—a role he argues their vice-ridden nature fits them for.[34]

While few people today accept the idea that some people are so deficient in reason that they qualify as natural *slaves*, there is still widespread support for the idea that some groups of people ought to dominate others by virtue of these others' inability to rule themselves well. Such arguments are often mounted to justify control of women by men and of some racial groups by other racial groups (e.g., blacks by whites). The details of these arguments differ, but the gist of all of them is that in virtue of one or more deficiencies possessed by some group of people, it is both possible and desirable that persons without this deficiency have control over them.

Even though appeals to the idea of natural domination continue to be common in our world, they are also under attack. To be told that one is a member of a group that is seriously deficient and, in virtue of that deficiency, in need of being governed by a kind of caretaker who is from a superior group is deeply insulting to most human beings, often prompting anger and even violence against those who have delivered the insult. To be told, as Aristotle tells women, that one is permanently childlike and in need of a male father all one's life is to experience paternalism of the worst sort. To the extent that the idea of natural dominance is institutionalized and rendered part of the social or political system of the community, for example, via Jim Crow laws or sexist prohibitions on employment, it becomes an "insult" that shapes people's life prospects and affects their chances not only for happiness but also for living lives of dignity and respect.

But aside from the fact that this is a view many people today hate, why is it wrong? There are two reasons it has been widely rejected as not credible. First, critics of natural subordination insist that all the evidence suggests that people are actually equal *with respect to those properties relevant to governance.* Consider that the kind of inequality that is taken by supporters of the view to justify subordination of some by others is rarely defined with any precision, so that mere hand-waving about "inequality" or "differences" is often all that makes the case for dominance of one group by another. Now while it is undeniable that some people are smarter or more virtuous or stronger than other people, these differences by themselves do not seem relevant to establishing political domination. Think, for example, of all the ways in which people are different from one another, physically, mentally, and temperamentally. If someone has greater muscle strength than another, does that mean he gets to rule the other? No: Arnold Schwarzenegger is not considered, by virtue of his physical prowess, a political authority. How about intelligence? Should Albert Einstein's superior intelligence have entitled him to rule? No: That intelligence was usefully directed at understanding the world, and we do not think that by virtue of having it Einstein did or should have been granted political authority. Nor does extraordinary beneficence or superior bravery grant one political authority: Mother Theresa and Alan Shepard are good and brave people, but those attributes don't confer on them automatic entitlement to rule the rest of us not-so-good, not-so-brave people.

A natural subordination theorist (such as Aristotle) ought to agree with all this. His view is not simply that "better" people get to rule over "worse" people but rather that people better *in a certain way* are entitled to rule other people who are deficient *in a certain way.* And the most plausible candidate for the capacity that marks who should rule and who should be ruled is the capacity to rationally direct one's own life. So, for example, Aristotle, who admits that the free males who compose the class of natural masters differ from one another in virtue, intelligence, talent, and physical ability, nonetheless still insists that these differences are consistent with their *political* equality, because these people are, in his view, equal with respect to the one characteristic that matters to the issue of natural subordination: namely, the capacity for rational self-direction. Thus even if there were a free male in ancient Athens who was cowardly or rather stupid, Aristotle would still take him to be the equal of braver and smarter free men with respect to that capacity—the only politically relevant capacity. Aristotle would not advocate that such a person be made a general of the army or put in a position requiring substantial intellectual skills, but he would not place him in the category of people who were naturally subordinate to others, because such a person still has the capacity to rationally direct his life, making him "his own master."

Most natural subordination theorists other than Aristotle neglect to note that *only a certain kind of inequality* will suffice to ground their argument. Aristotle understands this point and tries to mark out two kinds of incapacities in rational self-direction that would warrant subordination, that is, an inability to deliberate (the slave's incapacity) and an inability to deliberate effectively (the woman's incapacity). But he fails to prove or establish the reality of either sort of incapacity with respect to these two groups (and also fails to show that the men he would make masters are not prone to either sort). Moreover, he fails to legitimate the existing practice of slavery in his time, because the economic tasks that women and slaves had to perform in the societies Aristotle knew require possession of just the sort of effective deliberative faculty that entitles them to political equality.

This last point is worth elaborating upon. With respect to slavery, Aristotle's problem is this: How can a slave have enough rationality to be a human being and to be capable of performing the many tasks (sometimes involving intellectual skills) required of a slave and yet have no self-direction? (A severely retarded individual might not be capable of rational self-direction, but note that he would not be useful as a slave either.) Many scholars of Aristotle's *Politics* have argued that Aristotle's doctrine of natural masters and natural slaves is internally inconsistent. A slave is supposed to have enough reason to understand and obey a rational directive, but if he has so much rationality, isn't that sufficient to allow him to construct such directives himself? Aristotle is walking a theoretical tightrope—trying to argue that there are human beings who have enough rationality to be of instrumental value to others but not enough to enable them to direct their own lives effectively or safely. Whether or not he is able to stay on that tightrope or falls off into inconsistency has been the subject of scholarly debate.[35] But given that Aristotle's ultimate motivation is to defend an institution of slavery that can serve the economic needs of his time, he must be considered to have failed, because Greek city-state economies required slaves to perform quite complicated tasks for the economic good of the city, tasks that required too much rationality and self-governance to make plausible the claim that one who could perform them was incapable of governing himself. Moreover, Aristotle faces the same problem with respect to women: How can he establish that women are any more likely to make mistakes about how to plan their lives and direct their actions than men, or have insufficient capacity to rationally direct their lives (as Plato believed of many), when Aristotle must rely upon women to rear the free male children in Athens so as to be capable to assume a leadership role in the city? Again, Aristotle seems to require that the group he wishes to subordinate, in this case women, has the rational self-direction necessary to perform certain tasks vital to the city, even while he denies them that capacity in his argument for their subordination. This kind of inconsistency makes the arguments of Aristotle and other natural subordination theorists look suspiciously like arguments designed (with a certain amount of bad faith) to keep the ruling group in power.

As I noted earlier, Aristotle also fails to defend his claim that certain groups of people are inferior to others. Indeed, it is common for natural subordination theorists not even to *offer* proof that the particular group whom they wish to see subordinate actually is inferior in some particular way. So, for example, tracts written to defend the institution of slavery in America rarely if ever bother to show proof that those people who were slaves were, in some specified sense, "inferior" to those who ruled them. Knox and Rousseau confidently assert what women are like without any shred of empirical support. A dominant group's unsupported claim to the effect that "we all know what those people are like, and they are not as good as we are" is, once again, evidence that their argument is based more on wishful thinking and the desire to preserve power than on concrete evidence that the subordinate group needs or requires their rule.

Perhaps fearing the weakness of their empirical claims, supporters of natural subordination have frequently contrived to arrange the environment of those whom they wished to dominate, so as to try to make them into "inferior" creatures who would appear to need and who would accept and welcome such domination. By working to ensure that the class of people they wish to dominate has poor nutrition, poor educational opportunities, poor housing, little or no access to decent jobs, and so forth, they have attempted to turn these people into the sort of human beings that at least appear to need direction from others "for their own good."[36] It might be thought of as a kind of "protection racket" used by dominators against those whom they wish to subordinate. This protection racket can be hard for some people in the society to see: They may rightly attribute a failing to members of a certain group and claim that this is part of that group's "nature," not realizing that it is due to environmental circumstance.[37]

So what are the *facts* about our relative equality with respect to the one feature that is relevant to subordination, that is, the capacity for rational self-direction? According to virtually all modern moral and political philosophers, the facts are that with respect to this capacity we are all roughly equal, so that there is no significant difference among human beings that allows or justifies some of them to be ruling caretakers of others. "All men are created equal," proclaims the American Declaration of Independence, and it is a proclamation of the idea that "men" (generally understood to refer to all human beings)[38] are similar enough with respect to this single politically relevant characteristic that no group can be justifiably subordinated to any other. This modern view is based in part on what its proponents will claim are empirically confirmable facts: That is, they will insist that both observation and the experience of modern democracies show that despite all sorts of differences among us in physical abilities, mental abilities, temperament, and so forth—from skiing to doing mathematics, from musical talent to carpentry skills—there is no group of human beings (outside of those who are small children or severely mentally retarded or comatose or seriously mentally ill) who are so deficient in reasoning skills, life experiences, or ability to control passions that they cannot direct their own lives and must be subject to the direction of others. So we find women and men of all races, classes, and religions choosing how to lead their own lives and taking responsibility for doing so, voting successfully in democratic elections, raising children, earning money, and so on. The failure of some to lead lives that others would regard as "successful" (e.g., because they break laws or become impoverished or experience misery) is not a failure distinctive to any particular group of human beings. Moreover, I would argue that such a failure cannot be construed as arising from inferiority with respect to the *capacity* for rational self-direction but from the person's free choice to live a certain kind of life, for which we hold him or her morally responsible (in a way that we would not, and should not, do of a genuinely mentally incompetent person).

So on this view, even if there are substantial differences in physical or mental abilities among human beings, none of these has *political* significance because all mentally healthy adults are capable of rational self-direction and thus roughly equal in at least this area. Given this equality, the modern view is that there is no basis for any "natural" domination of some people over others. The acceptance of this view means that the natural subordination theory fails as an account of political authority because the view requires an inequality with respect to a certain natural capacity among healthy adults that simply doesn't exist.

Moreover, because it has become commonplace to accept the equality of rational self-direction, those who defend the sort of modern democratic regime in which most readers of this book are likely to live tend (usually vociferously) to reject any form of the natural subordination theory, even if some within those regimes are attracted to it and support vestiges (some of them considerable indeed) of the would-be dominators' protection rackets in those societies (e.g., racist and sexist practices that prevent people from enjoying equal opportunities in the society). The egalitarian underpinnings of these democratic states, argued for by opponents of natural domination as diverse as Thomas Hobbes and Thomas Jefferson, are clearly at odds with the assumptions of natural inferiority and superiority that are the foundation of the natural subordination view.

So the natural subordination theory also fails as a theory of political authority, which means that we still don't have an answer to the anarchists' worries. Hence if we are to understand and appraise the justification of political authority, particularly in modern democratic societies, we will need to look for a justification of political authority very different from that provided by the natural subordination theory, one that accepts a far more egalitarian conception of the ability of human beings to direct their own lives.

Authority from the Good

The third theory of political authority we will consider was originally advocated by Plato and historically called the *perfectionist theory of political authority*. This theory is an instance of a more general thesis about authority, namely, that a person has authority over another in any area if and only if that person has greater knowledge or expertise than the other person does in that area. According to this view, the authority of the parent over the child, the authority of the teacher over the student, and the authority of the scholar in her field over those who are not in that field all rest on the authoritative person's claim to superior knowledge. Similarly, argues the perfectionist, the authority of a ruler over the ruled can only be justified (and can only really exist) if the ruler has superior knowledge— of a specific sort.

But what sort? According to Plato, the ruler who rules with authority over a community knows how to make that community happy,[39] and he does so by implementing justice in all its affairs. Hence the knowledge of the authoritative ruler is the knowledge that the just man has—or alternatively, what the just man knows is what the ruler who rules with authority knows. So whereas the natural subordination view takes political authority to be invested in a person by virtue of his superiority, the perfectionist view takes political authority to be derived from the Good itself, treating anyone who holds political authority as a (mere) vehicle for the authority generated by the Good.

To explain in detail the features of this view, I will use Plato's masterpiece, the *Republic.* In this work Plato argues that each human being is composed of three parts: the reasonable part, the spirited part, and the appetitive part. While each of these parts is necessary and valuable for a happy human life, Plato argues that it is nonetheless important that the reasonable part rule the other two parts, else the person will end up out of control, pursuing the wrong things in the wrong way. The appetitive part of us can be wild and lawless,[40] and the spirited part can give rise to uncontrolled outbursts of anger and violence. But the reasonable part, if it is properly developed, can control and moderate desires and soothe the spirits. And most important, the reasonable part can do this, and do it properly, because it is that part of us which has the capacity to gain access to "the Good"—which Plato says all human beings are striving to understand and follow in their lives: "What the good itself is in the intelligible realm, in relation to understanding and intelligible things, the sun is in the visible world, in relation to sight and visible things."[41] So the just man has knowledge of the Good and rules himself via his reason in accordance with the dictates of the Good.

Plato's *Republic* is famous for its creative metaphorical representations of the human pursuit of the Good. There is, for example, the metaphor of the cave developed in book 6, which represents the plight of human beings: It is as if, Plato says, human beings lived in a cave, seeing only shadows cast by the sun but never the sun itself or the real objects casting the shadows that the sun illuminates. The sun represents the Good and the True, and the cave is the world of darkness in which most people, ignorant of the Good and the True, are forced to reside. Plato compares philosophers to those lucky souls who learn how to crawl out of the cave and see the sun directly. But to get out of the cave of ignorance one must learn to reason and thereby come to see things as they are and as they ought to be.

So the rational part of a human being has authority to rule to the extent that it knows or understands what is Good and can direct the person toward it, controlling the desires and the passions so that they help rather than hinder this pursuit. Analogously, a person has authority to rule a community if and only if he or she knows or understands what is good for the community and directs the community toward it, controlling wild or spirited parts within so that they help rather than hinder this pursuit.

Accordingly, on this view, the authority possessed by a ruler or by the rational part of each of us is actually from the object of our reasoning—the Good itself. The rational part doesn't have the authority to rule because it is (in some way) better than the other parts but because it has access to the Good—that is, "that which ought to be." And similarly, the persons who are rational and knowledgeable about the good in the community do not have authority to rule because they are "better" than other people but because they know, and can implement, "that which ought to be."

Clearly, this theory of political authority presupposes that there is an objective good to which all human beings are subject and that is capable of discovery through reasoning. Plato is no moral relativist. His view assumes that there are standards defining how people should interact with one another in a human community, where these standards are ones all of us should aspire to meet, exist independently of us, and define the content of just laws. He is also not an egalitarian: Not all human beings are able to achieve the knowledge of the just man, and those who cannot are those who must be subject to the rule of one who understands what the Good is and can control his desires and passions so as to pursue it effectively.

Indeed, Plato extends the analogy between the soul and the state by explaining that just as there are three parts to the soul, there are also three parts to a human community: the rational part, from which the rulers (called guardians) are drawn; the spirited part, from which the warriors are drawn; and the appetitive part, whose members make up the bulk of the population and are the community's craftsmen, farmers, and so forth. Plato compares each of these groups to different metals in order to represent their different importance and role within the community: The rational part is like gold, the spirited part like silver, and the appetitive part like iron or bronze.[42]

However, Plato's inegalitarian views are importantly different from those of Aristotle, and the Platonic theory of authority as arising from the Good is interestingly different from the Aristotelian theory of the natural subordination of slavish-natured people to masterly people. Unlike Aristotle, Plato does not take it that those who are subject to the legitimate rule of the guardian class are like slaves, without any deliberative capacity. Indeed, he even insists in the *Republic* "that the power to learn is present in everyone's soul."[43] What distinguishes the goldlike natures of the guardians from the bronze or silver natures of the other classes is the knowledge of the Good possessed by the guardians, which knowledge the bronze and silver classes have been unable to procure. And their failure to do so does not come from the fact that they are missing any aspect of the capacity to reason but from the fact that in their natures the appetitive or spirited parts can seize control and render the rational part unable to function effectively.

So in a way Plato diagnoses the need some people have to be ruled as arising from the same type of problem that Aristotle says women have, namely, the ineffectiveness of reason in subduing the spirits and passions that tend to usurp its control. So Plato's ruled people are not like Aristotelian natural slaves but like Aristotelian women—that is, they are in need of a ruler to make effective in their lives the dictates of reason that they can recognize as authoritative but cannot directly discover or implement by themselves.

However, most remarkable given the time in which he lived, Plato himself does not agree with Aristotle that all women's reasoning is ineffective, such that they require rule. Indeed, he argues at great length in book 5 of the *Republic* that there are women with the capacity to be guardians, in whom the rational faculty is just as capable of discovering and pursuing the Good as in any (fully rational) man. Plato's belief that the just soul can be present in women as well as men means that he is ready to allow that they can have the authority to rule in a community. It is a notable repudiation of the common belief in the ancient world that women are naturally subordinate to men.

Nonetheless, the most fundamental difference between Aristotle's views on natural subordination and Plato's perfectionism is their differing conceptions of the source of the authority to rule. For Aristotle, the source of the master's or male's rule is his superior rational nature. He has the capacity to reason effectively in a way that is likely to be beneficial, and because of that capacity he is licensed to control those who do not, by virtue of the fact that it is likely to be beneficial if he does so. But note that even if that rule is not beneficial, Aristotle assumes that a natural master is still a master and a natural slave is still a slave. It is the master's superiority and the likely (but not guaranteed) beneficial effects of that superiority that give him authority to rule over deficient inferiors. Hence there is no suggestion in Aristotle's *Politics* that women or slaves can rightfully rebel against the man or the master who controls them if his rule is not beneficial. While the good consequences that arise from the control of superiors over inferiors are important in justifying the practice of mastery, those consequences need not always be present in order for particular masters to have authority over particular inferiors. It is more the (rational) *nature* of the master rather than the actual knowledge he possesses that is the fundamental source of his authority over slaves and women. People who are natural masters may lack all sorts of knowledge and virtue, and yet their authority to rule natural slaves or women persists because they have the *capacity* to be rational (albeit perhaps not the wisdom that reasoning is supposed to yield).

In contrast, for Plato, the license to rule comes (only) from a knowledge that reason gives and not from the (mere) rational faculty itself. That rational faculty is necessary but not sufficient for authority; only actual knowledge of the Good is sufficient. Indeed, Plato maintains that those who have the capacity to be guardians but who nonetheless rule badly because they do not know the Good, do not rule with authority: Such people, he says, only *appear* to be guardians.[44] Hence it is of the utmost importance for Plato that those who have the capacity to be guardians receive a lengthy and effective education, which allows them to learn about the Good and to learn to control themselves so that they can develop just souls. In the end the guardians who actually make the laws for the city and direct its operations will, Plato says, be over fifty, since it takes that long to develop the knowledge and character (with the right temperamental, physical, and intellectual qualities) to lead a community toward the Good.[45] Plato also assumes that if they were properly educated and trained, this elite would be, by virtue of its knowledge, morally pure and incorruptible, an assumption that strikes modern readers as hopelessly optimistic. Indeed, many critics of the *Republic*, including Aristotle, have charged that Plato makes the guardians too "godlike" in their moral purity to be believable, and this may be because he was unreasonably convinced that rational human beings could learn to know the Good in a way that would guarantee the purity of their moral character. One might say that Plato requires of those in positions of authority a knowledge that precludes significant errors of factual and moral judgment, whereas Aristotle dismisses the idea that such godlike people exist and thus links authority with the capacity for wisdom, but not with its full possession.[46]

So in a subtle way Plato's theory is perhaps less elitist than Aristotle's, insofar as it repudiates the idea that one's nature *alone* is sufficient to render one "better" than another and, by virtue of this superiority, entitled to master the inferior. Instead, Plato derives governing authority not from innate superiority but from knowledge. According to Plato, however, that knowledge is possible only for a few, and his comparison of guardian people with gold suggests that he actually thinks the guardian class is, as it happens, better than other classes because its members are more useful (given their ability to direct the community toward happiness) than the members of any other class. Moreover, Plato's insistence on significant inequalities in effective reasoning means he is not egalitarian in any modern sense, and this is certainly one reason contemporary readers of the *Republic* tend to reject his view that an ideal state would be run by an elite privileged in its knowledge claims.

Aside from the offensiveness of the kind of inegalitarianism Plato does endorse, there is the problem of Plato's considerable optimism about the human capacity to know the Good: Modern readers tend to find it wildly unrealistic to believe that there is a person who can be said to have grasped the Good in the way that Plato demands of his guardians. And if no one can be said to have such knowledge of the Good, Plato's theory implies that there is no society now—or ever—in which the rulers have had real political authority. This means his theory forces him to the conclusion that every political regime on earth thus far has been illegitimately coercive, lacking any authority, since it has been ruled by people who have not been fully knowledgeable of the Good. So his theory ultimately collapses as an account of the legitimacy of real states in the real world.

Plato himself seems to be aware of this last problem with his view and in two later political works, *The Statesman* and *The Laws*, tries to develop a way of keeping his knowledge-based theory of authority while allowing that real political regimes can have authority as long as they are in some sense minimally decent. What he suggests in these works is that even if human beings are still individually ignorant of the Good, an authoritative regime is one in which the laws, developed over many generations, approximate justice. So as long as rulers in these regimes implement these just laws, Plato argues that their commands have authority, even if the rulers themselves do not have full knowledge of the nature of justice.

But Plato's modified theory doesn't work either, for how are these authoritative commands generated if there are no experts on justice to generate them? And how are the people to recognize when these commands instantiate justice if none of us qualifies (uncontroversially) as one who knows the Good? So even this modified Platonic theory of political authority seems impossible to apply to our world, given that we human beings do not know, and often disagree about, what the Good is or whether it exists at all. So neither form of Plato's theory succeeds in explaining political authority based on the idea that authority derives from knowledge of the Good, which means that Plato's theory also fails to give an answer to the anarchist.

We return to our original question: Where do actual rulers get their authority to rule? Consider this way of thinking about the question: Wouldn't any ruler in Plato's time or ours have to *convince* those whom she wished to rule that she had the authority to command them, in order to become empowered and to remain in power in a stable political society? She might, for example, convince the people that she was especially wise or morally knowledgeable (something that might or might not be true), but wouldn't the fact that the people were convinced (correctly or incorrectly) that she should rule (on whatever basis) be the source not only of her political power but also of the sense in the community that only she had authority to rule? To put the point succinctly, isn't a ruler's authority traceable to the people's decision to make her authoritative rather than to any (dubious) claims the ruler might make to know the Good or be more rational or be authorized by God? If so, the ruler's authority is actually derived from the people's consent to her rule. As we shall now discuss, such an appeal to the consent of the governed has been the basis of the most popular modern theory of political authority, and it is also an idea that even certain ancient Greek thinkers found attractive.

Consent-Based Theories of Authority

Both the Platonic and natural subordination theories of political authority are based on the assumption that there are significant inequalities in people's abilities to reason and live well that affect the question whether or not they or someone else will have the right to direct their lives. But what if one believes that people are roughly equal in their abilities to reason and live well? If one is convinced that whatever differences exist among human beings are not sufficient to render some so superior in reasoning or knowledge as to have the authority to rule over others, how does one defend the concept of political authority?

This is a critical question for political theorists in the modern period, almost all of whom repudiated the idea of natural subordination and almost all of whom believed human beings were roughly equal in their ability to arrive at knowledge of the Just and the Good. But it was also an important question for Aristotle. For although he recognized the existence of natural inferiors subordinated to natural masters, he also thought that the members of the class of natural masters were roughly equal to one another in their ability to direct their lives through reason. Since this class is fairly large, how do its members become subject to political authority? None of them is significantly superior in reasoning capacities, and all of them have a rational capacity that is roughly the same in terms of its effectiveness in determining action (which is not to say that all of them are equally rational but only that all of them have the same *capacity* to reason and act rationally). So how can we defend the idea that any of these roughly equal people should be subject to a political authority?

Aristotle notes that if there were a human being who was so good and so rational as to be close to divine status, then his superiority in virtue and reasoning ability would be sufficient to license him to rule everyone—including those free (nonslave) men who were themselves masters of natural slaves. This godlike person would be *their* master.[47] Clearly, Aristotle is adopting a Platonic perfectionist view here. But if no such god-among-men exists (and Aristotle seems dubious about the possible existence of such a divine man), how do we explain the existence and justification of political authority over free (nonslave) men?

In order to answer this question, Aristotle has to develop a new, nonperfectionist theory, since the presumption of the question is that there is no person specially knowledgeable about the Good who can rule authoritatively in the way Plato's theory describes. Without wishing to wade into the complexities of Aristotelian scholarship, I want to draw out this nonperfectionist theory, which I believe many interpreters of Aristotle's work have missed or insufficiently appreciated. As we shall see, this new approach provides the outlines of a consent-based theory of authority. Although that theory is not developed in great detail, we will nonetheless see that its rudimentary outlines are present in *The Politics,* that they build on previous consent-based ideas present in Greek culture, and that they serve as an important source for subsequent consent theorists.

Aristotle suggests in *The Politics* that we should explain the political authority to which these men are subject as something they *create.* This creation process is natural in the sense that, given human interests, it is virtually inevitable that those males who are not slaves will want to create such an authority. As Aristotle explains in book 3, people find that as individuals they are not self-sufficient. They have needs and desires that prompt them to desire association with one another. This is in part so that they can cooperate with one another to secure the necessities of human life and in part because they have affection and, more basically, sexual needs for one another. Conjugal relations give rise to families, families associate with one another in villages for their mutual advantage, and eventually villages associate with one another to form city-states in order to achieve a community that is self-sufficient: "A state is an association of kinships and villages which aims at a perfect and self-sufficient life—and that, we hold, means living happily and nobly."[48] Moreover, Aristotle takes it for granted that the process of creating a political association involves creating authoritative lawgivers, and presumably this is because in order to work effectively states require laws that are enforced through punishment.

He also says explicitly that the authority to issue and execute laws in a state can vary, recognizing a number of types of political association, called "constitutions," that differ from one another in how the authority to rule is structured and who has it. The people who are involved in creating the state are the ones who decide which kind of constitution to create, and what they decide depends, according to Aristotle, on their particular needs and interests:

> A state [polis] is an association of similar persons whose aim is the best life possible. What is best is happiness, and to be happy is an active exercise of virtue and a complete enjoyment of it. It so happens that some can get a share of happiness, while others can get little or none. Here then we clearly have the reason for the existence of different kinds and varieties of states and the plurality of constitutions. Different sets of people seek their happiness in different ways and by different means, and so make for themselves different lives and different constitutions.[49]

In this passage Aristotle clearly signals that both political authority and the form it takes in various constitutions are *created* by those (free men) who will live under them.

Throughout *The Politics* Aristotle works on the assumption that among free men political authority is not based on any natural subordination of some to others, nor on the superior knowledge of some, but on their mutual consent that there should be a particular system of political authority in a state for the mutual benefit of all free men. Their rough equality precludes any of them from claiming to be a natural master of the others (book 3, chap. 3), and that same rough equality means that none of them is so superior in virtue that he should rule (and Aristotle is dubious that any godlike superior of such men exists). Aristotle also argues in *The Politics* (book 3, chap. 15) that many men acting together make better decisions in political matters than even the best man, a claim that assumes that in most human communities the wisdom of any one man cannot be so significantly greater than any other that the wisdom of many men deliberating together will ever likely be exceeded by the wisdom of the very best person. (Aristotle also argues that the many are less easily corrupted than any single person, an admission that shows a kind of realism about the tempting power of evil that Plato was loathe to recognize.)[50]

We moderns, who are accustomed to reading Aristotle's *The Politics* through the lens of Plato's *Republic,* should not be surprised to see consent-based ideas in Aristotle's work, because such ideas were also part of his intellectual culture. Historians of political theory have shown that in Aristotle's time and during the century or so prior to his birth, the idea that government was not only created but also legitimated by consent was popular. Charles Kahn traces the roots of consent-based ideas back to the time of Archelaus in the middle of the fifth century, and closer to Aristotle's time he finds these ideas not only among pre-Socratic thinkers such as Protagoras but also among playwrights such as Aristophanes in *The Clouds* and Euripides in *Sisyphus.*[51] In the latter play, we find the following passage:

> There was a time when the life of mankind was disordered, like the life of wild beasts, subject to the rule of force, when there was no reward for good men nor any punishment for the bad. And then, I believe, human beings established laws for punishment, so that justice might rule and hold crime in subjection, and anyone was punished who did wrong. Then the laws prevented them from committing open deeds of violence, but they went on doing such deeds in secret.[52]

Moreover, as we discuss further in the next chapter, Plato himself suggests consent-based ideas in his dialogue *Crito* and returns to these ideas (albeit without developing them) in other dialogues such as *Protagoras, The Laws,* and *Republic.*[53] So Aristotle would have found it natural to take seriously a consent-based conception of state authority (he can hardly be thought to have invented it), and many of his audience would have found those ideas not only familiar but plausible.

Aristotle recognizes a number of different ways in which political authority can be structured within a state. If the people decide to have only one person invested with this authority, then they have created a king, whose regime will be called a *monarchy* if he rules well and a *tyranny* if he rules badly. If they grant that authority to a few people, then their constitution is an *aristocracy* if it operates justly (which generally occurs if the rulers are selected because of their virtue) and an *oligarchy* if it operates unjustly (which generally occurs if the rulers are selected on the basis of their great wealth). Finally, if they invest that authority in all the free men, then their constitution is a *polity* if it operates well (which happens when the society is structured so as to secure virtuous rule) and a *democracy* if it operates badly (and this generally happens if the majority—usually the poor—rule in a way that runs roughshod over the demands of justice).

Note that as Aristotle describes the different kinds of constitution, good and bad, he assumes something that Plato rejects, namely, that even the bad rulers in a given constitution still rule with authority. Since for Plato authority comes from the Good, if a ruler cannot implement the Good, he cannot have authority. But since Aristotle suggests that authority is created by those subject to it, even if a ruler cannot implement the Good, insofar as he is ruling within a system that the people have created, he still has authority. Aristotle's theory allows one to distinguish the issue of whether a ruler has authority from the issue of whether that (authoritative) ruler is ruling well.[54] Whereas on Plato's view someone who rules badly and unjustly simply can't have authority, it makes sense on Aristotle's theory to recognize that the authoritative ruler in a political society can be unjust (although such a ruler should not be surprised if the people decide to take away his authority).

There is a fascinating passage in book 4, chap. 11 in which Aristotle characterizes the nature of a political association as a kind of partnership (*politike kononia*) that operates best when people are treated equally. This conception of the ideal political society as a partnership among (relative) equals leads Aristotle to conclude that the best form of government is a "polity" in which the many participate in political rule but not in a way that makes the small number of rich hostage to a large number of poor. In a polity resources are distributed so as to maximize the number of "middle" people, that is, those who have a moderate amount of resources and who are neither rich nor poor. Aristotle condemns states that permit substantial inequality of resources because those who are rich act like masters toward their poor brethren, when in fact these poor are not natural slaves but their rough equals. A good state recognizes this equality in a way that facilitates a kind of civic friendship among the citizens:

> Sharing is a token of friendship; one does not want to share even a journey with one's enemies. The state aims to consist as far as possible of those who are like and equal, a condition found chiefly among the middle people. And so the best run constitution is certain to be found in this state [polity], whose composition is, we maintain, the natural one for a state to have.[55]

Indeed, Aristotle goes on to advocate the recognition of equality among the citizenry even in a monarchy: "Kingships are preserved by tending towards greater moderation. The fewer those spheres of activity where a king's power is sovereign, the longer the regime will inevitably survive undiminished. They themselves become less like masters, and more like their subjects in character, and therefore arouse less envy among them."[56]

These passages are interesting because they show Aristotle's attempt—relying on a consent-based theory of political authority—to characterize a *good* political system. In particular, a stable, effective, and just political society is one in which the political authority, however it is structured, operates in a way that recognizes the equality between the rulers and the ruled. Although Aristotle insists that there is such a thing as natural slavery, he is even more insistent that the political relationship among people who are equals in their capacity to reason effectively ought to be constructed so that this equality is acknowledged.

So Aristotle's consent-based theory of the nature and source of political authority implies a theory of good government. Political authority is something that is created by relative equals for mutual benefit (note that Aristotle doesn't consider the subordinating relationships between master and slave or between men and women as "political" insofar as they are not founded on equality). And this authority operates well, and achieves justice, to the extent that it treats people equally and fosters relative equality of resources.

However, Aristotle's theory also implies a theory of bad government. Because Aristotle derives political authority from the consent of (free) human beings, it accommodates the idea that there can be such a thing as a "bad" political authority, that is, one that is created by these men and thereby has authority but operates in a way that denies their mutual equality and fails to secure their common good. He would certainly argue that such regimes *shouldn't* receive the consent of those subject to them, but since what people ought to do and what they actually do are two different things, bad regimes are possible if and when they are supported by the consent of the governed. In contrast, Plato's theory of authority as that which arises (only) from knowledge of the Good makes impossible the idea that there can be a "bad" authority. But as we discussed earlier, Plato's view in the *Republic* also makes it difficult to recognize any real-life ruler as authoritative, insofar as no ruler can be said uncontroversially to know the Good completely in the way that Plato requires of his guardians. Aristotle dismisses the idea that such godlike people are likely to live among us (even while acknowledging that if they did, we would "naturally" obey them), and he develops a theory of political authority recognizing the flawed nature of the human pursuit of the Good, the possibility of corruption, and the relative equality of the rulers and the ruled.

So do we now have the outlines of a successful answer to the anarchist? Not yet: an anarchist would complain that Aristotle's development in *The Politics* of the idea that political authority is a human creation by relative equals is far from complete. If not only the state but also the political authority possessed by its rulers is a human creation, from *what* is it created? What "rights" do the people have, such that they can claim to have made one or more of their number into an authority? Do all people in a territory have to consent to the idea that such persons are authoritative in order for them to *be* authoritative (or at least authoritative over them)? If so, how must this consent be given? If not, how many people does it take to get genuine authorization? And should the consent be understood to come from each individual or from the community, understood as some kind of distinct whole over and above the individuals composing it? Finally, when the people invest such persons with political authority, what kind of authority is it? What is its scope and limit? And when can the people legitimately overthrow or rebel against it?

Only if these questions can be answered successfully can the consent view succeed as a complete theory of political authorization. If they cannot be answered well, the anarchist would seem to be right about the legitimacy of the state, in which case all of us who are subject to political authority would seem to have moral reason to oppose and destroy it. However, all these questions were tackled by early modern political theorists, particularly in seventeenth-century England, who sought to refine and further develop the idea that political authority is the creation of those subject to it. We shall see in the next chapter whether or not their answers to these questions are satisfactory.

Further Reading

The problem of justifying the state's authority is raised in a classic essay by G.E.M. Anscombe, "On the Source of the Authority of the State," in *Ethics, Religion and Politics: Collected Philosophical Papers, vol. 3*. Robert Paul Wolff's *In Defense of Anarchism* challenges the legitimacy of state authority. For an illuminating discussion of the practice of ancient slavery and Aristotle's argument for its legitimacy, see Bernard Williams, *Shame and Necessity*, chap. 5. Robert Filmer's views are discussed in Johann Sommerville's introduction to *Patriarcha and Other Writings* and in Peter Laslett's introduction to John Locke's *Two Treatises of Government*; note that in the first of these two treatises Locke mounts a sustained series of counterarguments against Filmer's views. Writings representative of the debate between divine rights theorists and consent-based theorists in the early modern period in England can be found in David Wootton, ed., *Divine Right and Democracy: An Anthology of Political Writing in Stuart England*. Within the voluminous literature discussing Plato's political views, the reader may find particularly valuable Gregory Vlastos's essays "The Theory of Social Justice in the Polis in Plato's *Republic*," in Gregory Vlastos, *Studies in Greek Philosophy*, vol. 2, and "Justice and Happiness in the *Republic*," in Gregory Vlastos, ed., *Plato: A Collection of Critical Essays*, vol. 2. For a discussion of Plato's political views in the context of his ethics, see Terence Irwin, *Plato's Ethics*. For specific discussions of Plato's political works, see Julia Annas, *An Introduction to Plato's Republic*; R. F. Stalley, *An Introduction to Plato's Laws*; and Julia Annas's introduction to Plato's

Statesman, trans. Robin Waterfield. For useful discussions of Aristotle's political views, see the essays in David Keyt and Fred D. Miller, eds., *A Companion to Aristotle's Politics*, and Fred D. Miller, *Nature, Justice and Rights in Aristotle's Politics*.

Notes

1. G.E.M. Anscombe, "On the Source of the Authority of the State," *Ethics, Religion and Politics: Collected Philosophical Papers*, vol. 3 (Minneapolis: University of Minnesota Press, 1981), p. 136.

2. For a discussion of the way in which governments are prima facie coercive and thus morally unacceptable, see Robert Paul Wolff, *In Defense of Anarchism* (New York: Harper and Row, 1970), chap. 1.

3. From W. S. Churchill, *The Gathering Storm* (1948), chap. 8; quoted in *The Oxford Dictionary of Quotations* (Oxford: Oxford University Press, 1992), p. 662.

4. For this definition, I am indebted to Joseph Raz's definition of political authority in *The Authority of Law* (Oxford: Clarendon Press, 1979) and in Raz's *Morality of Freedom* (Oxford: Clarendon Press, 1986). But I have not explicated at any length Raz's notion of "exclusionary reasons" and their connection to political obligation; I discuss this concept briefly in Chapter 3. For a discussion of Razian ideas of political authority, see Leslie Green, *The Authority of the State* (Oxford: Clarendon Press, 1984), pp. 41–42. For an interesting early discussion of state authority, see Anscombe, "On the Source of the Authority of the State," pp. 130–155.

5. Famous Russian anarchists include Mikhail Bakunin, Sergei Nechaev, and Pyotr Kropotkin. The French thinker Pierre-Joseph Proudhon was an anarchist, and in America the view was vigorously advocated by Benjamin Tucker, Charles Mowbray, and Henry David Thoreau. In his essay "Civil Disobedience" (1849), Thoreau advocates rejecting the control of the state because we can, he says, intuitively perceive what is right, and on the basis of that perception we should, he says, wage a "peaceful revolution" against our governments and all their abuses by withdrawing all of our forms of support from them. (He himself refused to pay his taxes.) For a discussion of well-known anarchists of the nineteenth and twentieth centuries, see Paul Avrich, *Anarchist Portraits* (Princeton: Princeton University Press, 1988). For a contemporary discussion, see Wolff, *In Defense of Anarchism*.

6. These three ways may represent a gradual progression of thought, from close identification of the ruler with God to a looser linkage in which the ruler is granted divine authority but is not himself divine, as people became more skeptical of a ruler's invocation of divine status or divine connections. I am indebted to Ken O'Day for suggesting this idea.

7. In ancient Egypt, Babylonia, and Phoenicia, legend made the gods the first kings of the people, and certain kings thereafter were often thought to have been gods. See C. J. Gadd, *The Ideas of Divine Rule in the Ancient East* (London: Oxford University Press, 1945), esp. pp. 33–36.

8. See ibid., p. 45.

9. Robert Filmer, *Patriarcha*, in *Patriarcha and Other Writings*, ed. Johann Sommerville (Cambridge: Cambridge University Press, 1991).

10. See John Dunn, *The Political Thought of John Locke* (Cambridge: Cambridge University Press, 1969).

11. Quoted in Bertrand de Jouvenal, *Power: The Natural History of Its Growth*, trans. J. F. Huntington (London: Hutchison, 1948), chap. 2; and in Robert Stewart, comp., *A Dictionary of Political Quotations* (London: Europa Publications, 1984). Believing such ideas probably didn't help Charles rule in a subject-friendly way, and he was eventually beheaded by revolutionaries in 1649. For more on the use of the divine authority by British kings, see John Figgis, *Divine Right of Kings* (Cambridge: Cambridge University Press, 1904).

12. Filmer's title raised a sticky issue for him: Can a woman be the absolute ruler? That England was ruled very successfully by Elizabeth I made it difficult for him to answer that question negatively. John Locke attacked the idea that political authority was like parental authority in the first treatise of his *Two Treatises of Government*, ed. Peter Laslett (Cambridge: Cambridge University Press, 1988). (Would you want your father to have the kind of power over you that Filmer credits to a king?)

13. From James's speech to Parliament, 21 March 1609.

14. Locke, discussing Filmer's position in *Patriarcha*, in the First Treatise of his *Two Treatises of Government*, chap. 5, sec. 10, p. 143.

15. In Morocco the ruler is supposed to have divine authority to rule by virtue of being descended from the prophet Mohammed. In claiming descent from the prophet, the king claims to possess *baraka* (roughly translated as "blessedness"), which is able to descend in genealogical lines. It is interesting that the title of the ruler is "commander of the faithful." For more on the origins and functions of Moroccan kings' claim to be divinely authorized to rule and the way it has contributed to the present king's highly autocratic regime, see Dale F. Eickelman, *Moroccan Islam* (Austin: University of Texas Press, 1976), pp. 25 ff.; and John Waterbury, *The Commander of the Faithful: The Moroccan Political Elite—A Study in Segmented Politics* (New York: Columbia University Press, 1970). I am grateful to Thomas Parks for providing me with information on Moroccan politics.

16. And yet King James tried to argue that the theory did place some constraints on the king. In his speech to Parliament in 1609, he maintains that a king is under an obligation to rule according to his own laws and not to rule using capricious ad hoc commands. If he does so, James says, "God never leaves Kings unpunished when they transgress their limits"—which is why, says James, no matter how godlike kings are, God still ensures that kings "die like men" and are thus vulnerable to divine punishment.

17. However, as I noted above, the view has persisted into the twentieth century. Even today the king of Morocco claims divine entitlement to rule (see note 15 above). And this view played a powerful role in twentieth-century political events in virtue of the way Japanese politics was influenced prior to and during World War II by the belief that the emperor of Japan was divine.

18. For discussions of these two types of position, see Lynn White, "The Historical Roots of Our Ecological Crisis," *Science* 211–212 (1967): 1203–1207; Lloyd Steffen, "In Defense of Dominion," *Environmental Ethics* 13 (1992): 63–80; Tom Regan, *The Case for Animal Rights* (Berkeley: University of California Press, 1983); Peter Singer and Tom Regan, eds., *Animal Rights and Human Obligations* (Englewood

Cliffs, N.J.: Prentice-Hall, 1989); and Peter Singer, ed., *In Defence of Animals* (Oxford: Blackwell, 1985).

19. William Shakespeare, *Macbeth* (speech by Lennox to Macduff), act 2, scene 3.

20. For a work that suggests this line of thought, see Steven Goldberg, *The Inevitability of Patriarchy* (New York: William Morrow, 1973).

21. Aristotle, *The Politics*, trans. T. A. Sinclair, rev. Trevor J. Saunders (Harmondsworth: Penguin, 1992), book 1, chap. 5, 1254b16–20, pp. 68–69.

22. Ibid., 1254b21, p. 69.

23. Ibid., chap. 13, 1260a12, p. 95.

24. In general Aristotle does not connect natural slavery with certain ethnic backgrounds, unlike many Greeks of his time, but there is some suggestion of these ideas in *The Politics*—for example, when he says that barbarians fail to treat women differently from slaves because everyone among them is like a slave (book 1, chap. 2, 1252a34, p. 57). See Bernard Williams, *Shame and Necessity* (Berkeley: University of California Press, 1993), p. 115.

25. From H. Manly, *The South Vindicated from the Treason and Fanaticism of the Northern Abolitionists* (1836; reprint, New York: Negro Universities Press, 1969), p. 105.

26. Aristotle, *The Politics* book 1, chap. 6, 1255b8–15, p. 73.

27. Manly, *The South Vindicated*, p. 105.

28. Bernard Williams has a discussion of Aristotle's attempt to legitimate slavery as not only socially necessary but also just to the individuals involved, if the roles of slave and master are assigned properly; see his *Shame and Necessity*, chap. 5.

29. Aristotle, *The Politics*, book 1, chap. 13, 1259a12, p. 95.

30. Ibid., chap. 5, 1254b10, p. 68.

31. Ibid., 1254b15, p. 68.

32. From *The Works of John Knox*, ed. David Laing (Edinburgh: AMS Press, 1966), vol. 4, p. 373.

33. Ibid., p. 374.

34. See Rousseau's *Emile*, ed. Allan Bloom (New York: Basic Books, 1979), especially the opening of book 5, pp. 357–363.

35. One scholar who believes Aristotle succeeds in walking this tightrope is William W. Fortenbaugh, "Aristotle on Slaves and Women," in Jonathan Barnes, Malcolm Schofield, and Richard Sorabji, eds., *Articles on Aristotle*, vol. 2 (London: Duckworth, 1977). For a powerful argument that he fails, see Williams, *Shame and Necessity*, esp. pp. 113–117.

36. In *A Vindication of the Rights of Woman* (1792; reprint, Harmondsworth: Penguin, 1978), Mary Wollstonecraft replies to the analysis of women that appears in *Emile*. She maintains that some women do seem to match Rousseau's description of the female to an extent because their society has reared them to have the characteristics he describes. She thus notes the power that socialization has to affect a person's "nature" in a way that will advantage those who wish to dominate over her.

37. John Stuart Mill makes this point in *The Subjection of Women*, in *Essays in Sex Equality by John Stuart Mill and Harriet Taylor Mill*, ed. Alice Rossi (Chicago: University of Chicago Press, 1970). See also Claudia Card, "Rape as a Terrorist Institu-

tion," in R. G. Frey and Christopher Morris, eds., *Violence, Terrorism and Justice* (Cambridge: Cambridge University Press, 1991).

38. But it is unclear the extent to which the author of the document, Thomas Jefferson, thought that "men" included women. It wasn't until 1920 that women were granted suffrage in the country that Jefferson's doctrine helped to found.

39. Plato, *Republic,* trans. G.M.A. Grube, rev. C.D.C. Reeve (Indianapolis: Hackett, 1992), book 4, 420b, p. 95.

40. Ibid., book 9, 572a–c, p. 242.

41. Ibid., book 6, 508b–c, p. 182.

42. Ibid., book 3, 415a–c, pp. 91–92.

43. Ibid., book 7, 518c, p. 190.

44. Ibid., book 4, 421a, p. 96.

45. Ibid., book 7, 540a, p. 211.

46. However, in his later dialogue *The Statesman,* Plato is more willing to recognize the likelihood that rulers will be not only fallible but even evil, and he is grudgingly appreciative of democracy insofar as rule by the whole people can provide a powerful check on the evil ambitions of a few.

47. See Aristotle, *The Politics,* book 3, chap. 17, 1288a15, p. 230; and book 3, chap. 13, 1284a7–9, p. 215.

48. Ibid., chap. 9, 1281a, p. 198.

49. Ibid., book 7, chap. 8, 1328a33–1328b1, p. 413.

50. See ibid., book 3, chap. 15, 1286a25, p. 222.

51. See Charles Kahn, "The Origins of Social Contract Theory," in G. B. Kerferd, ed., *The Sophists and Their Legacy* (Wiesbaden, Germany: Franz Steiner Verlag, 1981), pp. 92–108. Note that the author of *Sisyphus* may have been the writer Critias.

52. Quoted and translated by Kahn, ibid., p. 97; this passage can also be found in Kathleen Freeman, *Ancilla to the Pre-Socratic Philosophers* (Cambridge: Harvard University Press, 1948), pp. 157–158 (Diels-Kranz edition: DK 88, B 25).

53. See *Protagoras,* trans. W.R.M. Lamb (Cambridge: Harvard University Press, 1967), 322a–b; *Laws,* trans. A. E. Taylor (London: Dent, 1960), book 3, 678e ff., 680e ff., 681d7, 683a7; and *Republic,* book 2, 358e–359b.

54. This distinction is fundamental to what is called the "positivist" theory of law, the most prominent exponents of which are J. Austin and H.L.A. Hart. See Austin's *Province of Jurisprudence Determined,* ed. Wilfred E. Rumble (Cambridge: Cambridge University Press, 1995), and Hart's *Concept of Law* (Oxford: Clarendon Press, 1961).

55. Aristotle, *The Politics,* book 4, chap. 11, 1295b24–27, p. 267; and see 1295b34.

56. Ibid., book 5, chap. 11, 1313a19–21, p. 344.

2

Modern Social Contract Theories

> To understand Political Power right, and derive it from its Original, we must consider what State all Men are naturally in, and that is, a *State of perfect Freedom* to order their Actions, and dispose of their Possessions, and Persons as they think fit, within the bounds of the Law of Nature, without asking leave, or depending upon the Will of any other Man.
>
> **—John Locke, *Two Treatises of Government*, Second Treatise, sec. 4**

The idea that political authority should be understood as consent-based has enjoyed enormous popularity in modern times and is the foundation of a kind of political justification for the state called a *social contract argument*. Indeed, the consent-based view has been so thoroughly associated in the modern mind with the idea of a social contract that most philosophers unthinkingly identify them. (This is one reason Aristotle's use of consent-based ideas has been missed, since he does not link consent to the idea of a contract.) But a social contract argument is only one way to develop a consent-based view, albeit the most popular (and for many) the most plausible way of doing so. In this chapter we examine the structure of two of the most famous of these arguments, put forward by Thomas Hobbes (1588–1679) and John Locke (1632–1704), to see if either argument can provide a successful answer to the anarchists' challenge to the legitimacy of the state. Despite the considerable appeal and popularity enjoyed by social contract arguments—particularly the Lockean variant—we shall see after an examination of these arguments that this way of developing a consent-based theory of political authority is beset with problems.

Whether those problems can be solved is the topic of our next chapter, where we explore another version of the consent-based theory of political authority unlike either the Lockean or Hobbesian social contract theories.

Ancient and Medieval Contractarian Ideas

As I discussed in the previous chapter, the idea that political authority comes from consent was widespread in ancient Greece. But the most prominent person to suggest that political authority comes from the legitimizing consent of the people in the form of a social contract was (rather remarkably) Plato, who makes this linkage in the *Crito* and yet never seriously develops it further in his later political works. In the *Crito* one of Socrates' friends, Crito, tries to persuade Socrates to sneak out of prison and leave Athens so as to avoid the penalty of death to which an Athenian jury has (unjustly) sentenced him for the crimes of impiety and corrupting the youth.[1] Socrates explains to Crito why he believes he is under an obligation not to avoid the death penalty, despite the injustice of his sentence. And one of his arguments is that because he has consistently remained in and enjoyed the benefits of Athens as an adult, he has thereby implicitly entered into an agreement with the state to abide by its laws (and thereby accept its authority over him) in exchange for those benefits. To evade its authority now, says Socrates, would be breaking that agreement and behaving unjustly.

But who participates in this contract, and how does the conferral of authority arise from it? Plato doesn't explicitly say, and subsequently there have been two ways of explaining how that conferral is contractually delivered: In the first way, political authority comes directly from the people via a contract between them and the ruler (where different theorists will take different stands on whether each individual contracts separately with the ruler or whether the ruler contracts with the people as a single group). In the second way, the conferral of authority arises indirectly via a contract among the people (in which the ruler is not a participant) to grant the ruler authority, after which the authority is conferred by them.

The former development of the theory, in which the people make a contract with their ruler directly and promise to obey him in exchange for the benefits of such rule, became increasingly popular in the Roman world and was actually explicitly acknowledged in the *Digest* of Justinian in a famous passage that came to be known as the *lex regia:* "What pleases the prince has the force of law, because by the *lex regia,* which was made concerning his authority, the people confers to him and upon him all its own authority and power."[2]

In medieval times this idea was endorsed by prominent philosophers such as Thomas Aquinas and William of Ockham and became the dominant theme in the political writings of many Renaissance figures (such as Marcilius of Padua), Reformation thinkers (e.g., the Huguenots and Scottish revolutionaries such as George Buchanan [1506–1582]), and Counter-Reformation leaders (such as Francesco Suarez).[3]

But an interesting controversy developed even as the consent-based idea grew more and more popular: When the people confer the authority to rule upon the ruler, either directly via a contract with him or indirectly via a contract with one another, do they *lend* him their authority and reserve the right to take it away from him if and when they judge it necessary? Or do they *alienate* that authority to him, so that no matter what subsequently happens, his rule is permanent over them? Understanding their conferral in the first way makes the ruler into a kind of *agent* of the people, hired by them and capable of being fired by them if they judge his performance deficient given their agreement. Understanding their conferral in the second way makes the ruler into a kind of *master* of the people, insofar as his authority over them is permanent and rebellion against him is always illegitimate.

Henceforth I shall use the term *agency social contract* to refer to an argument assuming that political authority is granted by the people to the ruler as a loan, and I shall use the term *alienation social contract* to refer to an argument assuming that political authority is given as an irrevocable grant. Hobbes attempts the most sophisticated alienation argument in the social contract tradition; Locke is the most famous exponent of the agency argument in the tradition. But as we shall see, neither philosopher succeeds in developing these forms of contract argument in a fully plausible manner.

Hobbes

Hobbes's argument received its most complete development in his classic *Leviathan* (1651).[4] The general outlines of his view are quite simple: Imagine, says Hobbes, a world in which people live without being governed and indeed without even being in a society with one another. Such a "state of nature," according to Hobbes, would be a state of war, in which people would inevitably come into conflict and wage war on one another, so that their lives would be "solitary, poore, nasty, brutish and short."[5] To preserve their lives and achieve a comfortable existence, Hobbes says human beings have created and maintained (and were rational to create and maintain) political societies to secure peace and the conditions for commerce. However, he maintains, the only viable form of political society that can achieve these ends is one ruled by a sovereign absolute in power over the people.

The details of Hobbes's thought experiment are philosophically important: We can, he says, think of people in the state of nature as if they were "even now sprung up out of the earth, and suddenly, like mushrooms, come to full maturity, without all kinds of engagement to each other."[6] That Hobbes believed such a thought experiment possible and revealing of the ultimate nature of human beings shows that he disagrees with a philosopher such as Aristotle, who would insist that stripping people of their social connections is tantamount to stripping them of much of their humanity. Hobbes's thought experiment is anti-Aristotelian in another way: He insists that by performing it, we see that all human beings are roughly equal in physical and mental abilities, so that there are no natural masters or natural slaves and no fundamental differences between men or women or any group of people such that some of them are naturally subordinate to others:

> Nature hath made men so equall, in the faculties of body and mind: as that though there bee found one man sometimes manifestly stronger in body, or of quicker mind than another; yet when all is reckoned together, the differ- ence between man, and man, is not so considerable, as that one man can thereupon claim to himselfe any benefit, to which another may not pretend, as well as he. For as to the strength of body, the weakest has strength enough to kill the strongest, either by secret machination, or by confederacy with others, that are in the same danger with himselfe.
> And as to the faculties of the mind . . . I find yet a greater equality amongst men than that of human beings' strength.[7]

Hobbes's point is that even though we differ in strength and intelligence, there is no superman or superwoman alive among us who can dominate any or all of us through muscle or mind. Whereas the superman of comic- book fame had the ability (if he had only chosen to use it) to rule the world simply by his strength (something that other members of his home planet actually did in the movie *Superman 2*), real human beings have to sleep and eat and are vulnerable to sickness and mistakes in reasoning, all of which leave them open to conquest by others no matter how brilliant or powerful they might be.

However, this equal vulnerability has political import, namely, that there are no natural masters or natural slaves among us. By insisting on our rough equality, Hobbes does not mean to deny the very real differ- ences in talents and skills that we see manifested in the human commu- nity. Instead he is making a *political* point. He is saying that no one is so much better than other people that his or her superiority entitles him or her to rule over them. Hence these egalitarian remarks are Hobbes's way of rejecting (perhaps more thoroughly than any other early modern polit- ical theorist) the natural subordination thesis. Throughout his political writings, he is contemptuous of the idea that there is some kind of natural subordination of some people to others, and he explicitly rejects the idea that women are naturally subordinate to men.[8]

Hobbes argues that the roughly equal people in such a state of nature would be largely, but not exclusively, self-regarding. They would desire above all else their self-preservation, which would generate in them an interest in many material things. And they would have other powerful desires, in particular the desire for glory. How would people so described behave toward one another?

Not well, says Hobbes. In their attempts to satisfy their largely self-regarding desires, they would inevitably clash, and they would come into conflict with one another so often that the state of nature would inevitably become a state of war "of every man, against every man." Hobbes describes the generation of that war in chapter 13 of *Leviathan:*

> in the nature of man, we find three principall causes of quarrell. First, Competition; Secondly, Diffidence; Thirdly, Glory.
>
> The first, maketh men invade for Gain; the second, for Safety; and the third, for Reputation. The first use Violence, to make themselves Masters of other mens persons, wives, children and cattell; the second, to defend them; the third, for trifles, as a word, a smile, a different opinion, and any other signe of undervalue, either direct in their Persons, or by reflexion in their Kindred, their Friends, their Nation, their Profession, or their Name.[9]

The result is, eventually, a state of total war in which everyone claims a "right to all things" on the grounds that there is no object that might not be useful in their struggle for survival against their fellows.

Now initially readers may think Hobbes is being unreasonably pessimistic about people's disposition to engage in war in the natural state. Wouldn't people, even as Hobbes has described them, see the futility of war and the advantages of peace? And wouldn't this mean that they could negotiate some kind of truce among them, producing a cessation of overt violence and perhaps some kind of limited cooperation?

To see why Hobbes would insist that such a truce is not possible in a state of nature and why war would be inevitable no matter how desirable a truce might seem, we must appreciate how the psychology of Hobbesian people is such that it would be *irrational* for them to keep their promise not to attack the others in any truce agreement. The central (albeit not only) problem that Hobbesian people face in the natural state is what is called a *prisoner's dilemma,* or PD (after the example that originally illustrated it), a dilemma that has been much discussed in contemporary social science and philosophy since the 1950s, when it was first explicitly named.[10] A PD is a situation in which the rational actions of rational people lead inevitably to conflict. Figure 2.1 illustrates the PD faced by two

Agent A

Agent B		Do not attack	Attack
	Do not attack	2,2	4,1
	Attack	1,4	3,3

FIGURE 2.1

people in a Hobbesian state of nature who have made a truce agreement and are considering whether or not to keep that agreement. The numbers of the matrix correspond to the preferences of each of the agents for the outcome that would occur if each of them performed one of two actions: keep the agreement and refrain from attacking the other, or attack the other. There are four such outcomes, and the numbers rank them (1 is best; 4 is worst). A's preference orderings are on the top; B's preference orderings are on the left.

Agents who have preference orderings as they are depicted in this PD matrix will find that it is rational for them to attack no matter what the other agent decides to do. To see this, consider how each of them would reason. A notes that if B decides not to attack her, she can either decide to attack him, thereby getting her favorite situation realized, or else she can choose not to attack him, getting only her second favorite situation realized. So if B does not attack her, she concludes she should nonetheless attack him. She also notes that if B decides to attack her, then she can either refrain from attacking him, in which case she gets her least favorite situation realized, or else attack him, in which case she gets a better (third-place) situation realized. So if B decides to attack her, she should also attack him. But this means no matter which action B chooses, it would be better for A to attack him and not to keep their truce agreement; and since B's preferences are symmetrical, he realizes the same. In a PD situation, even though the cooperative outcome is best for the two of them considered as a collective, it is individually rational for each of them not to cooperate with the other. The irony is, however, that when everyone fails to cooperate, the outcome their actions produce is individually worse for each of them than the outcome that would be produced by universal cooperation!

This dilemma seems to capture the reasons why Hobbesian people in a state of nature persistently fail to cooperate and eventually aggress against one another. The advantages of aggression against (naive) cooperators (prompting what Hobbes calls "invasion for gain") and the advantages of aggression as a protective strategy against other aggressors (prompting what Hobbes calls "invasion from diffidence") make aggression the best action, even though each person in that state would rather be in a state of peace than a state of war. Add to this situation the divisive effects of the desire for glory, and it seems inevitable that the Hobbesian state of nature will eventually be a state of total war.

However, there are other passages in *Leviathan* where Hobbes suggests that PD reasoning is not quite accurate as an account of the way in which Hobbesian people would deliberate in the state of nature. To appreciate what these passages mean, consider how you would reason if you knew there was a good chance that you would be in a *series* of prisoner's dilemmas with another person. Suppose, for example, that you and this other person had neighboring farms, and in order to harvest all your crops each of you required the other's help. Deciding whether or not to keep an agreement to help one another before any particular harvest places each of you in a prisoner's dilemma, but the failure to keep such an agreement on any particular occasion will also mean that neither of you can count on the other's help in any future harvest because neither of you will unilaterally cooperate. So in a series of PDs, cooperation early in that series can make possible not only the benefits from cooperation in that situation but also benefits from cooperative interactions in future PDs, while the failure to cooperate can foreclose the chance of receiving all future benefits. If those future benefits are factored into your calculations about what to do now, cooperation may often turn out to be rational after all. Depicted in Figure 2.2 are preferences two individuals would have for cooperating in a prisoner's dilemma that they expect to be only the first of a series of such dilemmas.

In this situation each player's favorite outcome is that produced by joint cooperation, because that outcome will generate the benefits of cooperation in the present situation and make possible benefits from cooperation in future PDs. The favorite outcome in the original PD, in which the agent fails to cooperate but enjoys the other person's cooperation, is not the favorite here, because each agent knows the other agent will never cooperate in the future if he or she reneges now, in which case he or she will never be able to enjoy the cooperative benefits of future PDs.

		Agent A	
		Cooperate	Do not cooperate
Agent B	Cooperate	1,1	4,2
	Do not cooperate	2,4	3,3

FIGURE 2.2

I have been describing what is generally called an *iterated prisoner's dilemma*. If the parties in such a dilemma have preferences as depicted in Figure 2.2, they will reason as follows: If my partner cooperates, then it will be rational for me to cooperate also. But if my partner fails to cooperate, it would not be rational for me to cooperate (because the outcome of universal noncooperation is preferred to the outcome in which my partner fails to cooperate but I do). Hence I should cooperate if and only if I have good reason to believe my partner will cooperate also.

There are signs in chapter 15 of *Leviathan* that Hobbes believes people in the state of nature are often in iterated PDs, so that Figure 2.2, and not Figure 2.1, describes the preferences over cooperation they have in this state. For example, Hobbes says in that chapter that keeping contracts is rational in a state of nature, as long as one can be assured that one's partner is prepared to keep his contract, because such cooperative behavior reassures others that one is the sort of person who can be trusted to keep her side of a bargain in a confederacy contract in which each participant promises to come to the aid of the other if attacked.[11] This is a nice example of the way in which cooperation in one PD makes possible the realization of (even more lucrative) benefits from cooperation in a future PD.

But remember that reasoning in an iterated PD situation results in cooperation only if one concludes that there is good reason to believe one's partner will cooperate. With no assurance that this is so, the rational decision is not to cooperate, forgoing future benefits in order to ensure that one is not harmed by one's partner's folly. So Hobbes's state of nature would still be a state of war, even if most people expected to be in iterated rather than single-play PDs, for as long as they could not get reasonable assurance that their fellows would cooperate. And indeed, it looks as if that assurance would be very hard to get. Hobbes's state of nature is one in which people are disassociated from one another, such that they don't have reliable information about whether their partners in a PD are able to reason well. If you were in such a situation and you believed there was a good chance that your partner was shortsighted or the sort of person whose reasoning was often derailed by passion, then you would worry that she would be unable to appreciate the rationality of cooperation.

So even if many people in Hobbes's state of nature appreciate the rationality of cooperation, many people won't—in particular, those who are bad reasoners or ignorant or shortsighted or greedy for present gain. This leads to trouble, because if you were in that state, when you faced another human being you could not be sure that you were facing someone who appreciated the rationality of cooperation. And you would be a fool to cooperate with someone who might well respond by taking advantage of you—particularly if his doing so was dangerous to your future well-being. Hence "diffidence" (as Hobbes means the term) requires a defensive, uncooperative posture. Indeed, even if you thought the other person was likely to be a rational cooperator, if that other person feared that *you* were likely an irrational cooperator, then he would be likely to take this defensive posture and thus refuse to cooperate, in which case you would be rational not to cooperate either.

In another place I have used decision theory to try to capture the exact nature of the reasoning process of Hobbesian people in this situation.[12] It is a reasoning process that *can* result in a (rational) decision to cooperate if the reasoner has reasonable assurance that his partner will cooperate also, the gains from mutual cooperation are considerable, and the losses that would be suffered if the reasoner cooperated but his partner did not are not serious. But as the losses increase, then the assurance that each party needs to find cooperation rational must also increase. And in a Hobbesian state of nature the common knowledge that one's partners in PDs are rational is difficult if not impossible to come by, making it difficult to get the assurance one needs in most situations to make cooperation rational. This means that the single-play PD mentality would be the mentality that people in Hobbes's state of nature would feel forced to adopt.

Hobbes's discussion of what he calls "laws of nature" provides supporting evidence that this assurance problem, faced by people in iterated PD situations, precipitates a state of war. These laws of nature direct people to behave in various cooperative ways, including keeping contracts, refraining from invading or aggressing against another, and so forth. Hobbes calls these laws "Conclusions, or Theorems concerning what conduceth to the conservation and defence" of people in this situation.[13] Cooperation, he says, breeds a climate of trust and peace that makes possible self-preservation and the exchange of services and benefits necessary for a comfortable and peaceful life. In this way it is behavior that, although other-regarding, is actually in each person's self-interest. Yet despite promulgating these laws, Hobbes does not think they would forestall or in any way provide a remedy for the conflict in his natural state. This is because, on his view, the cooperative actions recommended in these laws of nature are only rational for a person to perform in the state of nature if others in that state are also disposed to perform them:

> For he that should be modest, and tractable, and performe all he promises, in such time, and place, where no man els should do so, should but make himselfe a prey to others, and procure his own certain ruine, contrary to the ground of all Lawes of Nature, which tend to Natures preservation. And again, he that having sufficient Security, that others shall observe the same Lawes towards him, observes them not himselfe, seeketh not Peace, but War; & consequently the destruction of his Nature by Violence.[14]

So each law of nature should really be understood to have attached to it a rider specifying that the cooperative action is directed only if the agent can be assured that the other player(s) will also behave cooperatively.

Hence because each of these laws correctly specifies cooperative behavior that in certain circumstances will further our self-preservation, they "bind to a desire to take place" (as Hobbes puts it in chapter 15) in that each of us would like to be in a situation where such cooperative action was rational. Nonetheless, in a state of nature, where the rider does not hold, such cooperative behavior could threaten the safety of the one performing it, so that even rational people would find their behavior risky to perform. Hence (for both good and bad reasons) human beings in that state do not follow the laws.

So what is the remedy? To achieve peace, says Hobbes, we need *one* judge with the power to settle any quarrel over anything. That one judge is what Hobbes calls the "sovereign," who is a political leader with the authority to resolve any issue and the power to enforce any resolution of any issue. Hobbes specifies that a sovereign can be one person or many persons: If it is one person, the government is called a monarchy; if it is many but not all persons, the government is called an aristocracy; and if it is all persons, the government is called a democracy. Hobbes believes that monarchy is the best and most effective form of sovereign rule, although he admits that he does not have a decisive argument to prove its superiority.[15]

How is the sovereign created? Hobbes does *not* say that his creation involves the people's conferring authority and power via a contract between them and the sovereign. Indeed, he insists that no such contract should take place, else there will be quarreling between the people and the sovereign about whether or not he has performed according to the terms of the contract. Because there can be no impartial judge to resolve this quarrel, it will likely lead to war and the dissolution of the political society: If the sovereign is designated to resolve such a quarrel, then he will never admit to breaching the agreement, in which case it is useless. And if the people are supposed to resolve the quarrel, then they will likely disagree with one another as well as with the sovereign about whether he has performed well or not. Both sorts of disagreements will lead to conflict and the "dissolution of the commonwealth."[16] For this reason, Hobbes says that the sovereign must be created by a process in which the people contract with *one another* about who shall be sovereign and then individually "authorize" that person in a way that makes them permanently bound to him.

So Hobbes's development of the consent-based theory of political authority does *not* endorse the idea that there is some kind of "deal" between the ruler and the ruled giving authority and power on condition that she rule "well." Instead, Hobbes argues that as a result of determining that the creation of a sovereign is to his or her advantage, each person will decide to agree *with one another* to confer authority so as to create a sovereign, but the actual investiture of authority and power is performed independently and noncontractually. Moreover, as I said before, Hobbes uses the language appropriate for an alienation social contract argument because he insists that this investiture is one in which each individual *gives up* his or her power and right to direct his or her own life. He argues that the investiture cannot be construed as a loan of authority or power from the subject to the ruler because such an understanding of the sovereign's authorization would imply the existence of an agency contract between the sovereign and those she ruled—which Hobbes argues will only precipitate more conflict rather than peace. In the end Hobbes says that peace can be achieved only if people in the state of nature accept the need for a ruler who is quite literally their master.

Hobbes's development of the consent-based theory of authority also differs from the development of that idea in Aristotle's *Politics*. As we've noted, Hobbes is far more egalitarian than Aristotle in that he insists that every human being is the rough equal of every other; in Hobbes's state of nature there are no natural slaves or masters, and women and men are not fundamentally different enough to make the former subordinate to the latter. But according to Hobbes, our equality means that in order to live in peace we must "invent" a master, that is, we must select a person or group from among us and artificially make him or them master with authority to settle all our disputes.

Problems with Hobbes's
Alienation Social Contract Argument

For generations, readers have found Hobbes's argument powerful. And yet most have thought his logic has gone wrong and have rejected his conclusions. Where is his mistake? As I shall now seek to explain, Hobbes's argument goes wrong in a way that is very important to us given that we seek to understand the best way to formulate a consent-based theory of authority.

Consider what is involved in authorizing the sovereign: According to Hobbes, the state of war prompts every person to claim a right to all things, and these entitlement claims lead to quarreling over everything. Hence he says that the sovereign's creation means every person but the sovereign-designate surrenders this entitlement claim, thereby making the entitlement claim of the sovereign-designate effective. In this way not only effective power but also *authority* is granted to this ruler, as Hobbes makes clear in the following passage from chapter 17 of *Leviathan*:

> The only way to erect such a Common Power, as may be able to defend them from the invasion of Forraigners, and the injuries of one another, and thereby to secure them in such sort, as that by their owne industrie, and by the fruites

of the Earth, they may nourish themselves and live contentedly; is, to conferre all their power and strength upon one Man, or upon one Assembly of men, that may reduce all their Wills, by plurality of voices, unto one Will: which is as much as to say, to appoint one Man, or Assembly of men, to beare their Person; and every one to owne, and acknowledge himselfe to be Author of whatsoever he that so beareth their Person, shall Act, or cause to be Acted, in those things which concerne the Common Peace and Safetie; and therein to submit their Wills, every one to his Will, and their Judgements, to his Judgement. This is more than Consent, or Concord; it is a reall Unitie of them all, in one and the same Person, made by Covenant of every man with every man, as if every man should say to every man, *I Authorise and give up my Right of Governing my selfe, to this Man, or to this Assembly of men, on this condition, that thou give up thy Right to him, and Authorise all his Actions in like manner.*[17]

So the idea is that this authorization process, in which all agree they will participate with respect to a particular person or assembly, results in the ruler's having power over everyone who participates in the process, as well as the goods each controls. But he holds this power rightfully by virtue of the fact that each person gave up the "right to govern" herself or himself and bestowed that right on the sovereign. So he can now rightfully command each of them because he now "owns" these governing rights.

Yet all this talk of "authorizing" and "rights" is abstract. What is it that people actually *do* to put the sovereign in this position of authority and power? We shall explore this question at great length in the next chapter, but for now, consider that a sovereign can have legitimacy and power in a society only when he is able to get his people to accept that they *ought* to obey him and when he has the personnel and technology to ensure that he can capture and punish those who do not obey his commands. Hence a sovereign's authority and power depends quite literally on his subjects' obeying him because they take him to be the sole political authority. In particular it is critical that they obey him when he commands them to capture, try, and punish someone who has violated those commands.

But what happens if the sovereign's rule is such that the people believe it is threatening their own lives? Will they persist in thinking that they ought to obey him and accordingly do so, even then? No. Hobbes has described human psychology such that inside or outside the commonwealth each person is concerned to advance his or her own interests, particularly self-preservation. But this means that Hobbes must admit that people in the commonwealth will disobey the sovereign if *they* determine that to obey him means endangering their ability to preserve themselves. And indeed this is exactly what he says: "The Obligation of Subjects to the Soveraign, is understood to last as long, and no longer, than [*sic*] the power lasteth, by which he is able to protect them. . . . The end of Obedience is Protection."[18]

If the people are always going to be concerned to preserve themselves and if the sovereign begins to rule such that their self-preservation is threatened, then their interests are such that they will do what they can to evade his commands, lest their lives be put at risk. Note that *the subjects* decide whether or not the ruler's commands are life-threatening; since it is *their* lives that are at stake, they are the ones who will (and must) make the determination about whether or not they are at risk. (Suppose the ruler decided this issue: He might well proclaim his rules were consistent with the people's well-being when in fact they were not. Only the subjects themselves have the right incentive to determine the preservation value of a sovereign's command because only they run the risk of dying if these commands turn out to be life-threatening.)

Now if only one person concluded that a sovereign's rule is inconsistent with her self-preservation and thus refused to obey one or more of the sovereign's commands, the sovereign's power and authority would not be threatened. But if many or most people make that determination and decide not to obey him, then the sovereign is in trouble. For such a massive refusal to follow his commands would effectively amount to rebellion. Not only would he lose all or most of the support of those parts of the society that enforce his commands (e.g., the police, the court system, the army), but he would also lose the compliance of the population on which any regime relies to function efficiently and cooperatively. Moreover, if all or most of the people decide to start obeying someone else, the sovereign would be effectively deposed, and this new individual would be invested with power and authority.

In the end, it is Hobbes's effectively granting that the people will (and ought to) judge the ruler's performance that is the ruin of his attempt to mount a viable alienation argument. This point was appreciated by some of Hobbes's contemporary critics. For example, one of Hobbes's most vociferous critics, John Bramhall, noted that after claiming subjects must give up their right to all things, Hobbes gives them a bailout clause in chapter 21, so that their authorization of the sovereign turns out to be something like: "I give you, the sovereign, the right to command me in any area, and I will obey you *except* when I decide my life is threatened if I do so."[19] But, asks Bramhall, who shall judge if a sovereign's commands are threatening to one's self-preservation or not?

> Either it must be left to the soveraign determination, whether the subjects security be sufficiently provided for, And then in vain is any mans sentence expected against himself, or to the discretion of the subject, (as the words themselves [in chapter 21] do seem to import,) and then there need no other bellowes to kindle the fire of a civill war, and put a whole commonwealth into a combustion, but this seditious Article.[20]

Bramhall's point is that if each subject judges when he is entitled to disobey the sovereign's commands and when he is not, then to all intents and purposes the sovereign's reign depends upon the judgment of the subjects that his commands are worth obeying, in which case he rules at their pleasure—a situation Bramhall is convinced will result in civil war. Is it any wonder that Bramhall derisively refers to *Leviathan* as a "rebel's catechism"?[21]

So although Hobbes argues that the people must "alienate" their right to govern themselves to the sovereign, in fact the only kind of investiture of power and authority that is possible for people as he has described them (and as we know them) is one that is contingent upon their determination that the sovereign is ruling in a way that secures their protection. This means that, in reality, *Leviathan* has two arguments: the "official" alienation argument and the real but unacknowledged agency argument. The official argument is supposed to end with the conclusion that peace can be achieved only by creating a ruler with absolute power through the alienation of the people's rights to him. But in fact Hobbesian people cannot rationally alienate anything. Although they "lay down their rights" to the person selected as sovereign when they authorize him, they are prepared to, as it were, pick those rights up again if and when the sovereign's behavior threatens them. And if enough people refuse to obey him and even take up arms against him if they see him as threatening their lives, then he will be ousted as sovereign. The unofficial "real" contract argument in *Leviathan* assumes, and must assume, that when the people create a ruler, they do so in a way that makes it possible for them to rescind their grant of authority and power if they believe the ruler is not governing in a way that will advance their interests in security and protection. In a sense, therefore, the assumptions of Hobbes's social contract argument commit him to the view that an "absolute sovereign" is hired and fired by the people he governs.

But if the sovereign rules at the people's pleasure, then his authority and power are a function of their having loaned him power and authority for as long as doing so is advantageous to them. This is, in fact, the essence of an agency social contract! Hobbes sets out to defend the alienation argument, but his conception of who human beings are and why they want to create government forces him to accept that the creation and maintenance of authoritative rule is something that is always in the hands of those who are subject to it, making the ruler the implicit agent of the people, hired by them and capable of being fired by them if they object to his rule. This implicit agency agreement is the essence of Locke's argument in *Two Treatises of Government*. In a very real sense, Locke needed to look no farther than *Leviathan* for the outlines of his own political theory.

Locke

Many of us will breathe a sigh of relief that Hobbes's alienation social contract argument fails and seems to collapse into a variation of an agency view. It would be morally alarming if the correct theory of political authority established that our rulers were masters and we were their slaves! In contrast, the agency social contract theory is morally appealing, representing rulers as the people's "employees" and insisting that they remain under our control. Hence generations of readers of Locke's *Two Treatises of Government* have wanted to believe that something like the agency social contract theory he develops in that book succeeds, and the impact of its arguments on the development of existing democracies (such as the United States, Britain, and France) has been enormous. Indeed, Locke wrote it for an explicitly political purpose: Not only did he want to refute Filmer's divine rights theory, which had been used to buttress claims of monarchical supremacy over Parliament in the Britain of his day, but more urgently he believed he needed to provide philosophical license for the rebellious activities he and his friends had undertaken against the British rulers Charles II and James II, which culminated in 1688 in the overthrow of the latter in what the rebels called the Glorious Revolution. Hence it is no wonder that unlike *Leviathan*, the *Two Treatises* is clearly supportive of revolution, explicitly incorporating the idea of an agency contract between ruler and people in order to justify the "firing" of unsatisfactory rulers by dissatisfied subjects. But does this appealing version of the consent-based view of political authority actually work? As we shall see, this Lockean variation, albeit far more congenial to modern readers, is at least as problematic as the Hobbesian version.

Locke begins his argument by sketching the outlines of a state of nature that is, in certain respects, a nicer place than Hobbes's state of nature. Locke thinks human beings are naturally more other-regarding—and thus more cooperative—than Hobbes takes them to be. In particular, unlike Hobbes's people, Locke's people can be motivated in the state of nature not only by self-interest but also by God's "Fundamental Law of Nature," which directs them to preserve the life, health, and possessions of others as long as their own preservation will not be compromised by doing so:[22] "The *State of Nature* has a Law of Nature to govern it, which obliges every one: And Reason, which is that Law, teaches all Mankind, who will but consult it, that being all equal and independent, no one ought to harm another in his Life, Health, Liberty or Possessions."[23]

Note the way in which this moral law assumes the equality of all people in the state of nature. Like Hobbes, Locke insists that people are *politically* equal, so that despite differences in talents and abilities, none of them is so superior as to be master of any of the others. Hence as the passage above makes clear, no person in the state of nature can use or abuse anyone by claiming such natural mastery. Both God's revelation and the teachings of reason are supposed to show us that we are free and equal, so that each of us must respect the person and property of others in just the way that we respect the person and property of ourselves. So the Lockean people who obey this law are more respectful toward others than Hobbes's people, who recognize no such law. Locke also insists that the law binds all people in that natural state regardless of how they might feel toward others. And he argues that its binding nature would be recognized and the law obeyed by all rational persons in the state of nature.

Hence it seems that were everyone in the state of nature rational, it would be a state of peace. But warfare in Locke's state of nature is precipitated by irrational members of society who either harm others for their own gain ("In transgressing the Law of Nature, the Offender declares himself to live by another Rule, than that of reason and common Equity"[24]) or fail (because of personal bias) to interpret the fundamental law of nature correctly, especially when they use it to justify the punishment of offenders.[25] Moreover, note the way in which Locke's statement of the law allows and perhaps even requires (he is not clear which it is) that people prefer their own interests when those interests are in competition with those of others. This suggests that in an iterated PD Lockean people would behave no differently from Hobbesian people, insofar as cooperating in a situation where other people may fail to reciprocate could result in damage to oneself—a worry that, according to Locke's law, licenses a person to prefer himself and his own interests over others.

So even though Lockean people are capable of "moral" concerns, the problems of conflict and warfare would be serious in his state of nature, perhaps just as serious as in Hobbes's natural state. Accordingly, Locke says that we need a state to secure peace, and he details three problems, or (as he calls them) "inconveniences," that the state would solve:

> *First*, There wants an *establish'd*, settled, known *Law*, received and allowed by common consent to be the Standard of Right and Wrong, and the common measure to decide all Controversies between them. . . .
>
> *Secondly*, In the State of Nature there wants a *known and indifferent Judge*, with Authority to determine all differences according to the established Law. . . .
>
> *Thirdly*, In the state of Nature there often wants *Power* to back and support the Sentence when right, and to *give* it due *Execution*. . . . [26]

But because Locke thinks people have the psychological capacity to be more other-regarding than Hobbesian people, Locke believes the political remedy for this conflict needn't be, and shouldn't be, as extreme as

Hobbes's remedy, insofar as he believes the creation of a ruler with clear limits on his authority and power is both possible and vastly preferable to the creation of an absolute sovereign.

The most important of these limits is the threat of rebellion unless the ruler's behavior is consistent with the terms that people set when they invest him with power. That investiture is importantly different from the authorization process that Hobbes (in his "official" alienation argument) describes. Like Hobbes, Locke makes individual consent the source of all political authority: "Men being, as has been said, by Nature, all free, equal and independent, no one can be put out of this Estate, and subjected to the Political Power of another, without his own *Consent*."[27] That is, because there is no natural subordination of some to others, the subordination of free human beings has to come about because they *consent* to it. And Locke says they consent to it via a two-stage process. First, they enter into an agreement with other people in the state of nature to create a civil (or political) society: "The only way whereby any one devests himself of his Natural Liberty, and *puts on the bonds of Civil Society* is by agreeing with other Men to joyn and unite into a Community, for their comfortable, safe, and peaceable living one amongst another, in a secure Enjoyment of their Properties, and a greater Security against any that are not of it."[28]

When they create this civil society, they become one body "with a Power to Act as one Body, which is only by the will and determination of the *majority*."[29] Locke insists that it is critical that people understand themselves to be "bound by that consent to be concluded by the majority,"[30] else they will not really be part of a unified community capable of taking action as a unified body.

Once such a community has been formed, it is this community that determines the form of government using majority rule and that invests with political authority any ruler(s) whom they select to govern them. As Locke explains in chapter 10 of the Second Treatise, if the majority decide to make, judge, and execute the law of nature themselves, they have chosen a democracy. If they invest these powers in the hands of a few people, they have chosen an oligarchy. And if they invest these powers in one person, they have chosen a monarchy. So there is a second agreement in Locke's story of the creation of government, one in which the majority decide on behalf of the community what form of government will be created and who will rule.

Finally, there is a third agreement that takes place between the majority and the rulers they have selected, in which those rulers are hired as "political authorities" for as long as they satisfy certain conditions of just and effective rule. It is in this contract that political authority is passed on to the ruler. Each individual starts out, in a state of nature, with political authority over himself. That is, each person has the authority and power to guide his actions by interpreting what the law of nature requires, judging if others have satisfied these requirements, and punishing those perceived to have violated it. But as we've discussed, when people in the natural state perform these tasks independently, their differing understandings of what the law of nature says can bring them into conflict with one another concerning what the law requires, how others should be judged to have satisfied it, and how much punishment someone should receive who is thought to have broken it. A state is created when a ruler is handed each person's right to interpret, judge, and punish according to the law of nature.

So a ruler is supposed to rule *using the rights of those whom he rules.* But a ruler gets those rights *not* from the individuals directly but from the political society they form in the first contract. When the people contract to create such a civil society, these rights are handed over to the society at large, and it is the society—via the will of the majority—that hands over these rights to the ruler via an agency contract "hiring" him or her to use these rights to govern the society to people's mutual advantage. Hence there is no agency contract between any individual subject and the ruler; instead, the ruler is hired and fired *by the civil society.* And Locke insists that the ruler is the "trustee" or "deputy" of this society, so that they have the right to rebel against someone they judge to be failing as an effective trustee:

> Here, 'tis like, the common Question will be made, *Who shall be Judge* whether the Prince or Legislative act contrary to their Trust? . . . To this I reply, *The People shall be Judge;* for who shall be *Judge* whether his Trustee or Deputy acts well, and according to the Trust reposed in him, but he who deputes him, and must, by having deputed him have still a Power to discard him, when he fails in his Trust? If this be reasonable in the Cases of private Men, why should it be otherwise in that of the greatest moment; where the Welfare of Millions is concerned, and also where the evil, if not prevented, is greater, and the Redress very difficult, dear and dangerous?[31]

Since political authority and power are the people's to give, Locke insists that they are the people's to take back as they see fit. As discussed above, this idea is already present, albeit covertly, in Hobbes's *Leviathan.* But unlike Hobbes, Locke *wants* to write a "rebel's catechism," and his book has been used as such for hundreds of years.

Problems with Locke's Agency Social Contract Argument

Modern readers of the *Two Treatises* generally find its political conclusions plausible. But that plausibility tends to blind them, in my view, to the highly implausible nature of Locke's social contract argument for those conclusions. This section reviews five problems with Locke's argument, the first two of which may not be fatal to Locke's overall view if the argument is carefully reformulated so as to avoid them, but the rest of which threaten the coherence of the argument itself. Since Locke's contract argument is often taken to be the best way of formulating a consent-based theory of political authority, these problems cast doubt on the plausibility of basing authority on the people's consent.

The Alienation Relationship Between Civil Society and the Individual

The first problem is perhaps hard to notice given the nature of Locke's emphasis on rebellion. The modern reader delights in Locke's insistence on the ruler as a trustee or deputy but tends to neglect his remarks about the deputizing entity. That entity is, as we've seen, a *group*—in particular, the civil society. As we've noted, the relationship between the civil society and the ruler is an agency relationship. But what is the individual's relationship to his civil society?

Locke's remarks appear to indicate that it is *not* an agency relationship. After stressing in chapter 19 the way in which every ruler is a deputy of the civil society he governs, Locke goes on to insist that each individual is *permanently* bound to his or her civil society in a way that precludes rebellion against *it*: "The *Power that every individual gave the Society*, when he entered into it, can never revert to the Individuals again, as long as the Society lasts, but will always remain in the Community; because without this, there can be no Community, no Commonwealth, which is contrary to the original Agreement."[32]

And he also says, "Men give up all their Natural Power to the Society which they enter into."[33] So it seems that the first agreement by which people fashion civil society involves their *alienating* their right to govern themselves to the society they create, so that none of them can ever take back those rights for as long as the society lasts.

Locke makes this same point in chapter 8, where he describes how we must understand the nature of the consent that makes us members of a political society. Unlike Socrates, Locke does not think that what he calls "tacit consent," understood as the mere enjoyment of benefits in a political society, is sufficient to make one a "member" of it. While it is sufficient to obligate one to obey the laws of that society, this obligation is no different from the one that any traveler has to respect the laws of the land he visits:

> Submitting to the Laws of any Country, living quietly, and enjoying the Priviledges and Protection under them, *makes not a Man a Member of that Society:* This is only a local Protection and Homage due to, and from all those, who, not being in a state of War, come within the Territories belonging to any Gov-

ernment, to all parts whereof the force of its Law extends. But this no more *makes a Man a Member of that Society,* a perpetual Subject of that Commonwealth, than it would make a Man a Subject to another in whose Family he found it convenient to abide for some time; though, whilst he continued in it, he were obliged to comply with the Laws, and submit to the Government he found there. And thus we see, that *Foreigners,* by living all their Lives under another Government, and enjoying the Priviledges and Protection of it, though they are bound, even in Conscience, to submit to its Administration, as far forth as any Denison; yet do not thereby come to be *Subjects or Members of that Commonwealth.*[34]

Enjoying benefits merely obliges one to obey the laws that make those benefits possible; it is not sufficient to *bind* one to the political society that is in effect the body that hires and fires ruler(s).

So how does one become a member of the civil society? Locke explains: "Nothing can make any man [a subject or member of a commonwealth] but his actually entering into it by positive Engagement, and express Promise and Compact."[35] And that "express Promise" binds one permanently to the civil society as long as that society remains in existence. Whereas someone who has only given tacit consent "is at liberty to go and agree with others" to create a civil society elsewhere, someone who has consented "by actual Agreement and any *express* Declaration" to be a member of a civil society "is perpetually and indispensably obliged to be and remain unalterably a Subject to it, and can never be again in the liberty of the state of Nature; unless by an Calamity, the Government, he was under, comes to be dissolved; or else by some publick Act cuts him off from being any longer a Member of it."[36]

But does this mean that the same alienation relationship Hobbes said prevailed between the sovereign and his subjects exists, in Locke's theory, between the civil society and the subjects? Locke certainly suggests as much in this passage, which should surprise the reader, because just as the alienation relationship between the ruler and each individual is problematic in Hobbes's argument, the same relationship between civil society and each individual would be problematic in Locke's argument.

There are a number of reasons to object to the idea of this relationship. One difficulty is that such a relationship precludes the legitimacy of emigration at any cost. But such emigration may be not only desirable for certain individuals but also required for them *by Locke's fundamental law of nature* if the civil society approves of governmental policies that are injurious to them. So Locke's interest in binding people so severely to their civil society seems morally misguided. Indeed, given the premises of his argument, I don't even see how he can consistently argue for it: Just as Hobbes's psychological views of human nature are such that he cannot insist that people not reclaim their right to govern themselves if obeying their ruler's commands puts them at risk, so, too, Locke's premisses preclude him from insisting that people cannot reclaim the right to govern themselves if the majority in their political society approve governments whose policies put them at risk. Locke appreciates this point when he insists on the agency relationship between political society and the ruler; yet, curiously, he misses the same point when reflecting on the relationship between civil society and the individual. However, the premisses of his argument commit him to an agency rather than an alienation relationship between individuals and their political society.

Another problem generated by a notion of membership that precludes exit is that it removes the leverage that the threat of exit provides for reforming political society. Contrast Plato's view in the *Crito:* Plato takes it for granted that one way the state knows that it is benefiting people is that they remain within its jurisdiction. Massive emigration, which Plato would permit, would be an indication that the political society was failing and an impetus for reform. Locke seems to assume that the only aspect of a society that needs reform is the government itself, but (as Plato seemed to appreciate) the political society itself can "go bad," in which case the right of exit is not only valuable as a protection for the individual but also as a means of reforming the society being spurned.

Nonetheless, just as Hobbes could not consistently sustain an alienation relationship between the sovereign and the people in his argument in *Leviathan,* so Locke cannot consistently sustain that relationship between individuals and civil society in the Second Treatise—and Locke seems to know it. He writes in chapter 9:

> But though Men when they enter into Society, give up the Equality, Liberty, and Executive Power they had in the State of Nature, into the hands of the Society, to be so far disposed of by the Legislative, as the good of the Society shall require; yet it being only with an intention in every one the better to preserve himself his Liberty and Property; (For no rational Creature can be supposed to change his condition with an intention to be worse) the power of the Society, or *Legislative* constituted by them, *can never be suppos'd to extend farther than the common good;* but is obliged to secure every ones Property.[37]

The implication of this passage is that each individual retains the right to refuse to be obligated not only to the legislative body in the society but also to the society itself, if either the society or the legislature behaves in a way that compromises or endangers his person or property. This passage therefore suggests Locke was aware that consistent with his premisses, he needed to construct his conception of membership in the society so as explicitly to build in an agency relationship between each individual and the political society: In this relationship the subjects lend to the society but do not give up their rights to govern themselves, which the society (through the determination of the majority) grants in a further agency contract to the ruler. But just as the society can recall this loan to the ruler if he fails to act appropriately as its agent, Locke must admit that each individual has the right to recall her loan to the political society if that society (in her view) fails to live up to its side of the bargain.

So why shouldn't we charitably reinterpret Locke as advocating agency relationships both between the individual and the society and between the society and government?[38] Alas, doing so is not quite as easy as it looks. We should reflect briefly on why Locke should have made the "mistake" of suggesting that subjects alienate their rights to the political society: Consider that Locke desires to reassure his readers that the recognition of a political right to rebellion is not tantamount to permitting or justifying political chaos. Hence he says that even if we recognize a right to change rulers, *a political society can persist* through the change in a way that will allow for peaceful, nonchaotic transfers of power when a government "goes bad." Moreover, this political society persists because each member of the regime regards himself as bound to it, come what may. Consider what Locke says in chapter 8 of the Second Treatise:

> And thus every Man, by consenting with others to make one Body Politic under one Government, puts himself under an Obligation to every one of that Society, to submit to the determination of the *majority*, and to be concluded by it; or else this *original Compact*, whereby he with others incorporates into *one Society*, would signifie nothing, and be no Compact, if he be left free, and under no other ties, than he was in before in the State of Nature. For what appearance would there be of any Compact? What new Engagement if he were no farther tied by any Decrees of the Society, than he himself thought fit, and did actually consent to? This would be still as great a liberty, as he himself had before his Compact, or any one else in the State of Nature hath, who may submit himself and consent to any acts of it he thinks fit.[39]

Locke is insisting here that civil society can work only if a person is genuinely *bound* to the determination of the civil society that grants rulers authority.[40] In particular, he argues (in section 96) that each person has to agree to be obliged by the decision of the majority as to who will rule, for otherwise those who supported losing minority candidates have the potential to wreak havoc in the community if they refuse to accept that their candidate has lost to a rival candidate. This "willingness to lose" is basic to the stability of a regime (we will discuss this point further in Chapter 6, in the section on secession), and Locke seems to think that the only way to secure this willingness is to require of those who enter civil society that they bind themselves so thoroughly to the majority in the civil society that they will regard themselves as bound by its determination of who shall be ruler no matter what their private preferences might be.

Nonetheless, the premises of his argument demand that he cannot bind them so thoroughly to the majority that he makes it impossible for them to withdraw their consent to it if they endorse a government that is genuinely dangerous to their preservation and well-being. A successful reformulation of Locke's argument must secure each subject's obligation to the majority's determination in the political society, even while maintaining an agency relationship between each subject and the political society. This is, I would suggest, no easy task, although on its face it is not impossible.

Property and Authority

The second problem with Locke's argument concerns the relationship between his consent-based conception of political authority and the territory governed by that authority. Consider that, on Locke's view, a person's property is under the control of a political authority *only through the fact of her consent to that authority.* As we shall discuss more fully in Chapter 5, Locke argues for the view that God's laws enable people to have property rights in a state of nature, so that property is something that is conceptually prior to political society. One of his principal objectives in making this argument is to establish that a ruler has authority over property only to the extent that he is granted that authority via the consent of the subjects whose property it is. Because the ruler is not the source of property rights in a society, he cannot claim to be the ultimate master of everyone's possessions (as Hobbes wanted to argue) by virtue of being the creator of everyone's entitlements. One implication of this position is that taxes on property cannot be raised, according to Locke, except with the consent of the majority of the people: "For if any one shall claim a *Power to lay* and levy *Taxes* on the People, by his own Authority, and without such consent of the People, he thereby invades the *Fundamental Law of Property*, and subverts the end of Government. For what property have I in that which another may by right take, when he pleases himself?"[41]

This passage raises two issues. The first connects with the problem we have already discussed above: If we alienate our right to govern ourselves to the political society, and the majority of that society sanctions a form of taxation that we believe to be very abusive and dangerous to us, then since Locke says we do not have the right to exit that society, hasn't he made our property subject to the potentially dangerous caprice of the majority? And isn't that just as potentially damaging to our interests as subjecting our property to the dangerous caprice of a ruler?

Second, even if the Lockean argument can be revised so as to somehow protect us from the caprices of the majority as well as the rulers, doesn't Locke's position on property show that a ruler controls property only if a person has expressly consented to become a member of the society? This means that if someone fails to consent to the political society at all, then even if she lived amid those who had expressly consented to it, her property would not be a part of the ruler's territory. And if she merely tacitly consented to this society and its ruler, it would seem her property would not be a permanent part of the ruler's territory and would remain under the government's authority only for as long as she continued to consent tacitly to it. And yet Locke describes the government as having "a direct Jurisdiction only over the Land," so that someone who merely tacitly consents to it, although free to leave himself, must leave behind his land insofar as it is under that government's authority.[42] Now this is a commonsensical thing for Locke to say, and yet this commonsense idea does not fit with his consent-based justification of authority. That justification puts land (and any other possession) under the control of a ruler only if a person consents to that rule. If he doesn't consent or, in the case of giving mere tacit consent, ceases to give it, then why shouldn't he be free to exit *with his land* and all his other possessions?

Robert Nozick, a twentieth-century philosopher attracted to Lockean ideas, actually experiments with the idea of a purely consent-based understanding of the extent of political authority: It could result, he admits, in a kind of patchwork political society, with territorial gaps resulting from some people's decision either not to join it or secede from it. The first part of Nozick's book *Anarchy, State and Utopia* is in part an exploration of whether such a conception of political society makes sense. I cannot detail Nozick's discussion here, but I suspect most readers will probably already have decided that it does not make sense! Our conception of political societies is deeply tied to the idea that, as Locke puts it, government has "direct jurisdiction" over land. And yet, remarkably, that idea seems to conflict with a consent-based justification of political authority as Locke has formulated it. Any plausible development of the consent-based idea must figure out a way of accommodating this direct jurisdiction over land and not try to explain it as deriving indirectly from the landowner's consent to government, or otherwise a patchwork state, which is so impractical as to be impossible, will appear to be the only legitimate state as long as anyone refuses to consent to be ruled by the state that their neighbors accept. This alternative consent theory will inevitably involve a very different conception of property rights (which will likely have to represent those rights as created by and dependent upon the state's laws rather than understood to be prior to them).

Stability and the Paradox of Being Governed

The third problem with Locke's argument cuts to the heart of the viability of any agency social contract view. Consider that one reason Hobbes tried to avoid espousing an agency relationship between the ruler and the people was because he thought that any such relationship would be unstable and inevitably degenerate into civil war. Ironically, as we saw earlier, Hobbes's conservative critics, such as Bramhall and Filmer, who were just as opposed to the idea of this relationship, opposed the political argument in *Leviathan* on the basis of what they took to be the agency implications of *Hobbes's* argument! We who approve of the Lockean idea that such an agency relationship exists between ruler and people ought to be able to allay these concerns if that idea is genuinely sound and thereby show that if rulers are empowered and authorized by the people whom they govern, the political society will nonetheless be stable.

Yet this is remarkably difficult to do. If there is such an agency relationship between ruler and people, how does it make sense to consider the people "ruled"? And if the people who are being "ruled" are themselves in charge of their rulers, how can their political society last? If babysitters are hired to supervise a bunch of unruly children and in reality the babysitters turn out to *be* the unruly children, the supervision is useless. And similarly, if the reason for creating a political institution is that people cannot govern themselves satisfactorily and the political regime that is created is one in which the people rule, the exercise appears useless. Moreover, the problem is exacerbated if there is an agency relationship between each individual and the political society, because then it would seem that the political society cannot hope to keep its noncompliant members in line if they insist that both the government and the majority of the society who supports it are failing to secure effectively the preservation of person and property.

In our time the economist and political theorist James Buchanan, whose own contractarian analysis of the state gives the people the last word in government, calls the problem of explaining how the people can be both the agent of their ruler and yet subject to him (and the political society authorizing him) "the paradox of sovereignty":

> Man's universal thirst for freedom is a fact of history, and his ubiquitous reluctance to "be governed" insures that his putative masters, who are also men, face never-ending threats of rebellion against and disobedience to any rules that attempt to direct and order individual behavior.[43]

But the idea that each of us lives in a political regime under a master whom the people believe they are both able and right to master themselves when he gets out of line is, for seventeenth-century political conservatives, not just a benign paradox but straightforward inconsistency. How, they ask, can we conceive of the state as one in which people have ultimate control over their rulers when the reason this argument gives for creating and maintaining the state is that the *people* need to be controlled?

We who live in regimes that accept the idea that there is an agency relationship between the people and the ruler dismiss the charges of inconsistency—without, however, understanding why we are justified in doing so or indeed why these regimes work despite their paradoxical character. That those of us who are lucky enough to live in stable democratic societies have so little to say to defend our regimes' stability shows that we don't yet understand how they work, why they cohere so well, and why they are capable of being highly stable. Those of us who wish to commend the agency aspect of Locke's social contract argument have work to do if we wish to defend the stability of the agency relationship.

Is the Appeal to a Social Contract Inconsistent?

A fourth problem with a Lockean-style contract argument that also challenges its coherence has to do with the argument's reliance on the idea of a contract. Consider that on this argument one important reason we need government is that people in a state of nature would be unable to keep contracts, because keeping contracts involves solving a prisoner's dilemma, and in a state of nature people are generally unable to solve either single-play PDs or iterated PDs. But if people in a state of nature can't keep ordinary contracts because they can't solve PD games, how can they keep the contract to create government? We can't very well explain the creation of government by appealing to a contract, if we have already explained that a central reason governments are needed is that people can't keep contracts! Such inconsistency is a powerful reason to rethink the whole contractarian approach to political authority.

Do People Actually Consent to Political Authority?

The fifth problem is the most serious, insofar as it challenges the way in which the argument derives authority from individual consent. The philosopher most famous for questioning the success of the contractarian derivation of authority from consent is the eighteenth-century Scottish philosopher David Hume (1711–1776). A social contract argument says that in the same way my doctor has authority to take out my appendix if we have contractually agreed that she should do so, my state has authority to dictate how I should behave in certain areas if we have contractually agreed that it should do so. Both the patient and the subject in these contracts confer authority to the doctor or the state in exchange for certain services. So on such a view the state has authority over me only if I have given it that authority. And just when, asks Hume, have most of the world's population undertaken this contractual obligation? People, he notes, generally obey the state because they think they are "born to it," not because they have promised to do so. As Hume wryly observes:

> Were you to ask the far greatest part of the nation, whether they had ever consented to the authority of their rulers, or promis'd to obey them, they wou'd be inclin'd to think very strangely of you; and wou'd certainly reply, that the affair depended not on their consent, but that they were born to such obedience.[44]

Proponents of contract arguments have defended their argument against Hume's criticisms by insisting that it isn't meant as a *history* of the creation of states but only as an account of the nature of political authority. Hence any objection to the effect that the argument is historically inaccurate is beside the point.

But so stated, this defense doesn't work. Locke's contract argument presumes that states are both explained and justified by the way they are created by the people who are subject to them. Hence if the argument is right, it must be possible to develop a historically accurate account of how states come into existence by the people's consenting activity (and indeed Locke himself tries to give such a history in sections 100–122 of the Second Treatise). If it turns out that throughout history states have been created in ways that have not involved subjects' consent and people have taken themselves to be subject to political authority for reasons other than that they have consented to such authority, then the consent that the contract argument requires in order to explain and legitimate that authority has simply not occurred—and the contract argument would have failed to locate the source of political authority.

Now we see why the historical implausibility of the contract argument is so worrisome. The contract tradition has been persistently ridiculed for failing to provide evidence that anything like the kind of explicit agreement analogous to the agreement that authorizes my doctor to treat me has ever occurred in a political context. And appealing to consent when it simply hasn't occurred fails to explain the fact of political authority.

In response supporters of the contractarian methodology have often insisted that the consent and the contracts in their arguments are only "hypothetical" occurrences and not historical events: The contract theorist is, on this view, using the contract talk not to give any dubious history lessons but merely to justify the state in terms of what people *could agree to* in an equal and impartial setting. Insofar as a state is the sort of institution that we believe people could have agreed to, then it is authoritative; otherwise it is not.

But one modern philosopher, Ronald Dworkin, has the appropriate rejoinder: "A hypothetical contract is not simply a pale form of an actual contract; it is no contract at all."[45] No one takes it that any of us is obliged by make-believe contracts but only by real ones. Hence whatever excellent use a hypothetical contract has in helping to illuminate the nature of justice (and we discuss such uses in Chapter 5), a contract that was never really made cannot explain real authority. To paraphrase movie mogul Samuel Goldwyn, hypothetical consent is not worth the paper it's not written on.[46]

Moreover, an appeal to hypothetical consent may be nothing more than covert reliance on a Platonic conception of political authority. Consider that if I say that a government is authoritative over you because you would have consented to it in ideal conditions, I'm implicitly saying that your ideal, hypothetical consent is deserved by virtue of the merits of this government. This sort of appeal therefore bases our political obligation to an authoritative political regime not on actual consent but on whether that regime is just or in some way good or desirable on moral grounds.[47] It must be these moral grounds that deliver the regime's authority, and talking about the consent any of us *would* give it in ideal conditions is simply a way of eliciting the judgment that the regime is sufficiently morally satisfactory to be considered authoritative. So authority is being derived from the morality of the regime, which in turn explains why it would be consented to by the right people; in contrast, a genuine consent-based theory makes the authority derive from the real consent itself—perhaps even in situations where the regime consented to cannot survive moral scrutiny. (So a real consent theory has to hold it out as possible that a political regime has authority even in situations where people in ideal circumstances would *not* consent to it, because in this world real people have consented to it.)

So what about the notion of tacit consent? Perhaps we can understand this form of consent as the source of political authority and successfully locate it in the historical actions of real people. If this is possible, then the consenting behavior of people could be taken, contra Hume, as the source of the political authorities throughout history after all.

However, it is difficult to know how to understand the notion of tacit consent such that it is both successful in authorizing someone to have the kind of control over human beings that governments are supposed to have and also present in history. Suppose, for example, that tacit consent is understood to be granted (as Plato suggests) when one remains in a society and enjoys its benefits. Yet the mere acceptance and enjoyment of benefits is usually not taken to obligate us in any way to our benefactor if we have not previously agreed to give that obligation in exchange for those benefits (it certainly wouldn't do so normally in a court of law— acceptance of benefits rarely if ever counts as making a promise).[48] And as Locke notes, it is hard to see how acceptance of benefits makes us *members* of the state—it certainly doesn't oblige any foreign traveler who enjoys the benefits of the state while she is here. So it seems we must have a beefier conception of consent to explain the fact of political authority. But the more we interpret consent as explicitly made or explicitly promisorial, the more difficult it becomes to argue that all or even most citizens of regimes around the world have ever given it.

I take this to be an extremely serious problem with the social contract argument's attempt to develop a consent-based theory of political authority, which will have to be resolved if the argument is to be plausible. I tackle this problem at some length in the next chapter. Suffice it to say here that unless a consent-based theory can develop a way of formulating a notion of consent that is both authority-giving and historically plausible, this approach to political authority is just not viable.

In view of these problems, it is fair to say that despite the enormous popularity of Lockean contract theory since publication of the *Two Treatises of Government*, his social contract argument is an unsatisfactory development of the idea that the political authority of a ruler is derived from the consent of those people who are subject to him. Can we come up with a better development of that idea? We had better be able to do so if we want to answer the anarchist. In this and the previous chapter, we have seen every theory of political authority fail. Unless we can come up with a new, successful account of political authority, anarchism is the only justifiable position with respect to the state. In the next chapter, I will attempt to generate such a theory, which will be a type of consent-based view, using tools of contemporary social science.

Further Reading

The development of social contract ideas in late medieval and early modern times is pursued in Quentin Skinner, *The Foundations of Modern Political Thought*. Hobbes scholarship has proliferated in recent years; for discussions of Hobbes's theory that relate it to contemporary political thought, see David Gauthier, *The Logic of Leviathan;* Gregory Kavka, *Hobbesian Moral and Political Theory;* and Jean Hampton, *Hobbes and the Social Contract Tradition.* Richard Tuck gives a useful summary of Hobbes's ideas, plus interesting biographical information, in *Hobbes.* For a discussion of Locke's political theory, see John Dunn, *The Political Thought of John Locke;* and James Tully, *An Approach to Political Philosophy: Locke in Context.* There is a sustained discussion of the role and nature of consent in a Lockean contract theory in A. John Simmons, *On the Edge of Anarchy: Locke, Consent and the Limits of Society.* For trenchant criticisms of contractarian ideas, see David Hume, "Of the Original Contract," in *David Hume: Essays; Moral, Political and Literary,* ed. Eugene E. Miller.

Notes

1. At least those were his official crimes; in reality it appears that many in the society were threatened by what they perceived to be the subversive effects of Socrates' philosophizing and wished him silenced. Note that this tragedy occurred while Athens was democratically ruled, which is one likely reason Plato was never an enthusiastic supporter of democracy.

2. From the *Digest* of Justinian, I, 4, I, in John B. Morall, *Political Thought in Medieval Times* (London: Hutchinson, 1971), p. 46.

3. For an excellent discussion of the Renaissance and Reformation roots of early modern social contract arguments, see Quentin Skinner, *The Foundations of Modern Political Thought*, 2 vols. (Cambridge: Cambridge University Press, 1978).

4. This book was preceded by two others in which the major lines of the social contract argument of *Leviathan* were prefigured: *The Elements of Law: Natural and Politic*, ed. Ferdinand Tönnies (Cambridge: Cambridge University Press, 1928), originally published in 1640, and *De Cive*, originally published in 1642, in *Man and Citizen*, ed. Bernard Gert (Atlantic Highlands, N.J.: Humanities Press, 1968).

5. See *Leviathan*, ed. Richard Tuck (Cambridge: Cambridge University Press, 1991), chap. 13, par. 9, p. 62 (original edition).

6. This phrase occurs in *De Cive*, chap. 8, sec. 1.

7. Hobbes, *Leviathan*, chap. 13, pars. 1 and 2, p. 60.

8. See his discussion of this point in ibid., chap. 20.

9. Ibid., chap. 13, pars. 6 and 7, pp. 61–62.

10. The game was invented by Merrill Flood and Melvin Dresher; see Flood, "Some Experimental Games," *Management Science* 5 (October 1958): 5–26. It was given its name by A. W. Tucker.

11. This discussion appears in a passage of *Leviathan* known as the "Answer to the Fool" (chap. 15, pars. 4–5, pp. 72–73). I discuss this passage at length in Jean Hampton, *Hobbes and the Social Contract Tradition* (Cambridge: Cambridge University Press, 1986), chap. 2.

12. See Hampton, *Hobbes and the Social Contract Tradition*, chaps. 2 and 3.

13. See *Leviathan*, chap. 15, par. 41, p. 80.

14. Ibid., par. 36, p. 79.

15. In *Hobbes and the Social Contract Tradition*, pp. 105–107, I develop an argument on Hobbes's behalf to support this hypothesis.

16. Hobbes discusses the causes of the dissolution of the commonwealth in chap. 29 of *Leviathan*, but his detailed criticisms of the idea of a contract between ruler and people are in chap. 18, par. 4, pp. 89–90.

17. Ibid., chap. 17, par. 13, p. 87.

18. Ibid., chap. 21, par. 21, p. 114. See also *De Cive*, "English Works" ii, 6, pp. 74–75.

19. For example, see *Leviathan*, chap. 21, par. 10, p. 111.

20. John Bramhall (bishop of Derry and later of Armagh), "The Catching of Leviathan or the Great Whale," appendix to *Castigations of Mr. Hobbes . . . Concerning Liberty and Universal Necessity*. Printed by E. T. for John Crooke, at the sign of the ship in Paul's churchyard, 1658.

21. Ibid., p. 515. See Hampton, *Hobbes and the Social Contract Tradition*, pp. 199–200, for a discussion of the passages in *Leviathan* that prompted Bramhall to

make this remark. In that work I also discuss the way in which rebellion is nonetheless difficult because it poses a collective action problem for the disgruntled subjects. I discuss many of these themes in Chapter 3 of this book.

22. See Locke's *Two Treatises of Government,* ed. Peter Laslett (Cambridge: Cambridge University Press, 1988), Second Treatise, chap. 2, sec. 6, p. 271.

23. Ibid.

24. Ibid., sec. 8, p. 272.

25. Ibid., sec. 13, pp. 275–276.

26. Ibid., chap. 9, secs. 124, 125, 126; p. 351.

27. Ibid., sec. 95, p. 330.

28. Ibid., chap. 8, sec. 95, pp. 330–331.

29. Ibid., sec. 96, p. 331.

30. Ibid., p. 332.

31. Ibid., chap. 19, sec. 240, pp. 426–427.

32. Ibid., sec. 243, pp. 427–428.

33. Ibid., chap. 11, sec. 136, p. 359.

34. Ibid., chap. 8, sec. 122, p. 349.

35. Ibid.

36. Ibid., sec. 121, p. 349.

37. Ibid., chap. 9, sec. 131, p. 353.

38. This is the interpretation that A. John Simmons advocates in *On the Edge of Anarchy: Locke, Consent, and the Limits of Society* (Princeton: Princeton University Press, 1993); see chap. 3, esp. pp. 65 ff.

39. Locke, *Two Treatises,* chap. 8, sec. 97, p. 332.

40. John Dunn has an interesting discussion of this appeal to the majority's will in his *Political Thought of John Locke* (Cambridge: Cambridge University Press, 1969), pp. 129–135. Dunn stresses (and I agree) that this appeal was not meant to be a recommendation for the internal political organization of the society but rather is part of his analysis of the concept of political legitimacy.

41. Locke, *Two Treatises,* chap. 11, sec. 140, p. 362.

42. See ibid., chap. 8, sec. 121, p. 349.

43. James Buchanan, *The Limits of Liberty* (Chicago: University of Chicago Press, 1975), p. 92.

44. David Hume, *A Treatise of Human Nature,* ed. L. A. Selby-Bigge, rev. P. H. Nidditch (Oxford: Clarendon Press, 1978), book III, part ii, sec. viii, p. 548.

45. Ronald Dworkin, "The Original Contract," in Norman Daniels, ed., *Reading Rawls* (New York: Basic Books, 1974), p. 17.

46. Popular legend has it that Goldwyn's original remark was, "A verbal contract isn't worth the paper it's written on." The paraphrase I give is often attributed to Robert Nozick.

47. See Simmons, *On the Edge of Anarchy,* p. 78.

48. To quote Nozick, "The fact that we partially are 'social products' in that we benefit from current patterns and forms created by the multitudinous actions of a long string of long forgotten people . . . does not create in us a floating debt which the current society can collect and use as it will." From *Anarchy, State and Utopia* (New York: Basic Books, 1974), p. 95.

3

Consent and Democracy

If Hobbes's and Locke's social contract arguments fail to develop a consent-based theory of political authority, can we do better by theorizing about these questions ourselves? This chapter attempts to do just that, drawing on ideas that Hobbes, Locke, and Aristotle suggest and using the tools of modern social science to help develop a new and better kind of consent-based theory.

The theory I propose distinguishes among three kinds of power structures that can exist in a territory: mastery, political authority, and morally legitimate political authority (the third being a species of the second). As I explain in this chapter, anarchists tend to confuse the first two, whereas consent theorists tend to confuse the second two. To show that the anarchist is wrong to think that political power is simply a form of coercion, we need to explain how political authority is different from systems of mastery. But de facto political authority can be exercised in all sorts of unjust and morally unacceptable ways; so there is a difference between de facto political authority and political authority that is just and morally legitimate. Political authority exists even if it is bad or unjust; an unjust state is still a *state*. And yet there is a difference between unjust states and systems of mere mastery. There is also a difference between an unjust state and a just state, necessitating a distinction between mere political authority and *just* political authority. By making these three distinctions, we will be in a position to offer an explanation of what political authority is and how it is connected to the notion of the subjects' consent.

In order to pursue the nature of a morally legitimate political authority, we must understand what justice is and thus what a just exercise of political authority is like. The second half of this book is devoted to analyzing and exploring different philosophical conceptions of justice, so we reserve for later chapters a discussion of the nature of a just political authority. Our goal in this chapter is to get an analysis of political authority, to which a theory of justice can be appended to achieve a fully justified conception of the state.

The plan of this chapter is as follows: First, I present the nature of the problems facing people in any "state of nature" where there is no political authority. Second, I discuss how political authority, if it existed, would provide a remedy for these problems, thereby showing what political authority is. Third, I develop a model explaining how political authority is created. This model is not meant to be a detailed historical account of actual state creation: Histories are complicated, messy, and full of irrelevant contingencies. A model of state creation allows us to cut through the historical undergrowth and see the deep structure of state generation underlying all histories of state formation. The model I develop is called the *convention model of the state*, and it allows us to distinguish between a state holding political authority and a system of mere mastery holding coercive power but no authority to command. In the end I argue that creating a state amounts to creating a certain kind of authoritative structure that holds the right to command and powers necessary to enforce those commands. Fourth, I examine the kind of "consent" that is present in this model and discuss the way in which it can be used to explain why rulers in a genuine state command with authority while tyrants in a system of mastery hold power but no authority. Finally, I show how this analysis illuminates the structure of modern democracies and the way they are guided by "the rule of law."

A note of warning: this chapter is by far the hardest in the book, and some readers may find it a little daunting. If so, they can skip to the concluding summary to get the gist of its contents and continue with Chapter 4. However, for the hardier or more curious or more philosophically experienced reader, this chapter attempts to provide a new solution to an old problem using ideas drawn from recent work in philosophy of law, economics, and game theory. For these readers, I hope it will be worth the work.

Why Do We Need a State?

The claim that the state is desirable to all is a constant feature of consent theories, which paint life without government in a "state of nature" as problem-ridden, so that people decide the state is a remedy (either the best or the only remedy) for these problems. In Chapter 2 we reviewed some of these problems. For example, there is the single-play prisoner's dilemma, in which the rational action for every participant is noncooperation. There is also the iterated prisoner's dilemma, in which it is rational for all parties to cooperate, but only if each can be assured of the cooperation of the other—an assurance that would be extremely difficult to get in a state of nature. There are also what are called coordination games: In a coordination game there is at least one coordination equilibrium, defined as an outcome where the combination of the players' actions is such that no one would be better off if any one player, either himself or another, acted differently.[1] Coordination games frequently have no conflict in them; for example, you would be in a coordination game if you and your friend became separated while visiting Disneyland, and both of you had to figure out where to go to meet up with one another. In a state of nature, such games might exist when two people needed help from one another but had no way to achieve the coordination necessary to gain that help. There are also coordination games that include some conflict: For example, a "battle-of-the-sexes" game is a coordination game in which each player prefers a different coordination equilibrium, so that achieving any of them becomes more difficult. (The name comes from a famous example by R. Duncan Luce and Howard Raiffa of a husband and wife who each prefer different evening activities—he prefers a prizefight, she a ballet—but who would also rather go with the other to his or her preferred evening activity than to go to his or her own favorite alone.[2]) To illustrate this kind of game, suppose you and I wanted to achieve coordination on which side of the road to drive on, where you preferred the right side and I preferred the left side. Both of us would be better off if one of these sides were chosen, but we have different preferences about which side should be chosen. This game is illustrated in Figure 3.1. (For a population of n people in the state of nature, the matrix representing their deliberations will be n-dimensional, with n coordination equilibria, but that game will be closely analogous to this two-dimensional game.) This type of game is more difficult to solve than pure coordination games, because conflict must be resolved before coordination can be achieved.

Aside from conflict and coordination problems, there is the sort of antisocial behavior that can result from passion, the violence that can result from various forms of vice (greed, malice, etc.), and the disruptions that can occur when people reason or act irrationally. None of these problems requires a specific game-theoretic context; they can erupt at any time in all sorts of situations, and in a state of nature there is no systematic way to deal with them nor any systematic way of trying to remedy or prevent them.

These problems do not merely threaten people's ability to preserve their lives. They ensure impoverishment insofar as they make fruitful cooperation impossible, and they make impossible the sort of interaction and exchange necessary for all sorts of valuable activities, from artistic pursuits to sports pursuits. Without a state that will address these problems, not only personal safety but the foundations of a valuable life will be missing. Hence the quality of life in a state of nature would be consistently miserable and insecure.

The convention-based model makes an important assumption with respect to these problems, namely, that people in a territory are justified, on grounds of both morality and rationality, in generating a remedy for them. There are rational grounds for generating such a remedy because these problems damage each person's ability to satisfy her own self-interested desires. And there are moral grounds for generating such a remedy because these problems have a severe negative impact on the well-being of other people. Moreover, in order to work, such a remedy must be *collective* in the sense that all or most people in a territory must approve of and participate in it so that the warfare will end and constructive and peaceful interaction will begin.

So to review: on this model, people are justified on both moral and rational grounds in instituting a collective remedy for the resolution of problems of conflict and coordination that would otherwise exist in a state of nature. As we shall see, this collective remedy involves the construction of a political society.

Political Authority

All the problems I have just outlined can be either prevented, ameliorated, or addressed through the creation of a political authority. Whether or not political authority is the only way to deal with these problems is an interesting question, and one that I take up briefly later in the chapter.[3] But for now, we will focus on understanding what political authority is and how it can be used to resolve problems of conflict and coordination.

From Aristotle's time to the present day, philosophers have detailed the kinds of social problems that could be solved by a political authority that could demand obedience. A political authority legislates so as to solve coordination and PD problems in the community (via rules of property, contract, or marriage or rules of the criminal law); it adjudicates disputes, enforces the resolution of these disputes, and enforces law generally. To put it succinctly, political authority is understood by most philosophers to be an authority that demands obedience in order to *secure order*. All of the game-theoretic problems and the problems created by antisocial behavior

	Me	
	Right side	Left side
You Right side	1,2	3,3
Left side	3,3	2,1

FIGURE 3.1

are problems of order, requiring an institution that can enable people to achieve coordination, get the assurance necessary to make cooperation rational, and provide sanctions that encourage cooperative behavior in situations where it would otherwise be either irrational or at the very least unwelcome. While securing order in these various senses is surely not the only task of the state (and indeed the point of the second half of this book is to reflect on other purposes of the state), nonetheless we think that this task is required in order for us to call any system of power and authority a genuine state. So what exactly is political authority and how does it help a community to secure order?

When she gives you an order, a person who has political authority doesn't expect that you will take that order as some kind of mere suggestion. Nor does she regard her order as merely giving you a reason to do something that you are free to factor into your decisionmaking along with other reasons and that you are free to ignore if those other reasons oppose it. Instead, a person with political authority takes herself to be giving you *the* reason on which you ought to act. She takes it that her commanding authority is such that her reasons are, for you, supposed to be decisive, no matter what other reasons you have to act. Or to use Joseph Raz's term, political authorities give subjects reasons that are "preemptive": "The fact that an authority requires performance of an action is a reason for its performance which is not to be added to all other relevant reasons when assessing what to do, but should exclude and take the place of some of them."[4]

For example, most states require their citizens to file an income tax return. That such an action is required by the political authority is a reason *in and of itself* to file that return, over and above the avoidance of any penalties one will pay if one does not file a return. It is a reason that has a certain kind of power: It is supposed to preempt other reasons, especially opposing ones. That you are commanded to perform this action by the state is a reason that excludes other reasons that you may have not to do it.

Raz's analysis indicates that in a way King James was right to say that there is something godlike about a ruler—but (only) in the sense that a ruler's political authority has this "trumping power": To say that a ruler has political authority is to say that the ruler's reasons are supposed to preempt the variety of reasons we may have that conflict with the ruler's commands. However, to say the ruler's reasons *should* exclude others is not to say that they *will;* and because they don't always do so, we give the ruler punishment power, so that she can secure obedience through coercion when authority gives out.

As long as she possesses both authority to command and the power to enforce those commands, the ruler can designate salient solutions to coordination games, change incentives (using sanctions) to secure cooperation in PD games, deter and redress criminal behavior via punishment, and use her power either to encourage or at least make possible the wide variety of pursuits that human beings enjoy in a peaceful society.

Of course it is hard, and probably morally wrong, for any subject to suppose that the reasons given to him by his political authority "trump" *all* his other reasons (which is why Raz uses the words "some reasons" rather than "all reasons" in the quote above). For example, we may insist that they should not preempt certain *moral* reasons: Most of us believe that no political authority may command us and thereby give us a decisive reason to kill off all the babies in a village or massacre all members of a certain ethnic group. So in most real political societies the people and their rulers accept that there are *moral constraints* defining the possible content of the commands of someone holding such authority, which means that in these societies rulers' commands can't preempt *all* reasons. (Hence we do not accept the excuse given by those Germans during World War II whose behavior was supportive of the extermination of the Jews that "they were just following orders.") By accepting different theories of the moral limits of political authority, different states circumscribe the bounds of justified political rebellion and of more isolated acts of justified civil disobedience against laws and lawgivers that one takes to be too unjust to obey. Indeed, the moral and rational license that people have to generate a collective political remedy for the problems of the state of nature requires that people construct that remedy so that it is not only morally better than the state of nature it is supposed to replace but also morally desirable and hence promotive of justice and well-being.

Differences in moral worldviews will mean that different political societies will understand these moral constraints differently, reflecting another important fact about political authority, namely, that although in all societies it will have this preemptive character, its scope will be defined differently by different societies, so that they will disagree about which "domains of decision" belong to the ruler. We can think of the process of creating, sustaining, or reforming the nature of this political authority as one way in which people "mould their moral world."[5] There are three aspects of this creative process: First, the issues over which the ruler has jurisdiction must be defined (this involves defining the "domains of decision" in which her reasons are preemptive); second, the purpose of her exercise of power must be specified; and third, the structure within which this authority will be exercised must be constructed. People may create a very expansive authority or a very limited one. That authority may be constructed as perfectionist in its ambitions (attempting to make the subjects good and help them to attain the truth, as Plato advocated and as we discussed in Chapter 1), or it may be construed as antiperfectionist and limited only to ensuring that people do not injure one another. And this authority may be "housed" in a monarchical or oligarchical or democratic form of government. In the case of the United States, there are detailed records of this construction process; in other countries that process has been a slow evolution, the recording of which is sketchy at best. The point is that the extent of political authority is as much a matter of design as any of the political offices in the state. Or to put it another way, when people "invent" political authority, they agree that in order for it to work as a solution to state-of-nature problems, it must have a preemptive character, but they can structure in a variety of ways the scope and strength of the preemptive commands that the political authorities are permitted to make.

I used the word 'invent' deliberately here, because on the analysis I'm proposing political authority is indeed invented by the people rather than derived from them. The point is that the people don't have it naturally as individuals; rather, they have to create it in order to solve certain kinds of problems that would otherwise plague them were such an authority not present. This means that in the analysis to follow I reject Locke's claim that political authority is something that has to be transferred from a subject to a ruler (via a political society), in the way that, say, a patient transfers authority to her doctor, allowing him to treat her. There are two good reasons for rejecting that claim. First, since most of us can never remember giving such explicit consent, this explanation was (as we saw in Chapter 2) a poor model for explaining the reality of political authority, and it is hard to think of a form of tacit consent that would suffice to make a person authoritative. But a second reason to reject that claim (which I did not discuss in Chapter 2) is this: Locke's account assumes that prior to her consent, political authority resides innately in the individual, such that she can confer it (as a loan) on the ruler. But is it really plausible to think that the authority with which a ruler legislates or punishes offenders or conducts foreign affairs is something that each of us *naturally* has? Take, for example, the right to punish: It is hard to believe that each adult prior to her consent naturally possesses the right to use a trial procedure of her choice to convict the offender and the right to inflict retributive or deterrent forms of punishment on the offender. Imagine if someone claimed such a right over you, hauling you into her court, declaring you guilty using her rules of evidence, and sentencing you to some punishment that she found plausible. No matter what you had done, wouldn't you be outraged, claiming that she "had no right" to treat you in this fashion? Such a person would be treating herself as a "ministate" in a way that strikes us as absurd. But on the Lockean view, every person is a ministate until she gives her consent to transfer her authority to a ruler.

Do people in existing states who decide to take the law into their own hands and exact revenge or retribution against those who have harmed them act as ministates by doing so (whether they act alone or as part of a group or vendetta)? No: The actions of such people are importantly different from the authoritative actions of a state administering a criminal justice system. In particular, they lack the impartiality, the objectivity, and the evenhandedness that are the hallmarks of genuine criminal justice. Vendettas are highly personal, nonobjective, and extreme—often brutal and often degrading. One reason people decide they need a state is that they want to create an authority that can judge and punish fairly and impartially, respecting the rights of all parties. Although there may be occasions when the state is so corrupt or degenerate that we would understand a private citizen's decision to resort to private acts of punishment, such private acts would not have the impartial character that would mark them as dispassionate rulings of a political authority. This shows that such an authority is not something that any of us has in ourselves but something that has to be (with some difficulty) constructed by us.

Such reflections on what it means to say that each person "naturally" possesses political authority as an individual expose what a strange idea this is. Indeed, insofar as it incorporates this idea, Locke's theory doesn't really recognize a prepolitical state of the world at all; instead, his "natural" state is populated by as many states as there are individuals in it! That even Locke doesn't appreciate the existence of ministates in his state of nature shows that he found it difficult to shake the idea that a state, with the authority to command, resides only in an *institution* that is the creation of the people who live in it, and not in these individuals themselves.

However, the conception of political authority I am proposing obviates the need for locating a historically implausible *explicit* consensual promise from each individual in which he transfers "his" individual political authority to the ruler. Instead, I am arguing that political authority doesn't preexist in each person but is actually *invented* by a group of people who perceive that this kind of special authority is necessary for the collective solution of certain problems of interaction in their territory and whose process of state creation essentially involves designing the content and structure of that authority so that it meets what they take to be their needs. So on this view, political authority does not already exist within each of them but is created de novo by people who see it as a solution to problems of disorder that, for moral and self-interested reasons, they are required to solve.

To explain this idea further, consider how G.E.M. Anscombe originally suggested the idea that the state was the people's invention.[6] Anscombe starts from the fact that political authority is markedly different in both scope and content from the kinds of authority wielded by, say, parents or teachers or religious figures: A ruler with political authority demands virtually unconditional obedience for the domain of issues over which her authority extends, and depending on how that domain is defined, she takes herself to be justified in ordering people to do a wide range of things, some of them very dangerous, even including (in some societies) ordering them to death. We can, says Anscombe, understand *that* political authority is invented and *why* it is invented by reflecting on what purposes such an extensive and strong form of authority can serve: "The ground of authority is most often a task. Authority arises from the necessity of a task whose performance requires a certain sort and extent of obedience on the part of those for whom the task is supposed to be done."[7] Since the correlate of authority is obedience (as Anscombe puts it, "authority is a regular right to be obeyed in a domain of decision"[8]), the invention of political authority so understood must have to do with the desirability of nearly unconditional obedience in a wide range of areas, some of which involve a threat to life. The sorts of game-theoretic problems we reviewed and, more generally, the problems of violence and noncooperation, solutions to which are necessary to create peace, would seem to require exactly the kind of preemptive authority we attribute to a ruler, such that she can "lay down the law" and thereby prevent bloodshed, fraud, and mutually disadvantageous estrangement.

As I discussed earlier, this invention process is morally and rationally licensed. But what is this invention process? Does it have anything to do with the idea of "consent"?

The Governing Convention

How is political authority invented or created by the people? And how does it involve consent? As we reviewed in the previous chapter, real states don't seem to have been created by explicit promising among the citizens, and make-believe promises in hypothetical contracts don't confer authority. So we need a way of understanding the process of inventing political society that is both historically plausible and yet also authority-generating in order for this approach to political authority to be successful. The trick to developing such an account is to look for consenting activity that is not explicit, promisorial, or overtly directed at some ruler but rather implicit, nonpromisorial, and directed at developing what I call a "governing convention"—that is, a convention defining not only governmental offices and officeholders but also the nature of the authority held by those in office. Such consenting activity can take a variety of forms, so in order to look for it we must understand, at some basic and abstract level, its convention-creating form. I also attempt to clarify what is involved in a subject's consenting activity, resulting in a governing convention; then, as I show, we can use this model to understand the dynamics of actual histories of state creation.[9]

So far we have established the kinds of problems facing people in a state of nature and the way in which a political authority would provide a remedy to those problems. The people thus have moral and self-interested reasons to create a government. Consent theorists take it that people inside or outside a state would at least be agreed on *this*. However, were they outside a state and desirous of creating one, they would presumably still face considerable disagreement on the nature of the rulers' authority, the kind and number of offices the government should involve, and who should hold these offices.

Their disagreements have a certain structure. To specify it exactly, suppose there are three people in a state of nature who accept the argument that the warfare in this state can be remedied only by the institution of a sovereign. To simplify the problem for the time being, let us also suppose that they are in agreement about the kind of state they want to create: For the sake of argument, let's suppose they want to create a monarchy. Their preferences over the various possible outcomes in this situation are as follows. First, each party will rate lowest the situation in which she is not a member of the state while the other two are, because here she is a lone individual in a partial state of war facing a unified group of two who can likely beat her in any conflict. Each of them will rate the partial state of war in which she is a subject in a two-person state higher than this, because here she would enjoy the increase in security that association with another person brings. She would prefer even more being subject in a state in which all three of them are members because in this situation peace finally prevails. Assuming that individuals would rather be rulers than subjects in any state,[10] each would prefer being ruler of a two-person state rather than a subject in it, and each would prefer even more being ruler in a three-person state. But the importance of avoiding war and imminent death or injury is such that (assuming these people are not vainglorious) each individual would prefer being a subject in a three-person state to being the ruler in a partial state of war.

These preferences, however, define the conflict-ridden coordination game known as the battle of the sexes, which I have depicted in Figure 3.2. To simplify matters, I've presented the problem using a two-person matrix. However, for a population of n people in the state of nature, the matrix representing their deliberations will be n-dimensional, with n coordination equilibria, but that game will be closely analogous to this two-dimensional game. Hence the major problem people with these preferences face in their efforts to create a commonwealth is a coordination problem with considerable conflict of interest on the issue: "How shall we be governed?"

This problem really has two components. In the example above, the players agreed that only one of them would rule—amounting to an agree-

B

	Install A as ruler	Install B as ruler
Install A as ruler	1,2	3,3
Install B as ruler	3,3	2,1

A

FIGURE 3.2

ment to create a state with an absolute monarch. But of course there can be a dispute over whether to invest political authority in one person or a group of persons, which is, in effect, a dispute over what form of government to institute. Resolving this dispute involves determining how many leaders will rule them and what power they will have, and it, too, would likely have a battle-of-the-sexes structure. So the first problem people in a state of nature face is the problem of defining the offices in the government and the extent of the authority held by each officeholder.[11]

Second, the people must decide (as in the example above) *which* person or persons to choose as leader to fill whatever offices in the government they have defined. If there is no disagreement on these questions, the people's dilemma is an easily solvable coordination problem with only one coordination equilibrium. Disagreement makes the coordination problem conflict-ridden, but unless it is so severe that people would rather remain in the state of nature than accept someone other than their favorite candidate as ruler (a preference driven by the desire for glory that both Hobbes and Locke would condemn as irrational), it will not destroy the coordination character of the game.[12]

Granted that a series of conflict-ridden coordination games underlies the state's creation, how are these games solved? The social contract tradition speaks of people's making contracts or covenants to create a government, but are contracts necessary for the resolution of battle-of-the-sexes games?

Although the word 'contract' is sometimes used loosely to mean any sort of agreement, it is generally understood to be a certain kind of agreement, one in which one or more promises figure. The species of contract the traditional contractarian invokes is known as a bilateral contract, in which a promise or set of promises by one side is exchanged for a promise or set of promises by the other side. As we pointed out in Chapter 2, the prisoner's dilemma nicely represents the game-theoretic structure of this situation and is depicted in Figure 3.3. In circumstances such as the state of nature, in which no law exists to enforce the contract, per-

B

	Keep contract	Renege on contract
Keep contract	2,2	4,1
Renege on contract	1,4	3,3

A

FIGURE 3.3

formance would occur only if the parties to it were able and willing to keep their contractual promises.

So if people in a state of nature needed a contract to institute the state, that institution would occur only if people had the ability to keep a contractual promise to perform collectively rational but individually irrational actions. But as we have discussed, it seems people do not have the ability to keep contracts in the state of nature, which means that were contracts necessary for the state's creation, that creation would be impossible.

Fortunately, however, the exchange of promises is not necessary for the solution of the coordination games underlying the creation of the state. To see this, consider how participants of a coordination game with no conflicts would achieve coordination on one equilibrium point. An effective way of doing so, if circumstances permit, is to communicate with one another so as to *reach an agreement* to pursue only one of the equilibria. (For example, players in a traffic coordination dilemma might specifically agree with one another to drive on the right rather than on the left.) Such agreements work as solutions to these problems because they give each party the "common knowledge that each prefers to conform to [the equilibrium chosen] conditionally upon conformity by others involved with him in [the game]."[13] How does that common knowledge help to effect a solution to this dilemma?

There has recently been much research attempting to answer this question in detail.[14] But for our purposes we can develop the following rather simple answer: The fact that the agreement is commonly known causes each player to make a high assessment of the likelihood that the other player(s) will choose the agreed-upon equilibrium, such that each player's calculation of the extra costs, benefits, and probabilities of the actions open to them (which economists call an "expected utility calculation") will dictate that the player take the action that would realize a particular equilibrium. Henceforth I call such agreements "self-interested," or SI, agreements, because self-interested rational calculation, rather than the sense of "duty" arising out of a promise or fear of a coercive power, is the motive for each person's performance of the act agreed upon.

But it may not be necessary to make an explicit SI agreement in order to resolve a coordination problem.[15] As Hume discussed long before contemporary game theory,[16] this sort of problem can also be resolved by the generation of a *convention* governing which equilibrium to realize, and that convention can be generated even without agreement if there is an obviously salient equilibrium, one that stands out from the rest in some unique respect. For example, imagine that you and your friend know, and know that the other knows, that both of you regard the haunted house as the best ride in Disneyland; such knowledge can make it the salient solution to your problem of where to meet, so that you will both go there, despite never having made an explicit agreement to do so. In such situations it is "as if" there were an agreement on the pursuit of that salient outcome; hence it is common to hear people speak of there being a "tacit agreement" in these situations. Literally, of course, no one explicitly agreed with anyone on anything, but each did act by making reference to the beliefs and preferences of the others in the pursuit of a particular outcome, just as she would have done if there had been an explicit agreement among them to pursue it. If this coordination problem persists and is repeatedly solved in this way (e.g., whenever you get separated from your friend at Disneyland, both of you always go to the haunted house to meet up again), the participants have developed (without explicit agreement) a *convention* to solve their coordination problem.

So in order to solve the leadership problem, people who want to create a state must generate a governing convention. How should they do so? First, they can use voting (an approach suggested by Hobbes),[17] a method that democratically organized states in fact employ to select their rules (although they use it in a situation where there is already a convention on how these leaders will rule, what powers they will have, and how long their terms of office will be). Consider the problem facing any political party of selecting a viable candidate to represent the party in a general election. All members of the party realize that it is overwhelmingly in their interest to select someone from among their ranks to represent them, but there is often considerable disagreement as to who should do so. Political parties such as the Democratic Party in the United States or the Labour Party in Britain resolve this type of controversy by holding successive elections (either in different geographical areas at different times or successively at one national party convention), with those who get the majority of the votes staying in contention and whose who get small percentages of support dropping out. As the process continues, there is a gradual snowball or bandwagon effect, with one person usually emerging as the clear-cut favorite. The snowball effect in these elections is a clear indication that they are tactics for effecting a solution to a conflict-ridden coordination problem. The results of each successive election give people a way to determine the probability that their favorite leader will be able to receive support from the rest of the electorate and thus allow them to calculate whether or not it is rational for them to hold out for that leader's selection. Those people who find themselves supporting candidates with little or no support from the rest of the electorate will find it rational to switch to a more popular candidate they prefer less in the interest of getting a resolution to this coordination problem.

If this election technique ever fails to effect a solution to a leadership selection problem, it is because a significant number of those whose favorite candidates lose refuse to accept that their candidates are effectively out of contention for selection, in just the same way that the loser of a coin flip might repudiate that coin flip as a strategy for solving this sort of problem. Such a refusal in a political context can produce stalemate and even civil war, but this refusal is generally both immoral and irrational. Holding out for a better deal means risking no solution to the problem and thus a return to the state of war; it is a risk that an expected utility calculation in the state of nature would likely tell one not to take (unless, of course, the winning candidate posed a threat to one's life).

Historically, people have not been so rational or so moral and have frequently resorted to warfare to choose their leaders and their governmental structures. But warfare is actually a second device for achieving coordination in a battle-of-the-sexes problem. To see this, imagine a prepolitical situation in which war has gone on for some time and consider the plight of a very unsuccessful inhabitant. Unless he is vainglorious, such a person knows that he will never score a complete win over all the others in this state. Such a person will be attracted by the following offer from a more successful inhabitant whom I will call a "sovereign-entrepreneur." This entrepreneur says, "Look, you're getting nowhere on your own, but if you join forces with me and *do my bidding* (so that I am your ruler), then you will have more security than you now have." If the person doesn't accept this rather attractive-looking positive incentive by the sovereign-entrepreneur, he might be "offered" the following negative incentive: "Do my bidding or else I'll harm you!" And this threat will be real since, as we said, the sovereign-entrepreneur is a better warrior.

In general, both of these incentives are important tools for successful warriors to use in attracting subjects. The advantages of submission to this sovereign-entrepreneur are substantial: The subject will receive greater protection from other members of the confederacy, he will have a greater chance of warding off attacks from outsiders if he is allied with this leader than he would have on his own, and he might receive a share of the spoils of any victory achieved over the forces of these outsiders. However, negative incentives are useful as a method of encouraging some reluctant members of the state of nature to give in and accept the sovereign-entrepreneur as leader. Hence the threats help to resolve the battle-of-the-sexes problem over who should be declared ruler.

As entrepreneurs attract subjects in these ways, a certain number of powerful confederacies may emerge. But with their emergence comes a real market choice for the people in this state, as Nozick noticed in his own attempt to construct a scenario of the creation of government.[18] In Nozick's scenario the forces of the two competing "protection agencies" do battle. One of these agencies will emerge as the usual or continual winner of these battles. And since the clients of the losing agency are ill protected in conflicts with clients of the winning agency, they leave their losing agency to "do business" with the winner. Eventually, one confederacy emerges as winner over all others and is thus the "best buy" in protection for everyone in this state. So the inhabitants of the state of nature looking for a protection agency are in a market. Heads of different confederacies essentially say to them: "Buy me if you want protection." And the confederacy that wins more often than any other will be the best buy for the people in that state.

There are two important points to notice about this scenario. First, coordination on who should be leader is being achieved *not* via explicit agreement among the inhabitants of the state of nature but via a series of independent choices of a salient sovereign candidate by each inhabitant. Second, the negative incentives in this scenario are particularly useful in solving the *sort* of coordination problem that leadership selection presents: In particular, these incentives break the conflict over who should rule (and how). Nor does the sovereign-entrepreneur have to threaten *everyone* in the state of nature. He need only threaten enough people to get a cadre of support enabling his confederacy to dominate in the state of war. Thereafter his confederacy will be the "best buy" in the state of nature and, as such, the salient choice for subjugation by everyone else.

That warfare isn't generally regarded as a *legitimate* way to solve this type of conflict-ridden coordination problem doesn't alter the fact that it can succeed in effecting a solution to it. Nonetheless, most philosophers interested in state creation haven't used this warfare scenario in their arguments because it does not serve their justificatory interests. Any theorist interested in showing what kind of state we *should* create and maintain does not want to use stories of state creation such as the warfare scenario in which the mightiest but not necessarily the most just leadership faction would prevail. It is natural to present a just government, which takes account of the rights of each individual subject, as the product of an agreement process in which those rights are respected. But even an unjust scenario is appropriate if that scenario is a way of understanding the structural forces that have actually precipitated the creation of states, and hence political authority, in human communities throughout history. Remember we must distinguish between theories of the creation of political authority (which may be just or unjust) and theories of political justice. Social contract theorists have wanted to pursue both at once, but this confuses two quite different philosophical projects. And if one is interested merely in state creation, warfare is an effective albeit unjust way of resolving conflict-ridden coordination problems and thus explains why throughout history warfare has played an important part in the emergence of new governments. It is also the more historically plausible way of explaining the creation of real governments, since real people have always disagreed about the nature of justice and hence would likely be unable to reach explicit agreement on which coordination equilibrium point is most just.

The warfare scenario also tells us something else. In my restatement of Nozick's scenario, I attributed to people the intention to leave the state of nature and create a government. But I needed to attribute to them at each moment only the intention to subjugate themselves to the best confederacy leader at that moment, and given the structure of the situation, this intention on the part of each of them would more than likely lead to the creation of a confederacy leader with a monopoly of power. Insofar as this "invisible hand" explanation need make use of only this limited intention, it not only has certain desirable explanatory features[19] but is likely much closer to what actually occurred in the generation of most existing political conventions than explicit-agreement scenarios.

Third and finally, *something like* a contractual process can also generate a governing convention. If each member explicitly agrees with the others on who should rule and how, where that agreement involves a compromise by members of the group whose favorite outcome was not selected, then the conflict in the situation is resolved and coordination achieved. (Such an agreement might also work by specifying a lottery or similar device that would pick out the ruler and the form of government in which she would rule.) However, notice that this compromise agreement *is not literally a contract* because promises would not be necessary to keep it. Once the agreement is made, it is in each party's interest to realize the coordination equilibrium agreed upon. This agreement would only be more difficult to make, requiring capitulation or compromise by some or all of the parties.

So now we see how the convention model can be used to explain the underlying structure of actual historical events involving the construction of states. Whether those events were peaceful or violent, involving voting, explicit agreements among some, or war among all, this model represents the events as sequences in the construction of a governing convention, in which people in a territory take part by virtue of their decisions about whom to support and whom to obey. That traditional social contract theorists all resorted to the notion of an explicit agreement to construct a scenario of the state's creation has confused the more fundamental point about state creation: namely, that creating the state involves solving a conflict-ridden coordination problem via the generation of a certain kind of complicated convention.

Because this model makes the creation of government a result of people's participation in a convention and not the result of some sort of explicit promisory act, it has two important advantages over traditional social contract accounts. First, it seems to be a historically plausible model of state creation because it assumes that the state's creation comes from the kinds of actions that people actually seem to engage in throughout history (although I will leave it to historians to determine how far the actual facts of state creation accord with this model). Second, the model avoids the inconsistent appeal to a promisorial contract (with a PD structure) as a solution to PD problems in the state of nature. That is, instead of explaining a state that is supposed to ensure the possibility of contracts by appeal to a contract (thereby having to explain why the state-creation contract is possible when no other contract is), this model explains the state by appeal to convention-creating activities that people who had difficulty keeping contracts nonetheless *could* perform.

Still, philosophers will be worried about another issue: Does this model properly invoke the idea of *consent*? Those accustomed to a Lockean conception of consent will wonder whether mere participation in a governing convention provides a notion of consent that is meaty enough to generate the kind of authorization of rulers that results in genuine political authority. Participation in a convention may very well amount to an *explanatory* form of consent. But the contract tradition has wanted what might be called a *justificatory* form of consent, such that, having given it, a subject is obligated to obey the ruler who, after he has received the consent, is taken to have authority over the subject. So is there also a justificatory form of consent implicit in this convention story, such that we can use it to explain political authority and obligation?

Agency and Mastery

As I have presented it, the convention model represents the state as an institution whose role is to encourage cooperation and discourage conflict. For many, this will be too limited a conception of the role of this institution, ignoring the way it may properly be engaged in the redistribution of assets in the name of justice or in the education of its citizens or in the promotion of cultural opportunities and endeavors. Proponents of the convention model can and should argue for the addition of these duties to the state's agenda (as I discuss in Chapters 4, 5, and 6), but they should also argue that such additions do not change the fact that the state's power and authority to wield sanctions and issue binding commands are fundamental to understanding what it is and how it is created and maintained. This is because a person is a ruler—that is, has *authority and power*—only when her subjects do what she says, so people presumably make someone a ruler when they (or at least most of them) obey her commands. According to the traditional consent theorists, each subject gives the ruler the power of command over him: In Locke's words, "the first *Power, viz. of doing whatsoever he thought fit for the Preservation of himself, and the rest of Mankind, he gives up* to be regulated by Laws made by the Society."[20] But what does it mean to be "regulated by laws made by the society"?

At the very least, it means obeying *only* the person designated as ruler, which will be in each subject's self-interest if there is a convention established that makes this ruler the salient choice of the population interested in remedying the problems of a state of nature. But it also means being subject to the ruler's power to punish violations of these laws. With respect to punishment, a subject must, first, be disposed to obey *only* the punishment orders of the person or group chosen as ruler, which involves never coming to the aid of another who is being punished by the ruler. Second, a subject must also oblige himself to assist the ruler in punishing others (albeit perhaps not in punishing himself, on the grounds that this would be psychologically impossible).

The first action is easy to motivate: If we assume that the situation underlying the creation of a ruler is a battle-of-the-sexes dilemma, then once the subjects have agreed (implicitly or explicitly) that a certain person or group will be their ruler, obeying that person's punishment commands is the way to achieve coordination in this situation; hence to the extent that obeying the punishment commands of any other person or group would disrupt this coordination, people have good reason not to do so.[21] Moreover, people would not find it difficult to refrain from interfering with their government's punishment of people other than friends and relatives. Hobbes would point out that such punishment does not threaten their own well-being, and insofar as allowing it to happen is a way of instituting a remedy to the warfare in that natural state, it is in general desirable to let it occur. Locke would point out that for moral as well as self-regarding reasons, people are generally supportive of punishment of those who do not live by the law of reason and hence deserve the infliction of pain (indeed, they support such punishment in the state of nature). Thus any problems generated by those who do attempt to intervene on behalf of criminals for whom they care are small enough to be easily handled by a ruler who has sufficient police force to help him carry out the punishments.

With respect to the second action (i.e., assisting the ruler in punishing), in a community of any significant size the government will need help enforcing its edicts: Police, judges, and jailers will all be required to make possible effective enforcement of the laws. Therefore some percentage of persons in the community must be willing to assist in carrying out this enforcement. If (as Locke contends) people have the capacity to act in other-interested ways even at some cost to themselves, the ruler could appeal to them to volunteer their services. If (as Hobbes contends) they have no such capacity, a natural way for the government to receive their services would be to make individual contracts with each of them to become part of that cadre, giving them goods in exchange for service. Moreover, such a contract would not require either the ruler(s) or the members of the cadre to be fine, upstanding promise-keepers: It would only require that they be self-interested and smart enough to see the repetitive PD nature of the agreement.[22] That is, because the government will stay in power only as long as this cadre functions, it is in its interest to pay cadre members in order to ensure their future service. And because members of the cadre will get that pay only if they do what the government wants, it is in their interest to follow its orders. So we can expect these cadres to develop, and it is in the other subjects' interest not to interfere with their formation. The upshot of this discussion is that *no general social contract is necessary* for a government's empowerment. Hence our model is not inconsistent because it does not presuppose impossible-to-solve (PD-structured) contracts for the creation of government.

So participating in a governing convention involves, among other things, activities supporting the ruler's punishment activities. What kind of relationship exists between the ruler and the ruled when the ruler's power is generated and maintained by convention in this way? Although there is no literal contract between ruler and ruled, the people's convention-sustaining activities do establish what I have called (in Chapter 2) an "agency" relationship between them and the ruler. This relationship, which Locke says prevails between ruler and people, is one in which the ruler acts as the people's agent, hired by them to perform certain tasks and capable of being fired by them if they believe he performs those tasks badly. Although this relationship is not literally contractual either in nature or origin, it is nonetheless similar enough to actual agency relationships initiated by contracts to make forgivable any metaphorical talk of a "social contract" between ruler and ruled.

To see this agency relationship, consider the way in which revolution is both possible and justifiable on the convention model. Just as creating a state requires solving certain potentially conflict-ridden coordination problems, so, too, does changing it. Imagine that I am a disgruntled citizen who would like a new ruler. What reasons do I have for maintaining what I take to be a bad convention? Consider the reasons I have for maintaining any convention. Take, for example, the convention to drive on the right-hand side of the road. If there is no law requiring me to respect this convention, I will respect it anyway if I believe:

1. that I am in a coordination dilemma;
2. that in fact driving on the right is the conventional solution to that dilemma;
3. that it is a convention that enables the community to achieve a desirable coordination equilibrium, so that it furthers the interest of those in the coordination dilemma; and most important,
4. there is no other convention on a different coordination equilibrium that is rational for me to pursue (given the costs and benefits of doing so) by (in part) not obeying the convention.

Note that (4) presupposes that by acting so as to respect a convention, I also help in a very small way to maintain it through my respect for it.

These four considerations are also central to explaining why and when a citizen has reason to obey her ruler. I have reason to respect a governing convention about who should rule, and thus obey the ruler, when

1′. There are (conflict-ridden) coordination dilemmas about who should rule and how they should do so;
2′. in fact the present ruler and the present ruling structure amount to the conventional solution to those problems;
3′. it is a convention that enables us to realize a coordination equilibrium, so that it furthers the interests of those in the coordination dilemma; and
4′. there is no other governing convention that would realize a different coordination equilibrium whose adoption I believe it rational for me to pursue (given the costs and benefits of doing so) by (in part) not respecting this convention.

Again, this last point presupposes that when I act so as to respect the governing convention and obey the ruler's commands, particularly his punishment orders, I help in a small way to maintain this convention and keep him in power.

Now what happens when a subject believes (1′) and (2′) but denies (3′) and (4′)? He could deny (3′) for one of two reasons. First, he could judge the convention to be bad because, on his view, it fails to realize a coordination equilibrium at all (so that, barring exorbitant costs, changing it should be an improvement for everyone). Second, he could judge that there is a better coordination equilibrium available to the group. In either case the subject concludes that people have made a mistake and would be better off on the whole deposing the present leader and replacing her with another ruler. He therefore wishes to take from her the authority to rule that this bad convention grants her. If the rest of the community comes to agree with him that there is a better alternative, so that each person denies (4´), then neither he nor they will believe they should obey the ruler, and they will rebel. But if the people do not agree with him, then his unilateral action in support of another candidate will be useless.

In fact, in this situation a convention, albeit a bad one, does exist. And it is this fact that he is forced to take into account in his calculations. He might still draw the conclusion that he should obey the ruler if, for either moral or self-interested reasons, the consequences of acting to change the convention will be worse than the consequences of acquiescing in the bad convention. He may make this judgment when he finds the present government bad but believes (given what he knows) that so few others agree with him that an attempt to change the convention by refusing to obey the ruler would be futile, or when he believes that they do agree with him that the present ruler is bad but disagree among themselves about what convention should replace it.[23]

This analysis of the reasons a person has either to accept or reject a governing convention shows the implicit agency relationship between ruler and people in the convention model. In a quite literal sense, the ruler is "hired" by virtue of this convention, and if the people decide not to sustain that convention, then he will be "fired" and a new ruler "hired" via a new convention. The occasional disgruntled member of the community cannot disrupt a ruler's authority because the authority is sustained by the group, via a convention in which many members of the group participate.

Now compare a ruler whose political authority and power are sustained by convention to a person who commands as a master of the people, where that command is not given the imprimatur of authority by any popular convention. To be _mastered_ is _to be subject to the use of coercion in a way that disables one from participating in the process of creating or changing a governing convention_. Mastery, as I have defined it, is _not_ a form of political society; it is a nonpolitical form of coercive control in which the person exercising control, whom I call the master, lacks authority. Authority comes from the people; it is invented by them and bestowed upon rulers through the governing convention. But in systems of mastery no such convention exists, and the master rules not because he has been rendered authoritative by virtue of the people's participation in a governing convention but because of his superior coercive power. That coercive power may come about because of his superior technology or because of his control over a brutal enforcement cadre that is prepared to inflict terror on the population at his command. (Notice that there will have to be a convention within this cadre to follow only this master's commands, meaning that there will be a political relationship between the master and these henchmen. I discuss this point more fully later in this chapter. However, there is a nonpolitical relationship of mastery between the master and the rest of the population.)

A system of mastery can effect resolutions to problems besetting people in a state of nature, and so in this sense it is an alternative to the state as a solution to these problems. It is easy to argue, however, that it is a bad alternative, both on moral and on self-interested grounds. Masters are dangerous to oneself and to others. They need respect no limits—neither the limits of good sense nor the limits of morality. Arguably, mastery is a solution to the problems of the state of nature that is actually worse than those problems.

The use of coercion against blacks in South Africa until the election of Nelson Mandela, against left-wing Chileans by Augusto Pinochet in the 1980s, and against Tibetans in Chinese-controlled Tibet today has been substantial enough to inhibit severely these people's participation in the governing convention, rendering them mastered to an extreme degree in a way that we find morally odious. Such extreme mastery is possible when a master is effective in disabling all attempts by the citizenry to generate an alternative political convention. Indeed, as Kavka explains, even a tyrant who is universally disliked can, paradoxically, remain in power when the situation is such that the people do not have the knowledge of one another's dissatisfaction necessary to generate a new political convention, and hence obey the tyrant out of fear of one another. That is, each citizen is obedient

out of fear that some of his fellow citizens would answer the ruler's call to punish him if he were not. So citizen A obeys out of fear of citizens B, C, et al., B obeys out of fear of A, C, et al., and so on. In this situation, the beliefs of rational citizens that their fellows will punish them for not following the ruler's orders constitute a network of interlocking mutual expectations, a "net of fear," that provides each citizen with a sufficient motive of obedience.[24]

In this situation there is a convention empowering the ruler, but because he has the power to inhibit the passing of information among the disgruntled citizenry, the people's knowledge of the convention's existence and their uncertainty about receiving support from others to overturn it will likely make it irrational for them to risk opposing the ruler. Hence in this situation the ruler, by manipulating the people's access to information, disables them from effectively changing the governing convention and by doing so masters them, even though his rule is conventionally authorized.

Techniques of mastery are present not only in regimes we recognize as tyrannies but also in all Western democracies, as anyone whose name is on file at the FBI knows. A ruler has, and must have, significant coercive power over her citizens. That power makes her disproportionately more powerful than any of her subjects (or even fairly large groups of those subjects), and she may be able to use this power to disable, partially or totally, one or more of them from participating in or changing the governing convention. And it is so tempting for rulers to do so that there probably never has been (or ever will be) a regime in which such disabling doesn't go on to some degree or other.

Even worse, a portion of the population may approve of the mastery of the rest of the population and actively support their ruler's use of power to disable that portion from participation in the governing convention (again, think of South Africa before the election of Mandela). Those who are disabled may even be in the majority if the ruler and his supporters are clever enough or brutal enough to keep important technology from them, rendering them badly unequal (e.g., in South Africa).

So there are really two forms of domination that our discussion has revealed: the domination of a master and the domination of a "hired" agent. The convention model, which presupposes that every person involved in the creation of the state is the equal of every other, results only in the creation of politically authoritative agents. But in the real world equality can be upset not because of natural differences among people (for I agree with Hobbes that these are not terribly great) but because of technological superiority, and when that occurs, mastery is possible until that technological superiority is overcome by the mastered group. Moreover, insofar as the very empowerment of a ruler destroys equality by making her more powerful than those who are ruled by her, the seeds of political mastery are planted in the very act of generating a governing convention.

A pure form of mastery in a human community is very unlikely. Given human frailty and technological limitations (Superman and James Bond movies to the contrary), no ruler can hope to master people all by himself: He needs supporters to do so, and as I noted earlier, this means there must be at least an agency relationship between him and his supporters. In this sense Pinochet, Stalin, and Idi Amin, despite their mastery of subject populations, have all been agents; the power relationship within the ruling clique supporting them fits the convention model's analysis of a political regime. It is problematic to classify Stalin's Russia or Pinochet's Chile as a pure form of mastery or as a pure form of agency created by a governing convention precisely because these regimes are mixtures of the two, with some people in the regime sustaining it via a governing convention and others forced to obey it at the point of a gun.

And yet a pure form of agency seems just as unlikely. Aside from the fact that a portion of the population may approve of the mastery of others and actively support their ruler's use of power to disable the rest from participating in the governing convention, a ruler is always able to take advantage of his punishment power, which makes him disproportionately more powerful than any of his subjects (or even fairly large groups of those subjects), allowing him to partially or totally disable one or more of them from participating in or changing the governing convention. (Again, in the United States, think of the behavior of the FBI in the 1950s or 1960s or the obstacles preventing members of minority groups from registering to vote until the enactment of the Federal Voting Rights Act of 1964.) For better or worse, when people create a state, they create a "leviathan," literally, a powerful monster, over which it may not be easy to maintain control. Hence solving the problems of disorder in the state of nature means taking a moral and rational risk—because generating a political solution to these problems is potentially dangerous.

Given both the reality and the limitations of technological dominance, the explanatory truth about political regimes would seem to be that they are mixtures, to various degrees, of the agency and mastery forms of domination. So what the convention model "explains" is only one aspect of our political reality: that is, the extent to which rulers have ruling power because some or all of the subjects participate in a governing convention. The convention model fails to accommodate the reality of the nonagency aspects of subjects' relationships with the regimes that rule them.

But even if consent theorists have overemphasized this aspect of our political life, this is probably because they have intuitively sensed that only the agency aspect can be morally justified. The convention model gives us the form of domination we would create if we were and always remained equal. That state of equality is part fact and part moral ideal: It is factual to the extent that it describes our inherent natures, but it fails to account for the reality of technological inequalities among people (and among cultures). Nonetheless, because that technological inequality leads in general to morally reprehensible results, human equality, along with the kind of political regime it generates, should be regarded as an ideal.

So now we see the sense in which the convention model accommodates a notion of "consent"—albeit not the traditional Lockean conception of consent. Insofar as that model represents each person as a participant in the governing convention, she is involved in the creation or maintenance of her government in a way that the mastered person is not. The mastered person follows the orders of one whose power is in no way indebted to her obedience or assistance; a participant in a governing convention follows the orders of someone whose power and authority over her are a function of a convention in which she plays a role (albeit perhaps a small one) through her obedience and/or assistance, by virtue of the fact that she is, and is considered to be, the equal of other participants in this convention and of the person doing the ruling. Hence participants in a governing convention are in an agency relationship with those who rule, whereas those who are mastered are not. Moreover, note the way in which the convention model explains the creation and maintenance of government by reference to *each person's consent.* Although the political regime is sustained by a convention, this convention exists because of the preferences of individuals. Hence the analysis acknowledges both the social component of a political regime's authority and also each individual's involvement in that social component.

The conception of consent as participation in a governing convention, although considerably weaker than the Lockean notion of explicit consent, is still strong enough to capture the agency relationship that is the hallmark of the Lockean approach to understanding the state. This notion is explanatory in the sense that it explains what must happen in order for a state to occur, but it also has some justificatory force, insofar as it is a marker for an agency relationship that we believe is morally justified—unlike mastery, in which such consent does not occur. But is this notion of consent strong enough to provide the foundation for political authority?

Consent

We can now relate the convention model's analysis of political authority to the notion of consent. On the convention model, each subject of a regime gives a kind of "consent" to it as long as her behavior is either supportive of or at least not undermining of the governing convention of that regime. I call this *convention consent.* It is, in a way, an attenuated notion of consent whose moral justifying power is exceedingly limited. It is a notion that figures in at least part of the explanation of *why* the regime exists with the governing convention that it has. When I say that people create a governing convention when they consent to the creation of a state, part of what I mean is that they invent and sustain a certain form of political authority in that regime.[25] Nonetheless, it is not a consent that in and of itself shows the regime to be morally justified or legitimate.

Still, it does give us *some* moral information. Remember our analysis of mastery in a political regime: To the extent that a people is mastered, then to that extent they are prevented from participating in or undermining a governing convention. Hence convention consent, understood only as behavior supportive of a governing convention, is possible only when mastery is either nonexistent or very limited. In that sense, it is at least reflective of the extent to which the state eschews mastery and commits itself to the moral ideal of political equality. This is because such consent is possible only in a regime that does not use superior technology to disable the political activities of the citizenry and that therefore accepts that each citizen should be able to choose whether or not to participate in the governing convention maintaining that regime in power. Nonetheless, political authority isn't *conferred* by this sort of consent from particular individuals; instead, it is a consent that, insofar as it is involved in constructing and maintaining the governing convention, is part of the collective act of *inventing* that authority. Moreover, given that this authority will (in general) have been invented by our societies long before we are born, this analysis also allows us to admit that Hume is right to say we are all, in a sense, born into a political system whose authority over us is not of our own making. Yet when we reach adulthood, our participation in this political system—in particular, our support of the rulership conventions that compose it—is what will sustain this invented authority during our lifetimes. In this sense, each of us is involved in maintaining (and perhaps at times reforming) this system of power and authority.

Convention consent does not merely result in the empowerment of particular rulers; more fundamentally, it is responsible for the scope and structure of political authority in any particular regime. The empowerment convention giving any particular ruler the authority to command also defines the scope and limits of her commanding power. Moreover, this convention can be revised by the people over time. Britain in the seventeenth and eighteenth centuries underwent a shift in the way in which political authority was structured (moving from a system in which authority was very broad and centered in a monarch to a system in which authority was much more limited in scope and centered in Parliament). In the United States, the federal government has far more power now than it had in 1789. In Canada many people have argued that the scope of authority of the federal government has been changed by the enactment of the Canadian Charter of Rights and Freedoms in 1981. These examples illustrate the point that political authority itself is not only invented but also molded over time by the people to meet what they take to be their changing needs and interests. That is, while political authority is always going to be defined as that which a ruler has such that she can issue commands with (what I have called, following Raz) a preemptive character, nonetheless the persons holding that authority and the issues that can appropriately be the subject of their commands are constructed (and can be revised) by the people by whose convention this authority comes into existence. This means that while we can define what political authority is in the abstract (as I have done above), nonetheless different political regimes can develop different conceptions of the scope of that authority and of the political structure in which to house it.

Convention consent is inconsistent with revolutionary activity, but it can be (and in my view usually is) consistent with civil disobedience. Someone such as Martin Luther King Jr., even when he openly disobeyed certain laws, conceived of himself as committed to the political society he challenged—indeed, he challenged certain of these laws because he said he was committed to his country.[26] The strategy of the loyal but disobedient citizen is to express his commitment to the authority of the lawgivers even while rejecting what he takes to be the particular immoral laws they have legislated. Accepting the legitimacy of punishment for his disobedience is one way King demonstrated his commitment to his state's authority. In general, civil disobedience shows that convention consent is a complicated phenomenon, the giving of which cannot be equated with mere obedience to the law.[27]

Even if convention consent is responsible for creating and sustaining political authority, it is important to note that such consent may not express a person's *approval* of her regime. To accommodate the notion of approval, we need a meatier idea of consent that expresses not merely acquiescence in a political regime but also explicit approval of and support for it. A regime that receives what I call *endorsement consent* gets from its subjects not just activity that maintains it but also activity that conveys their endorsement and approval of it. A regime that has endorsement consent from most of its citizens will do more than simply survive: The considerable support from its subjects will make it vibrant and long-lived, capable of withstanding attacks from without and within. Beyond a kind of *attitude* toward the state, endorsement consent is a *decision* to support it because of one's determination that it is a good thing to support. By giving this form of consent, the subject conveys her respect for the state, her loyalty to it, her identification with it, and her trust in it.

It is very likely true that a state cannot receive such endorsement consent from its subjects unless it is reasonably just.[28] People generally don't approve of regimes unless those regimes behave well. However, endorsement consent doesn't *make* the state reasonably just; it is instead a (reliable but not infallible) sign that in its dealings with its subjects and others outside it, it (probably) is reasonably just. Note also that endorsement consent can be given only by those who take themselves to be "members" of the state; it cannot and will not be given by foreign visitors or alienated rebels. Locke's idea that a special kind of consent is associated with political membership is, I think, right, but it is not that such consent by itself *creates* membership, but rather that it is a consent that is indicative of a preexisting special relationship between a state and those of its members who are loyal to and highly supportive of that state. One might also call it loyalty consent. (There is also, I believe, a third kind of consent that can be involved in establishing membership in some states. I discuss this form of consent in Chapter 6.) Armed with these notions of consent, we are now in a position to show how they illuminate the nature of political authority.

Political Authority

According to the traditional social contract analysis, which assumes that each individual possesses the authority to rule himself that he then confers on the ruler, a political regime has authority only over those who have, in effect, given it to them. As we discussed in the previous chapter, this is a very unsatisfactory model of political authority, not least because it fails to capture the commonsense idea that political authority extends over a territory rather than only over those who happen to have given authority through their explicit consent (an event that, in any case, rarely seems to have occurred in the history of real states). Albeit a kind of consent model, the convention model works much differently and represents the conceptual topology of political authority as far more complicated than the (overly simple) social contract model represents it.

In order to see that topology, imagine, first, that we are anthropologists seeking to determine whether a political authority exists in a territory. We would look for two conditions that are jointly necessary and sufficient for the existence of such an authority in this territory:

1. the existence of a convention to treat the orders of one or more persons (i.e., the rulers) as both preemptive and final (i.e., the last court of appeal) in a wide variety of domains of decision (indeed, maybe even all domains), where these orders may contain directives that may mandate unpleasant and even highly dangerous behavior.
2. the existence of an enforcement cadre ready and willing to use force to ensure compliance (or else to punish noncompliance) of commands of this convention-sustained commander that some people in the territory might otherwise be reluctant to obey.

Now, imagine that you are a resident of that territory; how might you be related to this system of political authority? The resident who believes herself to be *politically obligated* to that system accepts not only 1 and 2 but also 3—which might be called a personal condition of political obligation:

3. the person designated as ruler issues commands that are preemptive for *me*, that is, I believe these commands preempt any other reason I have to do something other than what she commands.

Only a person who has given the ruler convention consent accepts condition 3 (although she may not always be able to sustain her commitment to 3—for example, when on particular occasions self-interest may tempt her to flout certain laws to gain an advantage over her fellows). Hence only such a person recognizes herself as politically obligated to the ruler (although this may sometimes be an obligation she has trouble sustaining, which is why a ruler always has an enforcement cadre available).

People who accept 3 are those who, by their behavior, give convention consent to the regime. But they may or may not give their endorsement consent. Fulfilling one's political obligations may be joyless and without enthusiasm; one may accept that one ought to obey a regime that one otherwise quite dislikes. The failure to give endorsement consent may prompt behavior aimed at reform—which, in the extreme case, may result in actions of civil disobedience. But all such reformist action presupposes that the regime to be reformed is authoritative and needs to be improved rather than deposed.

People who do not accept 3 do not give their regime their convention consent (or their endorsement consent). They understand that by virtue of the empowerment convention, a political authority exists in their society, but they do not support it and seek to oppose it. The traditional social contract analysis says that by virtue of their refusal to give convention consent to the regime, the regime is not authoritative over them, but the convention model represents the plight of such people rather differently. It maintains that they are indeed subject to the power of an authoritative regime in their territory—a regime that is authoritative because it has been made so by the actions of others rather than themselves, but it also recognizes that they will not believe they are politically obligated to the regime. Hence on this view, political obligation is correlated with condition 3, but not with conditions 1 and 2, which together define the existence of a political authority in a certain territory.

So this account distinguishes between the existence of a political authority and the various relationships that authority has with its subjects.[29] It has an agency relationship with all those who engage in and support the empowerment convention that invented and now maintains it as an authority. This agency relationship may be more or less positive with each subject-principal, depending on the extent to which the subject-principal has given the regime her endorsement consent, reflecting the extent to which she is pleased with its performance. However, it does not have an agency relationship with those who do not give it their convention consent. But if it isn't an agency relationship, then what kind of relationship is it? Mustn't it be a relationship of mastery? And if mastery is, as I've argued earlier, a relationship that is morally illegitimate, how can a political regime be morally justified so long as there are people in its territory who refuse to accept that they are politically obligated to it, and who are therefore (it seems) mastered by it? Have we located the morally unacceptable element to which anarchists object in political regimes as we know them, namely, their inevitable attitude of mastery toward those who do not give them convention consent? While this analysis preserves the sense in which the political dissident must reckon with the real authority of the political regime he rejects, it does not establish that the regime is authoritative in a way that justifies it in using force to insist on the dissident's compliance—indeed, the analysis suggests precisely the opposite, insofar as such force seems to bear all the hallmarks of mastery. And haven't real states continually behaved like masters toward the dissidents in their midst, inflicting on them everything from harassment to torture and death?

These questions show that gaining a clearer understanding of the consent-based nature of political authority doesn't, by itself, provide a justification of that authority sufficient to answer the doubts of an anarchist. So how is the defender of political society going to defend the institution, given that as long as there are dissidents, that institution will, it seems, have a relationship with them that cannot be morally defended?

One way of doing so is to use what in moral philosophy is called a *consequentialist* defense. This kind of argument defends an action, policy, or institution by saying that its consequences are such that its moral benefits outweigh the moral costs. A consequentialist defense of political authority would go something like this: Even though there are moral costs and moral risks involved in creating and sustaining a state, there are even worse moral costs and moral risks in a world without a political authority—at least as long as that political authority operates in a minimally just way. And the more just the authority and the better designed its governance, the fewer the number of discontents will be and the greater the number of people in the territory there will be who give it their convention consent. This means that the state can minimize the number of discontents over whom it has a relationship of mastery, and if it truly operates well, our sympathy with the complaints of the discontents may be virtually nil. (We wouldn't conclude that a state wasn't justified if Al Capone rejected it.) So on this view, the carnage and misery it prevents as well as the moral advantages and gains to self-interest that a good state makes possible are important in morally justifying the authority of any state that works (at least reasonably) well.

This analysis accepts, however, that the state is a dangerous institution that can operate in ways that make it morally indefensible in particular cases. It therefore refuses to offer a justification of all states qua states but rather offers justifications of particular states dependent upon how good their overall moral performance is—a test that some states may well fail.

Hence this analysis does not assume that all political authorities, by virtue of being authorities, are morally defensible. Instead it gives a descriptive account of what a political authority is and guidelines for assessing the extent to which it is a morally defensible political authority.

Note that this distinction between political authority on the one hand, and *good* political authority on the other, is a very un-Platonic feature of the convention model.

For Plato, in order to be authoritative, a state has to be good. But on my view a state can be authoritative and also wicked or unjust or inept. Political authority is (merely) the artifice of people, created and sustained by a convention. You as an individual might disagree with that convention, either because you think that the system of authoritative offices that make up the state is ineffective or tends toward unjust results or because you despise the injustice of the rulers' commands. These conclusions might lead you to withhold your endorsement consent but to persist in giving the regime your convention consent because you see no reasonable alternative to that regime. Or it might lead you to withhold both forms of consent and attempt to change the ruling conventions, perhaps even through violence. But even in this latter case, the convention model assumes you will realize that change is necessary precisely because the inept or unjust government has this (convention-granted) political authority.

Moreover, the Platonic view that political authority is a matter of goodness has serious problems brought out by Anscombe, who characterizes the Platonic position as the view "that you 'only' need to add justice to force—i.e. to postulate that what is enjoined or aimed at by those exercising the force is what would otherwise be just—to render the state just. But there is the question what renders it just to exercise force in, say, requiring what is just."[30] Only by saying that political authority is something created and maintained by people who will be bound to it—no matter the justice of those who are ruling—can one distinguish political institutions from systems of mastery, thereby giving an account of why in the former, but not in the latter, people take themselves to be bound to their rulers and why they believe that *only* those rulers are entitled to command them, even if there happen to be individuals who are more just than the rulers residing in the community.[31]

So have we succeeded in developing a consent-based model of political authority that captures what political authority is and also answers the anarchist's worries, at least in the case of certain particular (well-ordered) states?

Not yet. Two problems—one descriptive and one moral—remain. First, this analysis represents the state as the product of those who are governed by it, and as we discussed in the foregoing chapter, it is paradoxical how political authority, so understood, can be stable and persist for any length of time. Of course not all political societies are stable or long-lived, but some are, so how is such persistence possible on this view? I take up this paradox in the next section. Second, this account seems to represent as virtually inevitable a relationship of mastery between a political authority and a person in its territory who refuses to give it his convention consent. But such a relationship taints, perhaps substantially, the moral legitimacy of even good political institutions, and some may regard that taint as so considerable that the consequentialist defense of the institution that I constructed earlier fails to remove it. Simply saying that states can minimize this moral stain if they behave justly is not as much help as one might like, given the extent to which the nature of justice is in dispute (as we will explore at length in Chapter 4). Hence it is possible that there can be dissidents who truly believe that their state is behaving unjustly and therefore refuse to give it their convention consent, even while the supporters of that state are equally convinced that it is just. In such a situation, the state masters people who object to it on moral grounds, and since each side believes in the morality of its own argument, their disagreement is hard to adjudicate. Such mastery is particularly objectionable from a moral point of view because of the way it is directed against people who may be right in their criticisms but who nonetheless suffer for it. The convention analysis cannot deny that many states engage in techniques of mastery against those who oppose them, but I believe it can suggest the outlines of a kind of state that tries as far as possible to repudiate techniques of mastery against those who object to its operation. Such a state tries to allay the anarchist's concerns and hence may be the best answer to the anarchist's worry that no political institution can be morally justified. This state is essentially the modern democratic society. How such a state tries to accommodate rather than master political rebels is the final subject of this chapter.

Solving the Paradox of Being Governed

We are left with a practical question: Why does a political system work if the people who are ruled by the state are ultimately the ones who empower it and authorize it? As we discussed in Chapter 2, if people need a state because they are inclined to be unjust, greedy, prone to violence when quarreling with their fellows, and biased in their own case, then how can any state survive if these same people are the ones who, via convention, create and maintain the states that rule them? In the previous chapter, I called this the paradox of being governed. It is raised by any analysis of the state that posits an agency relationship between ruler and people, and that relationship is still at the heart of the convention model, even if it no longer retains the idea that the people lend power to the ruler. So can we dispel the air of paradox?

I offer a solution to that paradox here,[32] using the same device that philosophers have used to solve linguistic paradoxes, namely, by differentiating levels of inquiry and analysis. Consider the famous "liar's paradox," illustrated with the sentence, "This sentence is false." The sentence cannot be true when it tells us it is false; but if it is false, then given the assertion it is making, it would seem to be true. Alfred Tarski resolved this paradox by distinguishing two kinds of language, which he called the "object language" and the "metalanguage." The metalanguage is used to talk about the object language but is not itself part of that language. By understanding the predicates "is true" and "is false" to belong only to the metalanguage, we avoid the paradox. An assertion in the object language may not involve these words, which are properly employed only as part of evaluations at the metalevel.

We can employ the same "stratification" solution to the paradox of being governed. Let us start by distinguishing two levels of government, the object level and the metalevel. The object level is the level of laws made by those with legislative power in a regime: Call this the level of the "legal system." That which defines this system is the governing convention—itself a collection of rules that are part of the metalevel, not the object level. So (as H.L.A. Hart noted)[33] there are two kinds of rules in the legal system, the kind that define what the system is and the kind that are created in the system as specified by the system-defining rule. This system-defining rule must operate by identifying who the makers, interpreters, and enforcers of the primary (or "object") law are. Those who are not authorized by the governing convention to perform some aspect of governing would be appropriately considered "the ruled," pure and simple.

But who is the person or group that shall judge whether those who are ruling have respected their role as defined by the governing convention? The answer generated by the convention model is "the people." Their activities collectively create and maintain a state with authoritative power, which is the equivalent of creating and supporting a governing convention, and it is they who determine whether the state will continue or undergo change or be deposed, insofar as the state only persists through their support of it. But if the people are the source of the state, aren't they also the source of its rules, and so mustn't they also be the ones who should judge whether to obey these rules? And if so, how can the state be stable when the ones being ruled are in charge of the rules? However, here we must beware: To say that "the people who are ruled are also the ones who rule" is just as misleading as to say, "This sentence is false." To answer this question, we must specify *which* rules we're talking about.

The people in most societies don't have the job of interpreting any of the primary or object rules. That job is performed by someone who occupies a certain legal office. But the people *do* interpret rules constituting the governing convention, and as they do so they are performing a metalevel action—that is, they are engaged in an action that is about the operation of the object level.

Some might fear that this way of solving the paradox of being governed uses a mere verbal trick, but that is not so. The analysis I have just given doesn't simply generate labels but does so in a way that allows us to *describe and understand the relationship between fundamentally different kinds of political activity.* Think of a group of children playing a game of baseball in a vacant lot who periodically stop the game to argue about the rules (they might want to make up new rules, argue about the interpretation of existing rules, or object to the application of the existing rules by the person they've appointed umpire). We know the difference between "playing baseball" and "arguing about the rules of baseball." And similarly, this analysis helps us to see the difference between "being subject to object rules" and "participating in activities that seek to change how such rules are generated" in political societies. We are engaged in being ruled when we follow the law and experience sanctions set by legal authorities. And we are engaged in interpreting the governing convention when we either participate in activities that create and maintain our governments or when we do what we can to overthrow them.

There are many activities that constitute creation and maintenance of political structures: They can include everything from voting to doing jury duty to assisting in the punishment of those who have violated the primary laws to attempting to make constitutional changes (a process in which we behave most like the children arguing over the baseball rules in the vacant lot). Perhaps most important, they include refraining from performing, advocating, or assisting in violent activities designed to overthrow the government.[34] Moreover, a political society is robust and stable in a way that a sandlot baseball game is not, because once a governing convention is established, it can be very hard to dislodge it. Not only do rebels have to overcome any obstacles to changing the governing convention placed in their way by the ruler, but they also have to be able to propose alternatives that sufficient numbers of people find good enough to persuade them it is worth the time and effort to depose their present ruler. This will be difficult to do if the present ruler is perceived by many people as ruling well. It also requires considerable expenditure of time and effort by the rebels and an information network that enables them to get their message across. Thus governing conventions can be very robust, hard for those who dislike them to dislodge. In the next section, I elaborate further on how changing a governing convention can be difficult.

So although no one in a political regime has the right to judge the governing convention defining the powers of government in the "object legal system," because at this level the rules are the foundation of government, nonetheless the people have the "metaright" to decide these rules in the sense that they have this right *outside* the object legal system as they scrutinize the government at the metalevel. But why does the stratification analysis assume that the people are the ones who decide how well the object game is going at the metalevel? Why doesn't it allow the possibility that it could be decided by a few individuals or a small group? The answer to this question, I would argue, is implicit in the consent theorist's methodology. One of the covert messages being sent by those such as Hobbes who justify the existence of the state on the basis of what we "could agree to" is that—in fact—a state exists *only* because enough of the people who constitute it have created it and/or continue to maintain it, where this involves behaving such that the governing convention does not change or else changes only minimally. Creating a political system is like creating a game: The creators set out the rules that provide for the roles each person will play in the game (and most of us play the role of "ruled" in the political system), and everyone plays his or her part for as long as a sufficient number are satisfied with how it's going. So contractarians are saying that in fact a political system is the "people's game" because (whether or not rulers wish to acknowledge this fact) the people will decide how well the game is going and, in particular, how well any ruler is adhering to the rules defining the extent of his jurisdiction and power. And this is not only a normative thesis but also a *descriptive* thesis. A political system isn't something built into nature, created by God, or designed and maintained by only a few individuals who naturally rule other human beings in the way that a farmer rules over the animals in his herds. It is a thoroughly human institution whose existence depends in a variety of ways on the behavior of those who constitute it.

Modern Democracies

One of the advantages of the convention model is that it enables us to understand the distinctive structure of modern democracies. The idea of a democracy is often thought to involve a certain internal political organization (parliaments or congresses, majority rule, and so forth), as well as a certain normative commitment to (something like) the equal participation in the political process of all persons in the state.[35] We discuss some of these normative commitments and conceptions of democratic political procedure in Chapter 4. But here I want to point out the extent to which modern democracies have a certain distinctive political structure, regardless of how many branches of government they recognize, how they organize the legislative branch, and how they allow voting by the people. Moreover, as I shall explain, this structure enables the modern democratic state to accommodate to a remarkable degree all sorts of political rebels and thus to minimize the mastery of political dissidents.

What is distinctive about modern democracies is that their structure explicitly recognizes that political power and authority are the people's creation. In the old days, theorists such as Hobbes or Locke who maintained, contra the divine rights theorists, that the people, not God, established and legitimized political power, also assumed that as a matter of fact (albeit perhaps not of right) when people didn't like a regime they staged a revolution, preferably bloodless, in which rulers were overthrown and if necessary (as in 1688) the political rules changed. But what if one could design a political system in which "revolution" was an organized and regular part of the political process? This is the idea that inspired the founders of modern democratic societies (and particularly the founders of the U.S. polity); it is at the heart of the structure of contemporary democratic states.

Defenders of modern democracy self-consciously recognize that *political societies are created and maintained by the people that are ruled in them.* And as I've discussed, this creation-and-maintenance process involves the creation and maintenance of a set of authoritative norms that define the legal system and the obligations of the officials who work within it. However, *modern democracies operate so that the people have continual control over the process of creating and maintaining the regime.* In modern democracies the people have created not only the "legal game" but also another game that defines how to play the "creation-and-maintenance game." Let me explain.

Consider the standard coup: Ruler X has power because there is a rule, accepted by the people, that he is authorized to do so. But when some or all of the people no longer accept that rule, they engage in various power-retracting activities, and if enough people (or enough of the people who have most control over the present rulership convention) engage in these activities, ruler X is gone. And if not enough do so, the coup collapses. (So in the Soviet Union in 1991, when too many people in powerful positions refused to obey the orders of the coup leaders—e.g., Russian and Baltic soldiers in the army, political officers in various Soviet states, and prominent leaders in the economic community—the coup failed.) How coups can be successful and how such successful coups are coordinated despite the opposition of rulers is a fascinating story—communication among opponents of a ruler is critical (and thus some pundits have argued that one reason the Soviet regime finally collapsed was the existence of the fax machine). Call this kind of revolutionary activity "convention-dissolving," since it unravels the convention defining who is authorized to hold power—which is just to say that it destroys the society's governing convention.[36]

The experience of England in the seventeenth century was that political convention-dissolving could be difficult, lengthy, and even deadly dangerous for those involved in it. This lesson was not lost on the American revolutionaries.[37] But what the framers of the U.S. Constitution essentially asked themselves was this: What if the people could get control of convention-dissolving activity—establishing rules that would actually allow such activity to occur on a periodic basis if the people so decided and that would regulate it so that the dissolution would be as peaceful and orderly as possible? If there could be a "system of revolution" that was attached to the legal system, both rules and rulers could be changed quickly with minimal cost and disruption to the people. And the possibility of replacing them peacefully and painlessly would increase the people's control over the shape of their political game and thus allow them to better supervise their leaders (who would know that their being fired was not a particularly costly action for the people and who would thus be under pressure, if they wanted to retain their jobs, to perform them as the people required). By and large, this "controlled convention-dissolving activity" involves what is commonly referred to as "voting."

Consider how the U.S. Constitution works. This document not only sets up a certain kind of government with offices that involve distinctive kinds of power and jurisdiction but also sets up rules for creating and dissolving conventions about *who* holds these offices. Through these rules various government officials are authorized and empowered, but through these rules they can also be peacefully and effectively deprived of authority and power. *Voting is therefore a form of controlled revolutionary activity.* Socialist radicals of the early twentieth century were right when they referred to votes as "paper stones."[38] Our elected "representatives" don't represent us in any literal sense—as if we were doing the ruling "through them." This is nonsense. They rule and we don't. But because we can easily deprive them of power—depose them, if you will—at certain regular intervals, they have (at least theoretically) the incentive to rule in a way responsive to our interests. Just like any other employee, if they want to keep their jobs they must work to the satisfaction of their employer. They therefore "represent" us in the way that any agent represents those who authorize her. In modern democratic regimes, representation is actually a form of agency.[39] Thus in a democracy those who would rule us are in continual competition with one another, attempting to gather votes each hopes will be sufficient, according to the rules, to hire him or her as ruler. In democracies more than in any other kind of regime, rulers don't have tenure.[40]

So our government is by the people, for the people, and of the people—except that this last preposition is misleading. Unlike in ancient Athens, in the United States most of us aren't actually in the government; only a few of us are. What makes this a government "of the people" is the fact that built into the governing convention are not only the rules that define the object political game but also rules that grant the people the power to create and dissolve portions of that object political game if they choose to do so at relatively little cost. Creating these rules is a novel way of extending the activity involved in creating and maintaining government. Such rules allow the people to play their "metarole" as definers of their political society in a more effective and controlled way. Those who fashioned modern democracies came to see that not only such activities as criminal punishment and tort litigation but also the very process of adding to or changing the political game itself could be made part of a larger conception of the political game. Or to put it another way, they discovered that revolutionary activity could be an everyday part of the operation of a political society.

To appreciate the precise structure of these regimes, we need to examine more closely the content of the governing convention defining them. Not only are there a variety of object rules, such as contract rules (which are rules about how to create "private" transactional rules between two or more parties) or rules about property or rules of the criminal law, there is also a set of rules that allow us to identify what is to count as the object law in this political regime. In democratic societies these rules operate by defining offices that perform legislative, executive, and judicial functions, offices that, taken together, generate the object laws in this society. They needn't be written down in some kind of explicit constitution but can be implicit in the traditions, practices, and normative beliefs of the participants of the state (consider the "unwritten" constitution of Britain). Let me call such rules "structural" in virtue of the way they set out the institutions that perform these functions. They are, in essence, a type of metarule.

However, there is another type of rule (one that H.L.A. Hart failed to recognize explicitly) whose addition to the preceding rules transforms any regime into a modern democracy. This type of rule (which, once again, needn't be explicitly written down) defines how it is that the people control and/or change the operation of the political regime as defined by the first type of rule. Call rules of this type *convention-revising rules.* They dictate how the people install or replace those who hold the offices defined by the structural type of rule just discussed, either through direct or indirect voting procedures. Second, these rules set out the procedures for changing the rules that define these offices and the procedures for filling them. (For example, the U.S. Constitution sets out an elaborate process for constitutional amendment.) By including these rules in the governing convention, the people not only define the object political game but also determine the system by which the people can revise that game and under what circumstances they will be warranted to do so. So with the addition of these latter rules, the overall governing convention now contains components that are *tertiary* as well as secondary: That is, it contains rules about rules about rules insofar as it defines not merely the object political game and the primary rules generated in that game but also the game of changing the object political game. Politics becomes a three-tier, not merely a two-tier, activity.

In a nondemocratic regime, then, the citizen's role as a member of the population that creates, maintains, or destroys the governing convention defining this object game is often ill defined, little understood, thwarted by the ruler to any extent possible, and something she and her fellow citizens make up as they go along. But in a modern democracy the citizen not only plays a role in the object game and not only plays a metarole as a member of the population that creates, maintains, and changes the governing convention defining the object game, but she also performs this metarole according to well-defined procedures laid out in other parts of the governing convention. These procedures can involve elections, plebiscites, constitutional conventions, and so forth. And indeed in some democracies, she even plays the fourth-tier role of creating, maintaining, or changing those rules that define these election procedures and that also define how to create, maintain, or destroy any other part of the governing convention. And when she plays either of these last two roles, she is part of a population that has taken it upon itself to structure and abide by rules it uses to "revolutionize" the government.

Now we see the way in which a modern democratic regime accommodates rebels. It allows people to withdraw their consent, at regular intervals, from particular persons holding power and particular rules or offices in the regime, even while keeping them within the overall political structure of the regime. It is therefore a system of political authority that attempts to maximize the convention consent it receives from residents of a territory by providing politically acceptable avenues for those residents to rebel against aspects of its operation. In this kind of state, disgruntled residents are confronted not with tools of mastery but with procedures laid down by the governing convention for changing their rulers or the offices they hold or these procedures themselves.

But they might not follow these procedures. And if they attempt to change the governing convention—including those rules that tell the population how to change the rules or offices in the regime—by taking certain actions (including violent actions) or by following procedures not laid down in those rules, they are engaging in what might be called "extralegal revolution." Such "old-fashioned" revolution is still possible in modern democratic states and occurs whenever citizens strive to revise or destroy the governing convention *without* respecting the rules it contains for carrying out a revision process. Against *these* sorts of rebels, the modern political state will use (and has used) techniques of mastery (e.g., modern Germany has done so against neo-Nazis, and the United States has done so against radical leftist groups in the 1960s and against radical right-wing militia groups in the 1990s).

But insofar as the governing convention's procedures for revision are perceived as reasonable and are endorsed by most of the population, such revolutionaries will appear as opponents not only of the present rulers of the regime but also of the vast majority who support and maintain the way the governing convention defines the process of overseeing the regime's operation. Such a position makes their revolutionary activity seem like an affront not merely to the state but to other members of the community, who will likely see that affront as a moral insult that reflects the rebels' unreasonable contempt not only for peaceful attempts at change but also for *them*, insofar as they suffer from the rebels' violence. In more pragmatic terms, it also means that the rebels' revolutionary activity is unlikely to succeed, which may help to explain what many see as the remarkable stability of modern democratic states.

This analysis presents modern democracies as committed, above all, to *the rule of law*, a phrase that on this analysis means government established by rules that define not only structure, scope of authority, and officeholder selection but also how the preceding rules can be changed. These rules are, in the end, interpreted and enforced by the people whose convention-creating activity generates, sustains, and revises them. As such, they are the people's rules. Nonetheless, political authority in modern democratic regimes is traceable to the operation of these rules and not to the arbitrary will of any particular governing figure (who in fact will only govern because of these rules).

There is one other type of rule that can be a constituent of a governing convention in modern democracies—but this type of rule need not be present in order for the regime to be appropriately called a democracy. It requires those who govern to do so in conformity to certain moral requirements. This type of rule is morally loaded to the extent that it partially articulates or partially points to a moral theory as the proper source of the content of object law created by the legislature. There is no reason such rules cannot be part of the governing convention, and Randy Barnett argues that the presence of the Bill of Rights (and particularly the Ninth Amendment) indicates that the framers of the U.S. Constitution were convinced that moral reality was sufficiently clear to enable the American people to recognize and operate from that part of it which these amendments circumscribed.[41] Modern democracies do not have to incorporate such moral rules in order to be democracies, since their democratic structure is basically created by the tertiary rules discussed above. Nor do they need these moral rules to be explicitly written down in order for them to play an operational role in defining the nature of the object political society established by the governing convention. But they are a common part of many such societies, especially in written form, because they help to provide a moral yardstick the people can use to judge the performance of those whom they are able peacefully to depose at the voting booth.

In my judgment the contribution of social contract arguments to the development of this modern conception of democracy is enormous. Even though the image of an explicit social contract as the basis of government is make-believe, nonetheless that image must surely have generated in the minds of those who constructed modern democracies the idea that a well-run polity is one that recognizes and allows for the control of the people over that which is their creation—the political regime.

Hobbes would certainly question how a political society with the democratic structure I have outlined could be either long-lived or stable. And indeed the types of rules that together constitute the governing convention in modern democracies can govern only because the people of the political society understand them in more or less the same fashion and are prepared to do what is required to ensure that they are followed. But one of the most important lessons we learn from the stratification analysis is that the particular kinds of behavior human beings must perform to ensure that a modern democratic political system survives are ones that all human beings—even the "bad" ones—are capable of performing. As I've described, these behaviors all come under the rubric "maintaining the governing convention." And as people engage in these behaviors, they are engaged in a metagame of controlling the political game, which in modern democracies now includes procedures for revolution itself.[42] The people's control over this political game need not be tight; if the political system and those who rule within it are perceived as performing satisfactorily, public apathy is likely. After all, why participate actively in meta-activities if the political game is going well and the officials are performing (in the people's view) ably in interpreting their role in the various components of the governing convention? However, such apathy can encourage power-hungry or incompetent government officials to make changes in the operation of that game or the interpretation of the rules defining it in ways that benefit them or the interest groups they represent, hurting the people's ability to supervise them. (This can involve everything from trying to pack the Supreme Court to manipulating rules about campaign contributions to make incumbents' reelection highly likely.) As anyone who has been hurt by a bad lawyer will recognize, if the people fail to supervise their agents properly, they may wind up at their agents' mercy. Nonetheless, the object political game is the people's to lose.

But Hobbes would wonder why that loss wouldn't be inevitable, given that effective control of these agents is possible only when the citizens of the democratic regime by and large share a common understanding of what these normative conventions mean, so that they are able to reach a consensus on when they are being followed and when they are being flouted. Despite the stratification analysis that we used to dissolve the paradox of being governed, this may seem problematic. Even assuming that the people are playing a metarole when they judge the officials of the regimes in which they live, nonetheless as they play this role they will have to cooperate and agree with one another to a large degree about what components of the governing convention mean and how well the officials are playing the roles that this rule sets out. But this means the rule will have to be interpreted and enforced by the very people whose inability to cooperate and agree with one another is the fundamental reason for installing a government in the first place. We might call this the "paradox of democracy." So how can such a regime last for any length of time?

We can reply to these Hobbesian worries by pointing out that a modern democracy is explicitly designed to deal with and resolve the sort of disagreements about the performance of the rulers that Hobbes thought were inevitable. A democracy controls these disagreements, channels them into peaceful political paths, and makes the deposing of leaders rather easy if dissatisfaction is great. Rather than rely on a sovereign to banish such disagreement (a solution that post-Hobbesians thought unlikely to work and in any case unacceptable), the framers of modern democracies set up rules that would resolve disagreements about the performance of rulers through the use of various voting procedures. And although there is no voting procedure that can by itself persuade everyone that the outcome of the vote is the correct one, voting can provide a means of evaluating the operation of various parts of the object game that can strike people as fair in the sense that it grants everyone a say and thus allows the opposition to state its case—even while leading in the end to a decision. And the opposition knows that this decision is reversible (in its favor) if it can garner enough votes for its side in the future, which encourages the opposition to remain supportive of the system that in its eyes produced a bad outcome. Moreover, a society has a *democratic culture* when every citizen, including those with large differences in political outlook, can nonetheless follow and agree on the interpretation of those tertiary (or quaternary) elements of the governing convention that set out procedures for resolving that controversy in favor of only one party.

Granted, in order for this style of government to work, the people must be in rough agreement about the correct interpretation of the metarules defining these voting procedures. And even if the interpretation of these rules is by and large relegated to "expert" officials, the people must generally support their interpretive practices if the regime is to be stable and peaceful. Of course one must remember that creating an object political game involves (as I've argued at length elsewhere[43]) the creation of a coercive policing power that, once installed, may be difficult to remove. (After all, those who govern are supposed to have more force than you, so they will be able to prevail upon you not to break the law. But such an advantage can also be used to undermine revolutionary activity against them.) So even considerable unhappiness in the population about how the tertiary rules are being interpreted may still be consistent with the stable and peaceful operation of the regime. Nonetheless, because the policing power of a state relies on people's either being actively involved in policing activities or else refraining from interfering with the operation of this policing power, the continued health of even this institution relies on the people's support of it and their ability to create and sustain at least some rough conventions about what rules mean and how rulers are doing. The success and stability of this style of government in the modern world are proof that at least this minimal cooperation is something human beings are quite capable of, despite Hobbes's cynical assertions to the contrary.

Perhaps the increasing capacity of human beings to communicate and thus coordinate with one another has made this type of regime not only possible but also inevitable, given that governments based upon unconstrained human will cannot survive in a society where it is commonly known that dissatisfaction among the people is rampant. There is, of course, no guarantee that all such governments will remain stable and unified indefinitely, in part because there is no guarantee that the people will be able to maintain a commitment to following and commonly interpreting the metarules defining how to reconcile their disagreements over its operation. But that such highly stratified states are not only possible but surprisingly robust permits us to be optimistic about both the future of fledgling democracies and the continued health of older ones.

Summary and Further Questions

This chapter has tried to show that the convention model of political authority can be developed in a plausible and robust form, in a way that sheds light on the structure of modern democracies. To summarize that model: It represents political authority as something invented by the people through their participation in a governing convention, by which they give what I call convention consent to their regimes. Such consent is insufficient to morally legitimate the regime in full, but it forms the foundations for such legitimation insofar as regimes that do not receive such consent and operate as systems of mastery in which the power structure is sustained purely by force and not by people's participation in a convention cannot be morally justified. The invention of political authority involves creating authoritative offices such that when officeholders issue commands, they give the rest of the populace reasons to perform actions that preempt other reasons these people have to do other things. And this authority must be exercised in ways that are at least minimally rational and moral, else people will not be able to give their convention consent to the regime.

If the political authority is not only minimally rational and moral but also substantially just, then it is a morally legitimate political authority. But full moral legitimacy is not necessary for the existence of political authority (so that there can be morally bad states). States that are just will likely receive the approval of their citizenry—although approval needn't track justice. Giving such approval is what I call endorsement consent (I have also called it loyalty consent). Such consent, if widespread, can make a state particularly robust, stable, and long-lasting. Probably no existing state in the world has ever completely eschewed attempts at mastery over some of its rebellious population, but states that we consider just are ones in which the use of techniques of mastery is rare, the convention consent of the members has generated an agency relationship between the ruler and the people, and most subjects give their endorsement consent. Finally, modern democracies are states in which the recognition that political authority is created and sustained by the people is explicitly built into the structure of the state in the form of voting (for officeholders and laws), constitutional provisions for exercising control over political institutions, constitutional amendment procedures, and so forth.

But there are still many questions we can ask about this model, and we must answer these before we can be assured of its adequacy. First, even if this convention model is more historically plausible than the Lockean or Hobbesian social contract story, is it plausible enough to be historically confirmable? Second, what kind of justice must a state display, such that its authority can be considered morally legitimate on the convention model? And finally, is this model too individualistic? The convention model represents power and authority as conventionally created by particular acts of particular people. But recall that Locke was convinced that political authority comes from a group, not from individuals. Even if the convention account is right that political authority "comes from the people," has it misrepresented the process of creating this authority by making it too reliant on individual acts of individual people, and not sufficiently responsive to the interests and activities of groups?

In the next three chapters, we shall pursue all of these questions as we reflect upon the nature of justice, the nature of the communities making up political societies, and the nature of political membership.

Further Reading

An excellent introduction to the issue of political authority is G.E.M. Anscombe, "On the Source of the Authority of the State," in *Ethics, Religion and Politics: Collected Papers,* vol. 3. A compelling recent discussion can be found in Joseph Raz, *The Morality of Freedom.* Raz's theory has, like virtually all recent discussions of legal authority, been influenced by H.L.A. Hart, *The Concept of Law.* Hart's book is critically discussed by Ronald Dworkin, *Taking Rights Seriously.*

The particular theory of political authority that I develop in this chapter is from Jean Hampton, "Democracy and the Rule of Law," in Ian Shapiro, ed., *The Rule of Law.* My theory is critically discussed in the same volume by Catherine Valcke, "Civil Disobedience and the Rule of Law—A Lockean Insight," and by Michael Zukert, "Hobbes, Locke and the Problem of the Rule of Law." For more readings on the nature of democracy, see the various essays in David Copp, Jean Hampton, and John Roemer, eds., *The Idea of Democracy,* and Thomas Christiano, *The Rule of the Many.*

Finally, students interested in studying further the game theory underlying this chapter should see R. Duncan Luce and Howard Raiffa, *Games and Decisions.*

Notes

1. From David Lewis, *Convention* (Cambridge: Harvard University Press, 1969), p. 24.

2. See R. Duncan Luce and Howard Raiffa, *Games and Decisions* (New York: John Wiley and Sons, 1957), pp. 90–94 and chap. 6.

3. For a book that pursues nonpolitical remedies to state-of-nature problems, see Michael Taylor, *Community, Anarchy and Liberty* (Cambridge: Cambridge University Press, 1982).

4. Joseph Raz, *The Morality of Freedom* (Oxford: Clarendon Press, 1986), p. 46.

5. This is Raz's term in ibid., p. 87.

6. G.E.M. Anscombe, "On the Source of the Authority of the State," in *Ethics, Religion and Politics: Collected Philosophical Papers,* vol. 3 (Minneapolis: University of Minnesota Press, 1981), pp. 130–155.

7. Ibid., p. 134.

8. Ibid., p. 132.

9. The analysis in this section draws and expands upon my reconstruction of the Hobbesian argument for state creation in Jean Hampton, *Hobbes and the Social*

Contract Tradition (Cambridge: Cambridge University Press, 1986). See especially chap. 6.

10. See *Leviathan*, ed. Richard Tuck (Cambridge: Cambridge University Press, 1991), ch. 15, para. 21, pp. 76–77.

11. In his contractarian analysis of the state, Gregory Kavka agrees, noting that people may also agree at this stage on a constitution, explicit legislation, procedural safeguards to be followed in the regime, and so forth. See his *Hobbesian Moral and Political Theory* (Princeton: Princeton University Press, 1986), p. 188.

12. See Hampton, *Hobbes and the Social Contract Tradition*, chap. 6.

13. Lewis, *Convention*, p. 83.

14. The work that began reflections in this area is Thomas Schelling, *The Strategy of Conflict* (Cambridge: Harvard University Press, 1960). See also Michael Taylor, *The Possibility of Cooperation* (Cambridge: Cambridge University Press, 1987); Russell Hardin, *Collective Action* (Baltimore: Johns Hopkins University Press, 1982); and Robert Sugden, "Thinking as a Team: Towards an Explanation of Nonselfish Behavior," in Ellen Paul, Jeffrey Paul, and Fred Miller, eds., *Altruism* (Cambridge: Cambridge University Press, 1993).

15. See Lewis, *Convention*, p. 35.

16. See Hume's discussion of conventions in *A Treatise of Human Nature*, ed. L. A. Selby-Bigge, rev. P. H. Nidditch (Oxford: Clarendon Press, 1978). Hume's ideas influenced contemporary thinkers such as David Lewis; see Lewis's *Convention*.

17. Explicit mention of voting and other democratic choice procedures occurs in Hobbes's *Elements of Law: Natural and Politic*, ed. Ferdinand Tönnies (Cambridge: Cambridge University Press, 1928), pp. 198–199.

18. See Nozick, *Anarchy, State and Utopia* (New York: Basic Books, 1974), pp. 16 ff. Nozick actually constructs three scenarios, but the second and third are not sufficiently different from the first to merit discussion here.

19. In Nozick's words: "Invisible-hand explanations minimize the use of notions constituting the phenomena to be explained; in contrast to the straightforward explanations, they don't explain complicated patterns by including the full-blown pattern-notions as objects of people's desires or beliefs. Invisible-hand explanations of phenomena thus yield greater understanding than do explanations of them as brought about by design as the object of people's intentions. It is therefore no surprise that they are more satisfying." Ibid., pp. 18–19.

20. Locke, *Two Treatises of Government*, ed. Peter Laslett (Cambridge: Cambridge University Press, 1988), Second Treatise, chap. 9, sec. 129, pp. 352–353.

21. Of course the state is continually threatened by those who claim to be higher authorities than the ruler, for example, religious figures. Hobbes was particularly contemptuous of and hostile toward the religious figures of his day who maintained their right to disregard the commands of their ruler because a higher authority (e.g., the pope, a Protestant leader, even their own consciences informed by God through prayer and biblical revelation) permitted them to do so.

22. The literature on iterated PD arguments is voluminous, but for a well-known discussion see Robert Axelrod, *The Evolution of Cooperation* (New York: Basic Books, 1984).

23. Hobbes argued that it was against reason for a subject to rebel against her government, but I have argued (in *Hobbes and the Social Contract Tradition*, chaps. 8

and 9) that the premisses of his argument commit him to the rationality of rebellion in certain circumstances. That discussion runs along roughly the same lines as the discussion here.

24. Kavka, *Hobbesian Moral and Political Theory,* p. 257.

25. I might also have used the term *rule of recognition,* made famous by H.L.A. Hart, instead of the term "governing convention." See Hart's discussion in *The Concept of Law* (Oxford: Clarendon Press, 1961). For Hart, a rule of recognition is one that allows us to recognize who the political authority is and thus what the authoritative commands are in a state. For a discussion of Hart's approach to authority, see Ronald Dworkin, "Model of Rules I," in Dworkin's *Taking Rights Seriously* (Cambridge: Harvard University Press, 1977).

26. See Martin Luther King Jr., "Letter from Birmingham City Jail," in Hugo Bedau, ed., *Civil Disobedience: Theory and Practice* (New York: Pegasus, 1969).

27. For a discussion of civil disobedience that relates to this analysis of convention consent, see Catherine Valcke, "Civil Disobedience and the Rule of Law—A Lockean Insight," in Ian Shapiro, ed., *The Rule of Law* (New York: New York University Press, 1994).

28. For a discussion of the importance of justice to trust, see Raz, *The Morality of Freedom,* p. 91.

29. Raz also recognizes differences in the relationships the state has with people in its territory; see ibid., pp. 104–105.

30. Anscombe, "On the Source of the Authority," p. 136.

31. Augustine once remarked that "without justice, states are but robber bands enlarged." (In Latin the saying goes: "Remota justitia, quid sunt regna nisimagna latrocinia." The saying is discussed in ibid.) On this analysis, Augustine's saying would be revised to read, "Without the people's convention consent, states are but robber bands enlarged."

32. This solution is based on the one that I offered in Hampton, *Hobbes and the Social Contract Tradition,* chap. 9.

33. See Hart's famous discussion of primary and secondary rules in his *Concept of Law* (Oxford: Clarendon Press, 1961).

34. See Hampton, "The Contractarian Explanation of the State," in Theodore Uehling, ed., *The Philosophy of the Human Sciences,* Midwest Studies in Philosophy, vol. 15 (Minneapolis: University of Minnesota Press, 1990).

35. For discussions on the nature of democracy, see David Copp, Jean Hampton, and John Roemer, eds., *The Idea of Democracy* (Cambridge: Cambridge University Press, 1992); and Thomas Christiano, *The Rule of the Many* (Boulder: Westview Press, 1996).

36. See Hampton, "The Contractarian Explanation of the State."

37. For a discussion of Thomas Jefferson's perspective, see R. K. Matthews, *The Radical Politics of Thomas Jefferson: A Revisionist View* (Lawrence: University of Kansas Press, 1984).

38. See Adam Przeworski and John Sprague, *Paper Stones* (Chicago: University of Chicago Press, 1986) for a discussion of this term.

39. This is not unlike Hannah Pitkin's view of the nature of representation in modern democratic societies, as put forth in her book *The Concept of Representation* (Berkeley: University of California Press, 1967). However, Pitkin tends to use the

metaphor of trust, and that metaphor is problematic. A trustor does not own that which is used on his behalf by the trustee. Moreover, unlike in an agent-client relationship, the trustee-trustor relationship is one in which the trustor does not have sufficient standing to fire the trustee and is generally regarded as inferior to or less competent than the trustee, such that he must be subject to the trustee's care. (So children are assigned trustees, and in nineteenth-century England married women could only hold property in trust, in virtue of what was taken to be their inferior reasoning abilities.) The assumptions of the rights of citizens in modern democratic societies are at odds with the presumption of the trustor's incompetence.

40. I am grateful to Pasquale Pasquino for the tenure metaphor here.

41. See Randy Barnett, "Unenumerated Constitutional Rights and the Rule of Law," *Harvard Journal of Law and Public Policy* 14, 3 (Summer 1991): 719.

42. So members of Western democracies can be considered "subjects" not to any political officeholder but to rules they have made, some of which give them control over the officeholder.

43. See Hampton, "The Contractarian Explanation of the State."

PART TWO

The Extent of
Just Political Authority

4

Distributive Justice

This book began with an issue that worries all political anarchists, namely, Why is the coercive power of the state justified? Thus far we have come up with a partial answer to that question: States are justified insofar as they are created via convention by people in a territory to fulfill certain roles considered to be extremely important for moral and for self-interested reasons. This creation process involves inventing a special kind of authority and a considerable coercive power that is then invested in those people who are said to "make up" the state. With this power and authority, these rulers perform the roles for which the state was created. Our analysis has also enabled us to distinguish between what are properly called "states" and (mere) "systems of mastery." People who are citizens of states play a role in maintaining (and have the sufficient freedom to engage in collective action to change) the leadership convention of their society; those who are subject to systems of mastery are dominated through the use of technology that leaves them relatively powerless to change the form of that domination for as long as that technological advantage exists. But as we noted, perhaps all states have some elements of mastery within them.

Nonetheless, this is not a fully satisfactory answer to the anarchists. We know that the state is something that people want, but people can want all sorts of bad things, and they can fail to want good things. Moreover, states throughout the world and throughout history vary enormously in what they have done and how they have functioned, how they have understood their role and how they have understood the role of their subjects. To answer the anarchists properly, we must acknowledge that some states, even if they do not properly qualify as systems of mastery, are still not morally justifiable in view of the kinds of laws they generate and the goals they pursue. And this requires us to specify what goals and laws characterize a decent or *just* state. Those political societies that are not systems of mastery and are therefore maintained by the convention of the people, that attempt to instantiate justice, and that are reasonably successful at doing so constitute on this analysis morally justified political societies and are in and of themselves an answer to the anarchists' claim that political coercion cannot be justified. Indeed, even those who are discontents in such societies could not bring the moral justifiability of such societies into question: How can we take seriously someone discontent with a society that is not only sustained because everyone else wants it but that is also reasonably successful at bringing about justice? Discontents in this society would seem to be those who are either opposed to justice or interested in dominating the people (as opposed to letting them sustain the political system of their choice) for their own (self-regarding) reasons.

There is only one hitch with this argument: There has never been, and is not now, agreement on the nature of justice. Hence political philosophers as well as citizens of existing regimes find themselves in all sorts of disagreements about what a morally justified state ought to be doing and whether any existing state is reasonably just. To the extent that a state is committed to a conception of justice that some individuals within it find morally dubious, they may be unable to recognize the moral legitimacy of their state, even in a society where the existing political forms are sustained by convention. If the majority likes the conception of justice the state is realizing, those who are in the minority are stuck with a political society that in their view is using political authority and power to do the wrong things.

The three chapters in Part 2 review disagreements people have had about justice. There are many aspects of justice in our political system: Each chapter in Part 2 looks at one particular aspect of justice, exploring philosophical controversies that have arisen with respect to it. In this chapter I concentrate on that aspect of justice in which the disagreements are most severe and that has been the most dominant part of political theory since the late 1960s: that is, distributive justice—which involves rules of property and exchange of property, inheritance law, taxation (particularly if it is proposed for purposes of redistributing wealth), and regulations on institutions that are wealth-creating or wealth-using. I review four different ways of defining distributive justice: utilitarianism, Rawlsian contractarianism, libertarianism, and egalitarianism.

In view of these disagreements, there is no way that the citizens of any regime on earth can unanimously agree that any one regime is largely successful at realizing justice, since adherents of any one of these views will object to states that do not endorse their favorite view. This seems to give the anarchists an advantage! Given all the disagreements about justice, anarchists can claim that no state uncontroversially qualifies as just, so that no extant state can be considered morally legitimate. However, this argument is unfair in many respects: As we shall see, there is sufficient overlap among these views to allow adherents to reach considerable agreement on those states that are clearly doing badly (those in which most of the people are badly impoverished fail everyone's test of a just state) and states that are doing well (those that have a well-nourished and happy population where individuals are treated equally and have lots of opportunities, political powers, and resources pass everyone's test of a just state). Nonetheless, there is at present no univocal answer to the question, What does a fully just state look like? At the end of this chapter, readers are left to reflect on the extent to which the states of which they are members satisfy the criteria of justice set out by the theory they take to be most plausible.

I conclude the chapter with a brief discussion of the views of a number of theorists, including Karl Marx, who argue that all attempts to define distributive justice so as to make a society distributively just are "too late," in that any distribution of resources in the state reflects and is generated by prior systemic (and largely economic) structures in that society. To ensure a better distribution, on this view, we must first change these structures, using conceptions of justice that do not directly bear on distributive matters. This discussion prepares the way for Chapters 5 and 6, where we examine theories that attempt to clarify other aspects of justice.

Utilitarianism

The theory of utilitarianism was outlined by the English philosopher Jeremy Bentham (1748–1832), who was intent on providing a political theory for the British Parliament and other governments to use in constructing sound, rational legislation. Bentham was discontent with (what he regarded as) the aimless and "unscientific" character of the legislation process in his day and critical of the idea that significant and genuinely reforming legislation could be based on the traditional (and in his view obscure) idea of "rights." (He once remarked, "Natural rights is simple nonsense: natural and imprescriptible rights, rhetorical nonsense—nonsense upon stilts.")[1] So Bentham argued that lawmakers should use what he called the "principle of utility" to construct morally sound legislation. While its concrete details are not likely to be familiar to many readers, Bentham's theory has been a powerful influence within the institutional structures of many states today, used in the decisionmaking of courts, government departments, and economic institutions. Bentham and many of his subsequent followers have argued that the principle of utility is also the best account of how individuals should assess the morality of their actions, but here I shall only be considering utilitarianism's success as a theory of justice for political institutions.

According to Bentham, just as we as individuals lead our lives by choosing to do things that we take to maximize our own happiness, a state should choose what actions to perform and what policies to adopt by determining what would maximize the happiness of the state. But what does "maximizing the happiness of the state" mean? Bentham argued that it means maximizing the happiness of members of its community.[2] Bentham's idea can be explained metaphorically as follows: Imagine that each person is a kind of well containing a certain amount of happiness (which might be equal to zero or, if she is in pain, might actually be negative). For any policy it is considering, the state, he says, should determine how that policy's adoption would affect each individual's personal well of happiness—either by increasing or decreasing the amount in it. And it should adopt those policies and perform those actions that affect these wells of happiness such that the total amount of happiness in all of these wells is as great as possible. Bentham thought of this as maximizing "utility," which he defines as follows:

> By utility is meant that property in any object, whereby it tends to produce benefit, advantage, pleasure, good, or happiness (all this in the present case comes to the same thing), or (what comes again to the same thing) to prevent the happening of mischief, pain, evil or unhappiness to the party whose interest is considered: if that party be the community in general, then the happiness of the community: if a particular individual, then the happiness of that individual.[3]

Bentham then defines the *principle of utility* as that principle which commands a state to maximize the utility of the community: "A measure of government . . . may be said to be conformable to or dictated by the principle of utility, when in like manner the tendency which it has to augment the happiness of the community is greater than any which it has to diminish it."[4] He defends this principle as a way to place legislation on a sound, rational footing, advocating that legislatures use its clear formula for testing proposed laws, rather than relying upon vague, inchoate, and perhaps biased intuitions. Indeed, utilitarianism can be formulated in a completely mathematical way, giving it an air of scientific authority, as follows:

If u_i stands for the utility of any person in a society of n people, then the principle of utility says that a just society should

$$maximize \sum_{i=1}^{n} u_i$$

This formulation constitutes what has been called *classical utilitarianism*.[5] In more recent years, that view has been modified so as to produce what is called *average utilitarianism*, which directs us to maximize the sum of the utility of the members of a society divided by the number of people in that society; to put it mathematically:

$$maximize \ \frac{1}{n} \sum_{i=1}^{n} u_i$$

Classical and average utilitarianism are highly similar, differing only in the stand they take on whether or not happiness can be increased via an increase in population. As the mathematical formulation of classical utilitarianism makes clear, if it is possible to maximize total utility by increasing the number of people in the community, then even if each of these people experiences very little happiness, it is nonetheless appropriate to do so. In contrast, because an average utilitarian will divide the sum of the utility of the members of society by n (the number of people in that society), he will refrain from maximizing utility simply by adding large numbers of new people to the society. To see why, consider what would happen if one tried to increase total utility by increasing the population. With every new person, the number n would increase, until eventually n would grow so large and the utility yield from each additional person would be so small that the sum of utility divided by n would start to decline. Increases in population, on the average utilitarian view, are dictated only up to this point. So average utility is *not* the view that society should maximize each person's "average" welfare but is actually identical to Bentham's utilitarian view, with the exception that it puts a brake on trying to increase total utility by massive unconstrained population increases.

Bentham's principle of utility, whether in its classical or average form, has been persistently alluring to generations of politicians, policymakers, and theorists ever since he promulgated it. It is not only simple and seemingly "scientific" in that it can be given a mathematical formulation (thereby pleasing social scientists who wish to have clear and rigorous foundations for the formulation of policy), but it is also centrally concerned with what many take to be the core of morality, namely, human welfare. It has also been very attractive to proponents of the modern welfare state, who like the idea of a government active in engineering societal institutions using a rigorous principle of reasoning that concerns itself with what (at least arguably) matters most to questions of justice, namely, human welfare.

Yet the principle of utility has been heavily attacked, so that over the years advocates of that principle have felt they needed to modify or redefine it so as to make it plausible. To appreciate these criticisms, consider the interesting theoretical assumptions built into the Benthamite principle of utility. First, Bentham takes it for granted that each of us can evaluate our own happiness. Second, he assumes that this evaluation can also be made by those who are determining policy in a state. Third, his principle assumes that this evaluation is *quantitative*, that is, that happiness is something inside each of us that can be measured and represented by a single (cardinal) number, as if it were "stuff" that came in degrees. Fourth, his principle assumes that the happiness of each person can be added to the happiness of any other person, allowing us not only to compare the happiness of persons (as we do when we say, e.g., that Jane is happier than Mary) but also to add their "happinesses" together to get a sum total of "happinesses" (as if the happiness in each of them was the same "stuff" and could therefore be added together to get a total amount).

It was not long before all of these assumptions were attacked. Consider the third assumption, that evaluation of happiness is (purely) a quantitative matter: Can we really measure people's happiness, assuming that happiness is only one kind of thing that comes in degrees but does not differ in quality or kind? Bentham insisted that happiness was not a word that denoted multiple (and hard-to-compare) experiences or feelings in a human being but only one kind of feeling—that is, the feeling of pleasure, which could be occasioned in people by all sorts of things, from Shakespeare to sports events, from fine champagne to jug wine. Hence evaluating happiness was, for Bentham, nothing more than measuring a person's experience of pleasure (similarly, measuring unhappiness was for him just the same as measuring a person's experience of pain).

But John Stuart Mill, himself a follower of utilitarianism, thought that this view clearly could not be right, since we intuitively think that experiences of "pleasure" not only differ in quantity but also in quality. Mill sympathized with critics of Bentham who contended that the idea that life has "no higher end than pleasure" was "utterly mean and grovelling,"[6] which would tell us it was better to be a pig satisfied than a Socrates dissatisfied. Because Mill says that very few human beings "would consent to be changed into any of the lower animals, for a promise of the fullest allowance of a beast's pleasures," he argues that this means pleasures differ in kind according to their value, so that a lower animal experiences only the low sort, whereas human beings have the capacity to experience the high and better sort: "some *kinds* of pleasure are more desirable and more valuable than others. It would be absurd that while, in estimating all other things, quality is considered as well as quantity, the estimation of pleasures should be thought to depend on quantity alone."[7] Hence Mill concludes that

it is better to be a human being dissatisfied than a pig satisfied; better to be Socrates dissatisfied than a fool satisfied. And if the fool, or the pig, are of a different opinion, it is because they only know their own side of the question. The other side of the comparison knows both sides.[8]

Yet note that if Mill is right, it is hard to reformulate the principle of utility so that it gives determinate answers. To do so we would have to formulate the different types of pleasure (differentiating the number and nature of high and low types) and define a way of measuring each type. Then we would have various numbers representing how much happiness each person would be experiencing. But once we do that, we become puzzled: Which numbers (of which types) would we use when we tried to "maximize utility"? Would we simply maximize higher pleasure? Lower pleasure? Some mixture of the two? Wouldn't we need some principle to tell us the answer, and wouldn't that principle have to involve moral ideas that are prior to the principle of utility (such as "higher pleasure is the only pleasure relevant to a just society"), making the principle of utility either dependent upon or derived from these more foundational moral ideas? Mill never directly confronted these questions, so many theorists since have thought that his way of "fixing" utilitarianism makes it even more problematic and obscure than Bentham's understanding of the theory.

Next consider Bentham's first assumption that each of us can evaluate how happy she or he is using a number that represents the total happiness each of us now experiences or would experience after the implementation of some policy. Yet critics have puzzled over whether such an evaluation is possible. Could any of you say right now exactly how "happy" you are? Are your experiences of yourself transparent enough to allow you to measure your pleasure (and pain) with even the remotest accuracy? Indeed, if your pleasure comes in different types, as Mill says, such measurement is even more difficult, because each type would have to be identified and separately measured. Moreover, if none of us can come up with a reliable measure of our own happiness, then Bentham's second assumption is in trouble—because if we can't know how happy any of us is, how can politicians or policymakers know how happy we are?

Bentham's fourth assumption is arguably the most troublesome, because even assuming that any of us can know how happy we are, how can it be possible for us to *quantitatively compare* our happiness with the happiness of others? While we make *ordinal* comparisons of happiness all the time (e.g., when I say that I am happier now than a person suffering great physical pain), we do not have the kind of access to other people's experiential states that allows us to know *exactly how much happier* we are than other people. That is, we do not know how to make *cardinal* comparisons of utility across people. But in order to implement the principle of utility, we not only have to be able to come up with an ordinal ranking of people from most happy to least happy, but we also have to know how much happier each person higher on the scale is than those below her on that scale.

The difficulty of coming up with comparable cardinal measures of the utility of many people in the society is called the interpersonal comparison of utility problem, and it has made many people conclude that Bentham's principle of utility, however appealing in theory, is impossible to implement and thus a false moral "science." After all, a real science would be able to give concrete, nonambiguous legislative prescriptions, but the interpersonal comparison problem makes this impossible. For if we don't know how to appraise the extent to which any person is happier than any other, how can we evaluate the impact of various possible policies on a group's happiness?

To see how this problem poses practical difficulties in applying Bentham's theory, consider the controversy that surrounds the purported phenomenon of "diminishing marginal utility." Proponents of the reality of this phenomenon will say that one dollar means far more to a poor person than it does to a rich person and, more generally, that the utility experienced by someone with few resources after being given a good is greater than the utility experienced by someone with far greater resources after being given the same good. If this phenomenon is real, goods should be distributed relatively equally. But how do we know whether or not it is real, given that we cannot get inside the minds of other people and compare their experiences with our own? Why can't there be people who experience steady and significant increases in utility despite great resources, so that the group's happiness would be maximized not by equal distribution but by giving far more to them than to others? A proper "science of justice" would tell us decisively how to maximize group utility, but utilitarianism does not seem to be able to do so, with the result that many critics have dismissed it as an unworkable theory.

Many people who are attracted to the principle of utility have argued, however, that we should not abandon Bentham's idea but only redesign it. They argue for a better way of identifying human welfare, such that it can be quantified, measured, and aggregated. In the latter half of the twentieth century, one proposal for doing so involves the idea of "satisfaction of preferences." On this view, human welfare is not to be identified with some notion of pleasure but simply with the satisfaction of (whatever) preferences a person happens to have, where those preferences can be those of a Socrates or those of a fool or some mixture of both. Maximizing the community's "happiness" or "utility" then simply involves the maximal satisfaction of preferences of people in the community.

Moreover, contemporary expected utility theory, developed by John von Neumann, Oskar Morgenstern, and Leonard Savage,[9] has generated a way of doing something like "measuring" the satisfaction of preferences, so that we come up with a number that accurately reflects how well a person has received what she wants (no matter what those wants are, whether "high" or "low"), showing the intensity of those wants. And while these "measurement numbers" are not, as they stand, able to be added together as the principle of utility requires (so that expected utility theory does not solve the interpersonal comparison of utility problem),[10] some people have argued that this approach is promising enough to enable us to postulate the possibility of using ideas from expected utility theory to come up with numbers that can be added together.[11]

Critics (such as Amartya Sen) argue that such an idea is wrong—and that expected utility theory is misused if it is seen as a source for the foundation of a notion of welfare that will be serviceable to the utilitarian.[12] Such critics raise technical issues about the nature of the "measurement" of preferences that game theory gives. I cannot pursue that argument here,[13] but I can explore a second issue: that is, whether game theory can be used to answer the interpersonal comparison problem defined above.

Critics have argued that the idea of "preference satisfaction" is unacceptable as an interpretation of what human "welfare" involves and hence the wrong notion to use in developing the idea of utility. After all, people can have preferences involving other's harm, for example, when a man wants to rape a woman or when a thief wants to steal another's possessions. Is it really appropriate to take these preferences into account in the determination of the happiness of the community? More generally, shouldn't a society be concerned with identifying and satisfying only the "important" preferences of people, where importance is not necessarily the same as the intensity with which they are felt? Yet how is "importance" to be defined, and, once again, isn't it a moral notion that must be prior to (and foundational for) the principle of utility (since that principle could, on this view, be stated only if we understand what "important" preferences determinant of a person's welfare actually are)? If this is right, then once again the principle of utility turns out not to be a foundational idea for the determination of policy after all.

Defenders of utilitarianism may reply that any evaluation of preferences so as to determine which ones are authentic or acceptable to include in the utilitarian calculus should not be performed, insofar as such calculations rely on inchoate (and probably unreliable) intuitions. On this view, all preferences must be admitted, no matter how immoral or nonsensical their content may strike us.

But bravely biting the bullet and allowing any and every preference into the utilitarian calculation won't work, because given that each person's preferences constantly change during her lifetime, the utilitarian will still need some way of determining which preferences at which time the society should take seriously, lest she include in that calculation inconsistent preferences that make the task of maximizing preference satisfaction impossible. But how do we make this determination? Do we ignore the preferences of a child, since such preferences often change, and satisfy only those we think she will have when she grows up? Similarly, do we ignore the preferences of young men and women, knowing they will also change? For example, suppose a committed atheist who has always said he never wants a priest to give him last rites on his deathbed changes his mind as he is dying and demands that a priest be brought to him. Which of his preferences during his life should we take seriously? Note that a form of utilitarianism that assumes happiness is pleasure has a way to generate determinate answers to such questions (that is, it can say: Take seriously whatever preference will lead to the overall maximization of pleasure in the community). But to answer the same questions, the preference-satisfaction theorist seems either to have to rely upon intuitions of just the sort she has previously dismissed as unreliable, or she must admit to having nothing to say to answer such questions, because she has no theory telling us *which* of a person's changeable preferences are important or authentically "hers" and thus no way of making the determination about what a person "really" prefers that the utilitarian state requires to formulate policies. Moreover, highly attentuated forms of utilitarianism that try to avoid these problems by merely requiring each person to express her ordinal preferences over various possible policies and then constructing a social welfare function from these preferences turn out not to succeed. Kenneth Arrow has proved what has come to be called Arrow's impossibility theorem, which says that there is no way to aggregate ordinal preferences of individuals in a society so as to produce such a social welfare function given suitably plausible conditions.[14]

These sorts of problems have eroded the popularity of utilitarianism in our time. Yet critics have argued that there are even more serious problems plaguing the theory, having to do with the kind of policy recommendations it would generate if its foundational assumptions could be better clarified and defended. Consider, for example, that the theory tells us to maximize *total* happiness. Now if maximizing total happiness depended upon impoverishing some members of the society, the principle of utility would nonetheless tell us to do it. Yet this intuitively strikes us as unfair. That is, if there are ten people in a society and policy A would have us distribute goods equally to all of them, resulting in (say) 100 units of total utility, whereas policy B would have us distribute goods to eight of them, leaving two with nothing but resulting in 110 units of total utility, the principle of utility would tell us to choose policy B. But how can this be just? The principle of utility seems to violate our intuitions about justice in a way that many people take to show that it cannot be the right moral theory for a state to rely upon in its efforts to generate just legislation.

Some utilitarians defend their theory from this example by pointing out that it is too fanciful to be taken seriously, because they believe in the phenomenon of diminishing marginal utility discussed earlier, in which a good is supposed to produce more utility in a poor person than in a rich person. If this phenomenon is real, it seems that maximizing utility in the distribution of goods should generally mean doing so in a way that leaves no one impoverished and that will result in fairly equal distributions of resources. So if the state has a choice between giving a dollar to a poor person and giving it to a rich person, diminishing marginal utility tells it to give the dollar to the poor person because doing so will generate greater total utility. Doesn't this accord with our intuitions about justice?

Critics of utilitarianism reply, however, that there is no *necessity* to this result: The phenomenon may not be real or may have only limited applicability. And if conditions are such that as a matter of fact maximal total utility can be purchased at the price of damaging a few, utilitarianism dictates doing so. It is the fact that utilitarianism does not have a *principled* commitment to equality to which critics object and that makes them reject it as a theory of justice. It is not enough that the theory may be able *usually* to generate egalitarian policies that eschew the impoverishment of some; these critics require a theory of justice that will *always* be committed to such policies. Note that the mere fact that utilitarianism may require some people to sacrifice something for the well-being of the community is not what these critics are objecting to: All theories of justice will sometimes have to require that (e.g., when a community needs land for highways that its owners do not wish to sell). Instead these critics complain that utilitarianism has no principled way of precluding sacrifices on the part of individuals for the benefit of the community that are *too great* and that cannot be morally defended.

There is another way that critics have made the same type of argument against the theory. Consider that, for a utilitarian, punishment in a political society is justified if and only if it will maximize total utility. Now in general it seems that punishing people guilty of some crime will maximize utility by deterring them and others from performing criminal actions (which are utility-subtracting) in the future. But what if punishing a person who is guilty of a wrongdoing will not, as it happens, bring about any increased utility in the society (let's suppose this person would never commit the crime again and that punishing her will have no deterrent effect). Given that inflicting punishment on her would lower her utility, it would seem that the principle of utility would tell us not to punish her, since doing so would only result in a cost to total utility and no gains. But again, it seems to be a violation of our intuitions of justice that we fail to punish a guilty person. Even more alarming, the principle of utility can dictate the punishment of an innocent person if doing so will maximize total utility. For example, suppose that the community is convinced that a person has committed a crime, despite evidence known to the government that she has not. Suppose further that the community will engage in violent rioting unless they see this person punished. Wouldn't the principle of utility dictate punishing this innocent person, insofar as doing so will prevent violent riots and cost only the suffering of one life? But once again, doing so violates our intuitions of justice, so that the principle of utility seems to yield the wrong results and thus be an incorrect account of the moral foundations of a just state.

Some utilitarians charge that these examples are misleading in the way that they focus on particular events rather than general rules. Societies, they say, formulate *general* policies in the form of laws. These laws address what is normally the case. So given that it is normally the case that punishing guilty people is a way of maximizing total utility, whereas punishing innocent people is not, we should understand the principle of utility as dictating a rule to punish only guilty people. So these theorists understand the principle of utility as dictating not particular actions but general rules or policies—and the general rules or policies dictated by the principle of utility, they argue, *do* accord with our intuitions. Such a position is known as rule utilitarianism, in contrast to act utilitarianism, which is the view Bentham suggests. Indeed, Mill insists (in *Utilitarianism*, chapter 5) that we can even understand how the principle of utility can yield a notion of "rights" if we appreciate the way a person's rights are defined by rules regarding the treatment of human beings that are by and large utility-maximizing for the community.

Yet critics of utilitarianism persist in saying that the proponents of the principle of utility have to argue for the violation of these "rights" and make exceptions to general rules and policies whenever doing so is utility-maximizing, or otherwise they will behave as "rule worshipers"—that is, they will care more about rules and rights than about total utility, in violation of their own theory. So it seems that as long as one uses a broad interpretation of 'acts' to refer either to laws or particular commands, only act utilitarianism is consistent with the injunction of the principle of utility. Since act utilitarianism allows exceptions to rules whenever total utility can be maximized, such exceptions can result in governmental action that strikes us as unjust.

Note how these criticisms of utilitarianism rely on our "intuitions." Some theorists have worried about what these intuitions are and why we should take them seriously. As I've noted, utilitarianism aims to place our moral reasoning on a sound rational footing—one that we can clearly understand and apply. Should it be defeated by examples that rely on ideas that may be inchoate and obscure and whose moral credibility is hard to determine?

Some people have actually put forward a moral theory called intuitionism. On this view, we have fundamental moral ideas within us that are the source of our conceptions of justice and to which any adequate moral conception must answer. However, such a theory has not proven popular: First, it has no resources within it to systematize or interpret intuitions if they come to us in an inchoate form. Second, it has no theoretical resources to prioritize among intuitions or decide between them when they conflict. Third, and perhaps most important, given that many intuitions held by people reflect the prejudices, injustices, and peculiarities of their culture, intuitionism must be able to identify which intuitions should be morally relied upon—and yet it does not have the theoretical resources to do so. We should not take seriously, from a moral point of view, or build into the political society the very ideas that a good theory of justice should be trying to combat and replace.

Hence philosophers critical of utilitarianism have attempted to formulate alternatives to intuitionism that could not only show the failure of the principle of utility in a way that relies less on intuition but also yield a satisfactory conception of justice based on reason. The most prominent of these attempts, by John Rawls, is the topic of our next section.

Rawls's Theory of Justice

In 1971 John Rawls published *A Theory of Justice,* and political philosophy hasn't been the same since.[15] Not only did Rawls set the stage for a large-scale reconsideration of the nature of distributive justice by philosophers critical of utilitarianism, but he also gave new life to the discipline of political philosophy, which was largely moribund in the Anglo-American world in the first half of the twentieth century. Influenced by the political turmoil of the 1960s, Rawls's vision of the just state is deeply egalitarian in spirit in a way that many have found compelling. Even critics of his vision have been excited and influenced by the argument Rawls uses to defend it.

That argument makes use of the idea of a hypothetical social contract, applied not to the nature of the state's authority over the people but to the nature of justice. We are, says Rawls, to imagine ourselves in a contract situation in which we must agree with all those people who will live with us in a society on the principles of justice that will govern it. Rawls argues that any principle of justice that results from this hypothetical agreement process should be understood to be the best defensible conception of justice available to us. But before we review the details of this contract argument and the way Rawls uses it to argue against utilitarianism and for his own conception of justice, we should appreciate how it is prefigured in the work of certain ancient and modern philosophers and yet importantly different in both form and aim from the social contract arguments of Hobbes and Locke.[16]

One of the first people to suggest the idea that a contract could be used to illuminate the nature of justice was Plato in book 2 of the *Republic*, although Plato suggests a rather Hobbesian version of that idea and plants it in the mouth of Glaucon, whom Socrates attempts to refute using the perfectionist ideas we reviewed in Chapter 1. It is also an idea explored by the Stoic Epicurus (341–270 B.C.), who says that "natural justice is a pledge of advantage, towards not harming or being harmed by one another," where this pledge is contractual: "There is no such thing as justice in itself; in people's relations with one another in any place and at any time it is a contract about not harming or being harmed."[17]

In more modern times, the contractual nature of justice was explored by Immanuel Kant (1724–1804), particularly in passages from *The Metaphysical Elements of Justice* that surely influenced Rawls. When Kant uses the idea of the social contract, it is *not* meant to illuminate the nature of political authority; instead, it is meant to be an "idea of reason" that can help us to determine the form and content of just legislation. In his later writings, Kant proposes that the "idea" of the "original contract" could be used to determine which policies for a society would be just. By asking what people could agree to, Kant does not try to justify governmental actions or policies by invoking in any literal sense the consent of the people; instead, he believes that this question generates a thought experiment that is morally revealing:

> We need by no means assume that this contract (*contractus originarius* or *pactum sociale*), based on a coalition of the wills of all private individuals in a nation to form a common, public will for the purposes of rightful legislation, actually exists as a *fact*, for it cannot possibly be so. . . . It is in fact merely an *idea* of reason, which nonetheless has undoubted practical reality; for it can oblige every legislator to frame his laws in such a way that they could have been produced by the united will of a whole nation, and to regard each subject, in so far as he can claim citizenship, as if he had consented within the general will. This is the test of the rightfulness of every public law. For if the law is such that a whole people could not *possibly* agree to it (for example, if it stated that a certain class of *subjects* must be privileged as a hereditary *ruling class*) it is unjust.[18]

So for Kant, thinking about what laws people could agree to reveals something about what sorts of law are just. To illustrate, he argues that laws allowing slavery or legal policies that make some people masters over others would be rejected by those people who would be dominated, so that they would refuse to agree to it. In contrast, he implies that policies recognizing the equal status of each person would be agreed to by everyone, which indicates that these policies are just. In this way, thinking about what people could agree to gives us a way to test the moral adequacy of policies that a state might adopt. One might think of the idea of a social contract as a kind of "moral proof procedure."[19]

Why does the social contract idea work as a test for the moral adequacy of policies or laws? Kant seems to think that this idea acknowledges the way in which, to use his language, people should be treated as "ends in themselves" and not solely as "means."[20] If someone is intrinsically valuable and not merely valuable as a tool or a means to someone else's ends, then her importance and interests should be acknowledged by other people and institutions—including the state. A social contract test of political policies is, in Kant's view, a way to secure that acknowledgment by hypothetically involving each member of the society in the assessment of those policies in a way that respects his interests and perspectives as an individual.

Rawls also believes that a contract test takes the individual seriously in a way that utilitarianism does not. Rawls argues that in the utilitarian calculation the boundaries of the individuals are merged, and what is morally important about them—that is, their welfare—is aggregated together. In the end it is this aggregated "stuff" that the calculation tells us to focus upon. It does not tell us to concern ourselves with how that stuff is distributed among individuals and even permits a highly unequal distribution of resources as long as this will maximize it. Yet for Rawls, justice is concerned not merely with human welfare but with each individual's welfare. Instead of endorsing a moral reasoning procedure that explicitly conflates individuals, Rawls argues that an adequate theory of justice must morally respond to, and preserve, the "distinction of persons":

> It is customary to think of utilitarianism as individualistic, and certainly there are good reasons for this. The utilitarians were strong defenders of liberty and freedom of thought, and they held that the good of society is constituted by the advantages enjoyed by individuals. Yet utilitarianism is not individualistic, at least when arrived at by the more natural course of reflection, in that, by conflating all systems of desires, it applies to society the principle of choice for one man.[21]

It is as if, says Rawls, the utilitarian reasoning procedure responded to the various bits of welfare experienced by people in a society as part of one large corporate person,[22] and yet a society cannot be considered in such a way, insofar as it is made up of many people, each of whom demands respect and concern for her well-being.

A reasoning procedure that invokes the idea of an agreement or contract, claims Rawls, will involve each individual in the assessment of the effects of any conception of justice in a way that secures the respect for each person that justice requires. The beauty of a contract argument is that it involves each individual in the selection of the best conception of justice, such that any conception that would allow the society to use (or sacrifice) some people for the benefit of others in substantial ways could not be agreed upon. Hence Rawls believes that a contractarian way of thinking about justice provides us with a way of specifying the nature of justice so as to determine what policies and laws a just state should implement, ones that are appropriately responsive to the moral claims of each person—in a way that we intuitively believe to be required by justice.

Unlike Kant, Rawls also argues that the contract procedure should test large-scale (and relatively abstract) conceptions of justice, rather than, say, particular laws or policies. We need, he says, a charter for a well-ordered society, not some kind of piecemeal approach to just legislation. Such a conception can then be used to assess and/or construct social institutions, economic frameworks, and structural features of a polity, as well as specific laws and governmental policies. This holistic rather than piecemeal approach to constructing a just society is required, on Rawls's view, because individuals are deeply affected (and their very identifies determined) by large-scale societal institutions. (Think of the effect on each of us of capitalism and institutions like the family, the church, and the legal system.) Rawls believes that only if those social institutions are appraised and revised from the standpoint of an overall conception of justice can we be sure that they will operate in a way that honors and respects each individual. To construct such a conception, he asks us to perform a thought experiment in which people have to decide among alternative conceptions of justice, the two most prominent of which he takes to be utilitarianism (he distinguishes between rule and act utilitarianism and classical and average utilitarianism[23]) and his own theory, which he calls "justice as fairness." He argues that the conception of justice the contracting parties would all agree upon is that conception of justice which best instantiates the concept of justice, at least until and unless a better conception is developed (in which case people in this hypothetical contract situation would agree on this better conception).

The winning conception, he argues, would be his own, and it consists of the following two principles:

First Principle: "Each person is to have an equal right to the most extensive liberty compatible with a similar liberty for others."

Second Principle (also called the "Difference" Principle): "Social and economic inequalities are to be arranged so that they are both (a) reasonably expected to be to everyone's advantage—and in particular, to the advantage of the least-well-off persons, and (b) attached to positions and offices open to all."[24]

Rawls also specifies that the first principle is prior to the second, meaning that equality of liberty must be pursued prior to the distribution of social and economic resources. Note that unlike utilitarianism, this conception of justice stresses equality and concern for everyone—including the least advantaged.

Rawls's basic idea is this: Primary goods are to be distributed by the state equally, unless an unequal distribution would be to everyone's advantage. Whereas unequal distributions of liberty are never desirable, he does accept that it may be possible that unequal distributions of, say, wealth could be desirable insofar as giving more to some people will result in their using these resources in a way that expands the "economic pie," yielding more for everyone. Not to allow some people to have more wealth than others even in a situation where they will use that wealth to increase the allotment of goods for everyone is, says Rawls, to be animated by an irrational (and morally disreputable) kind of envy. So Rawls is not a strict egalitarian. However, he does allow that if inequality in holdings becomes too extreme, there might be such a thing as "reasonable envy,"[25] reflecting the way in which extreme inequality can negatively affect some people's self-respect. In that situation Rawls is prepared to acknowledge that self-respect (which he holds to be one of the primary goods) puts a brake on acceptable inequality.

Rawls is not content simply to appeal to raw intuition to defend his claim that people would prefer, and agree on, his theory. He believes he has to describe the agreement process in sufficient detail such that the people's agreement on his conception of justice makes sense. He also believes that spelling out this agreement process involves defining the contractarian "moral proof procedure" in a way that will not only make it clearer what moral ideas are relevant to understanding the nature of justice but also exclude extraneous ideas that could morally distort or pervert the reasoning process.

So Rawls develops a detailed account of the social contract situation that people are in prior to the agreement process, spelling out the considerations that they do and do not take seriously in their consideration of alternative conceptions of justice. He calls this situation the "original position." As we shall see, many people who like Rawls's appeal to a social contract (and agree with his criticism of utilitarianism as insufficiently respectful of individuals) find things to criticize in his development of the original position and thus reason to question his conclusion that the contract methodology vindicates his conception of justice. Truly, when it comes to contractarian theories of justice, the devil is in the details.

The most important feature of Rawls's original position procedure is what he calls the "veil of ignorance." In order to ensure that people are sufficiently free of bias, prejudice, racist or sexist views—indeed, anything that could cause their preferences over conceptions of justice to be morally distorted—he makes each person in this position ignorant of her place in society, her particular religious or metaphysical views, her moral beliefs, her social theories, and so forth. In this way, he says, we create a situation where the contracting parties are able to form preferences over conceptions of justice in an objective and impartial way:

> The idea here is simply to make vivid to ourselves the restrictions that it seems reasonable to impose on arguments for principles of justice, and therefore on these principles themselves. Thus it seems reasonable and generally acceptable that no one should be advantaged or disadvantaged by natural fortune or social circumstances in the choice of principles. . . . One excludes the knowledge of those contingencies which sets men at odds and allows them to be guided by their prejudices. In this manner, the veil of ignorance is arrived at in a natural way.[26]

After the knowledge of "contingencies" is taken away, Rawls says that the individuals who remain can be considered "moral personalities," whose preferences, insofar as they will not be distorted or biased by these contingencies, have moral authority. Moral personalities, says Rawls, are rational, distinct individuals, nonenvious, normal in their attitude toward risk (neither risk averse nor risk seeking), possessing a sense of justice and a capacity to pursue a plan to achieve what they consider to be the good for them.[27]

Having taken away so much, Rawls must give the parties something to reason *with*. Hence, a considerable part of his description of the original position involves arguing for the introduction of certain ideas that he insists are appropriate for them to take seriously in their consideration of alternative conceptions of justice. First, the parties must know that (what are called) the "circumstances of justice" apply in their society, such that a conception of justice is required:[28] In particular, they must know that *goods are limited in number* (but not radically scarce), such that people will compete over them in a way that requires a principle of adjudication, and that *people are limited in their benevolence,* so that we cannot rely on their fellow feelings to provide a remedy for this competition without the help of a conception of justice implemented and enforced by a state.

Second, the parties must know something about what they want. Since they can't know the details of their desires (without violating the veil-of-ignorance condition and potentially introducing bias into their decision-making), Rawls stipulates that these people want as much as possible of what he calls the "primary goods." These are goods whose distribution the state can affect and that are means for achieving individuals' life plans—and are therefore instrumentally valuable. The primary goods are rights and liberties, opportunities and powers, and self-respect. By making the parties "heads of families," Rawls wants the parties to secure these goods not only for themselves but also for their children and their future descendants, ensuring that the conception of justice they select will serve not only the present generation but also future generations.

Third, the parties should regard their decisionmaking as subject to what Rawls calls the "constraints of the concept of right," where these are constraints that Rawls argues any conception of justice must satisfy in order to be adequate as an effective adjudication of competing claims among the citizens. These constraints require that a conception of justice be general, universal, understandable, public, effective at imposing an ordering on competing claims, and final—that is, the final theoretical "court of appeals" in the society.

Fourth, the parties should make the choice of conception using the "maximin rule," which tells the parties to choose so as to maximize their minimum prospects. This rule has been proposed as a rational principle governing decisionmaking when a person is in a "situation of uncertainty," a situation in which she cannot estimate the probability that any single possible outcome will occur. Rawls argues that the parties are in a situation of uncertainty because they cannot estimate the probability that they will be rich or poor, talented or untalented, and so on. Thus, says Rawls, they have to choose as if they might end up being the least-advantaged members of their society, so that they would want that conception of justice which would give them the best deal in that scenario.

Putting all these constraints, veils, and considerations together, the reasoning process of each member of Rawls's original position procedure can be specified in detail as follows:[29]

The Deliberation of a Party in the Original Position

Step 1: Submit oneself to the veil of ignorance, such that one is defined solely as a moral personality.

Step 2: Desire the maximum amount of primary goods possible for oneself and one's family.

Step 3: Know that the circumstances of justice apply in one's society.

Step 4: Subject any conception of justice proposed to the constraints of the concept of right.

Step 5: Because of the veil of ignorance, conclude that one could be anyone in a society; hence choose a conception of justice (satisfying the constraints of the concept of right) knowing that one might turn out to be the least-advantaged member of the society.

Step 6: To ensure that one will have an adequate amount of the primary goods even if one is a member of the least-advantaged class of citizens, choose that conception of justice using the maximin rule, which says that in an uncertain situation, choose so as to maximize one's minimum prospect.

Step 7: In a pairwise choice between (some form of) utilitarianism and "justice as fairness," choose the latter, insofar as the maximin rule dictates the selection of a conception of justice that does not permit the sacrifice of any individual for the community's benefit and distributes resources so as to benefit everyone—in particular the least advantaged (thereby maximizing one's minimum prospect).

By using this argument, Rawls hopes to persuade readers that he has good reasons for commending his theory as correct, without relying on undefended or ill-defined intuitions.

Yet intuition, as he notes, still plays a role in the justification of the principles to this extent: We must rely upon intuition to be sure that the components of the original position are correct, and we must rely upon intuition to determine the plausibility of the conclusions themselves. As Rawls notes, an argument that seems good and yet results in what intuitively strike us as highly implausible conclusions will not be successful, and we will want to revise the argument. We strive, he says, for reflective equilibrium, in which our intuitions, duly examined and considered (or what Rawls calls our "considered convictions"), match the theories (and their conclusions) that we construct.

Aside from the original position argument just given, Rawls also defends his conception of justice more directly as a conception that appropriately respects each person in a society. It is a conception that, he says, not only refuses to allow the unreasonable sacrifice of the resources (including wealth, liberty, and opportunity) of some for the sake of others but also insists that a system of justice not penalize some people because they are less well endowed with talents, skills, or luck than other people:

> No one deserves his greater natural capacity nor merits a more favorable starting place in society. But it does not follow that one should eliminate these distinctions. There is another way to deal with them. The basic structure can be arranged so that these contingencies work for the good of the least fortunate. Thus we are led to the difference principle if we wish to set up the social system so that no one gains or loses from his arbitrary place in the distribution of natural assets or his initial position in society without giving or receiving compensating advantages in return.[30]

So Rawls is eschewing not only inequality that is not to the advantage of all but, more fundamentally, all forms of (what might be called) "caste" thinking: He wants a system of justice that treats people as equal no matter their natural talents, life prospects, skills, temperamental assets, beliefs, ethnicity, or gender.

Both Rawls's original position argument and its conclusions have been the subject of enormous discussion not only in America but throughout the world since the publication of his book, and while many have supported them, many others have criticized them. Some critics simply attack his conclusions; others attack his argument, paying less attention to the conception of justice it is used to justify. It is worth reflecting on both kinds of criticisms.

Let us begin with the objections critics have made to Rawls's original position argument. First, there is the issue of whether it is really "contractarian" at all. Note that when I stated the argument above, I (deliberately) represented it as a reasoning procedure followed by *one* person in the original position procedure. Any single person, reasoning alone, would prefer Rawls's two principles if he reasoned in this way. So has Rawls presented his theory of justice as endorsed by *contract* thinking? While it is always possible for him to postulate a contract's occurring after each party has determined his preferences over the alternatives, in fact the *reason* the two principles are selected by each person in the original position seems to have nothing to do with such a contract but rather with the fact that each person, reasoning on his own, knows that "he could be any person" and thus chooses so as to ensure that the least advantaged do not lose out. It therefore appears that it is the idea that "I could be anyone," and not the prospect of having to agree with any other person in this position, that leads to the choice of the two principles.[31] Indeed, since every person in the original position, insofar as he is subject to the veil of ignorance, is defined in exactly the same way, Rawls has no basis upon which to ground any kind of bargaining among these identically defined parties. And he even admits this fact:

> It is clear that since the differences among the parties are unknown to them, and everyone is equally rational and similarly situated, each is convinced by the same arguments. Therefore, we can view the choice in the original position from the standpoint of one person selected at random. If anyone after due reflection prefers a conception of justice to another, then they all do, and a unanimous agreement can be reached.[32]

But if the choice of the two principles is not a function of any contract in Rawls's hypothetical contract situation, why should we take his argument to be contractarian? I have found this question intriguing and have pursued it at some length,[33] because it is a way of exploring the philosophical and moral ideas that are subtly motivating Rawls's original position argument.

Now perhaps there is a connection between the sort of acknowledgment of the individual that seems intuitively required by contract arguments and the "I could be anyone" idea animating the reasoning of Rawls's original position parties. If that is so, both forms of argument could be considered species of a more fundamental (and Kantian) approach to understanding justice (along with other moral matters) that stressed the importance and value of every individual. Each style of argument would then be a particular formulation of this more fundamental approach.[34] Alternatively (as some have argued), that Rawls fails to incorporate a contract into his argument might be thought to damage its credibility and deprive it of some (or all) of its moral power.[35]

One reason to take seriously this last criticism is the way it may be connected to what critics have regarded as a weakness in the argument. Consider the reliance in Rawls's argument on the maximin rule. Many critics (particularly utilitarians) counter that a much more rational way of proceeding in an uncertain situation—and indeed a way that many rational choice theorists commend to real people who are in uncertain situations—is to use the "principle of insufficient reason" to establish reasonable probabilities in this situation and then decide on the basis of those probabilities. The principle of insufficient reason tells a person to set probabilities equal to the number of prospects that might occur; so in the original position, if there are n people in the society, people should, using this principle, estimate the probability that they will be any particular person in this society as $1/n$. But note what happens if they do so: Each will say, "I should choose that conception of justice which will maximize the primary goods that I will receive, where I have a $1/n$ chance of being any person in the society." In other words, each should reason as follows:

$$maximize\left(\left(1/n\right)u_1 + \left(1/n\right)u_2 + \ldots + \left(1/n\right)u_n\right)$$

But note that this is a kind of utilitarian reasoning! In particular, it is identical to average utilitarianism, in which total utility is maximized subject to a constraint on population. So were the parties to reason using this rule of choice under uncertainty, then such a simple (and for many) highly plausible revision to Rawls's original position procedure results in Rawls's argument turning into a kind of utilitarian reasoning procedure. Indeed, John Harsanyi actually advanced something like this reasoning procedure as a way of defending average utilitarianism prior to the appearance of Rawls's book.[36] Advocates of Harsanyi's ideas thus see Rawls as having made a substantial theoretical error in departing from Harsanyi's formulation of a similar style of argument, the results of which vindicate utilitarianism rather than Rawls's two principles.

Rawls does mount some arguments to defend his use of the maximin rule, but all of them are problematic.[37] Accordingly, some critics have believed that his original position argument for the two principles is fatally flawed and that the use of the veil of ignorance, insofar as it kills off the possibility of having people in the original position with genuinely different interests and natures, also kills off the possibility of having a "real" contract argument that can provide a proper defense of his two principles. Yet Rawls might ask how we can construct such a "real" contract argument, using "real" people with all their differing views, talents, and so on, without introducing into the contracting process biases, prejudices, and differences in bargaining power that destroy the impartiality, and thus the moral authority, of the whole process. Some critics, for example, David Gauthier,[38] have tried to show that we can do so, constructing non-Rawlsian contract situations where people have some (or even complete) knowledge of their circumstances and who contract upon non-Rawlsian—and far more conservative—conceptions of justice. But these critics have in turn had their arguments attacked by those who question the moral acceptability of the starting points of their contracting parties.

So at the most fundamental level the quarrel between Rawls and these critics raises the issue of what a viable and genuinely morally revealing contractarian theory *is*. How can one construct such a theory so that it includes only morally relevant information and no prejudicial ideas and yet ensure that a genuine contract among the parties can take place? And what grounds does (should) one use to determine when information is "morally relevant"? Such questions remain live ones for contractarian theorists today.

Aside from attacking Rawls's arguments, many critics have focused on attacking his conclusion. There have been left-wing and right-wing attacks. On the right, critics have charged that Rawls has failed to acknowledge the proper role that effort, merit, and responsibility should have in the distribution of resources. Why should people receive roughly equal allotments when some work harder than others, when some invest more wisely than others, or when some are lazy and fail to contribute effectively to the community? They claim that a system of distributive justice that ignores differences in effort undermines individual responsibility, promotes sloth, and allows the lazy to free ride on the efforts of the industrious in a way that will likely lead to social unrest and eventual diminishment of the economic pie. Now if it produces the latter result, Rawls's own theory would disallow that distribution, because in this situation giving more to the industrious is justified in order to increase the economic pie and yield more for everyone. Hence he would allow unequal distributions in order to forestall a drop in productivity. In contrast, he would not allow them if the economic pie were increased but the only people to benefit from the increase were the most advantaged. Rawls's right-wing critics would object, however, that if the more advantaged created those increases, they should be allowed to enjoy their share of them, even if that added to the inequality of the society.

On the left, critics have been distressed by Rawls's willingness to depart from strict equality of holdings, and some have wished for a conception of equality that focuses more on the equality of people's welfare than the equality of their resources. Moreover, as we shall see, even some on the left have been troubled by his failure to incorporate more fully the idea of personal responsibility into his theory.

In the next two sections, we look at the alternative suggestions of both Rawls's right-wing and left-wing critics. But before we begin, we should note how deeply indebted these critics are to Rawls himself, not for their specific conclusions but for many of the theoretical ideas and argumentation they rely upon and for the philosophical inspiration to pursue the construction of a satisfactory theory of justice.

Libertarianism

Shortly after the publication of Rawls's book, Robert Nozick published *Anarchy, State and Utopia*,[39] which is in some respects a libertarian reply to *A Theory of Justice*. Noting that Rawls doesn't even allow his original position parties to consider a libertarian conception of justice, Nozick mounts a variety of arguments to defend his far more conservative and liberty-based theory. It is worth noting that Nozick's arguments are not contractarian: Although in part 1 of his book Nozick does invoke the social contract idea to explain and justify the state's authority—thereby following in the footsteps of Hobbes and Locke—his arguments on behalf of a libertarian conception of justice in part 2 of that book do not invoke any (Kant-style) appeals to a hypothetical contractarian "idea" or reasoning procedure. Instead, Nozick's arguments appeal in a variety of ways to what Rawls would call our "considered convictions" about justice, so as to show that, contra Rawls, those convictions endorse a conception of justice very different from the one advocated in *A Theory of Justice*.

Nozick argues against what he calls "patterned" and "end-state" conceptions of justice:[40] The former are conceptions that seek to implement a distributive scheme according to some patterning principle of the form "to each according to his ————." The latter are conceptions that seek to attain a certain kind of telos, or goal, via a certain distribution of resources. Nozick claims that Rawls's conception of justice is an end-state conception, requiring that the state arrange society so as to produce a certain result (maximizing the prospects of the least advantaged). But any such conception of justice is, Nozick argues, bound to be unfair to some people. To see this, Nozick asks his reader to choose her favorite patterned or end-state conception of justice and imagine the state's implementing (perfectly) that conception. Then he tells her to imagine that people who wish to better their situation start to engage in various trades, contracts, gifts, and so on. In a very short time that pattern will be disrupted, as transfers brought about by this kind of trading or gift-giving activity occur. So were a society to remain committed to its patterned conception of justice, it would have to forbid such transfers, yet doing so, says Nozick, would result in great injustice as well as economic ineffi-ciency. The state would be preventing people from aiding their children, bettering their situation through contracts, satisfying their desires through trades, and so on. How can this be defensible on moral grounds? It would result in substantial interference in people's liberty, damage to people's ability to further their own welfare, and, ultimately, economic ill health in the society.

To illustrate his argument, Nozick uses what has come to be called the Wilt Chamberlain example: Suppose that many people in a certain city in a society that implements a patterned or end-state conception of justice are eager to see Wilt Chamberlain play basketball for the team represent-ing their city. Indeed, they are so willing to do so that they would be happy to pay an extra quarter for tickets as long as this quarter would go directly to Wilt, assuming the promise of all this extra money would lure Wilt to sign with their city's team. If Wilt comes and gets all this money, he will be very rich—and his holdings will violate whatever conception of justice has been implemented in that society. Yet to preclude people from paying an extra quarter for their tickets as a way of getting Wilt to come to their city is not only to prevent them from getting what they want but interfering with their liberty to use their own resources to arrange the world as they see fit. And for what good? For the sake of some pattern? For the sake of some end? Why should liberty give way to some pattern or end, particularly if, as many people (including Rawls) claim, liberty is a fundamental political value that any acceptable concep-tion of justice must endorse?

> The general point illustrated by the Wilt Chamberlain example . . . is that no end-state principle or distributional patterned principle of justice can be con-tinuously realized without continuous interference with people's lives. Any favored pattern would be transformed into one unfavored by the principle, by people choosing to act in various ways; for example, by people exchanging goods and services with other people, or giving things to other people, things the transferrers are entitled to under the favored distributional pattern.[41]

So Nozick's ultimate concern is with the way end-state and patterned conceptions interfere with liberty. In a sense, he agrees with the impor-tance and priority of Rawls's first principle of justice, but in Nozick's view that first principle, requiring equal liberty for all, has implications for the kind of conception of justice that can be endorsed by a liberty-lov-ing society. It must be one that allows people maximal (and equal) free-dom to do with their property what they choose to do, without being sub-jected to interference by the state.

Hence Nozick argues in favor of a historical principle of justice, that is, one that credits someone with a property right in an object depending upon the history of that person's acquisition of that object, not depending upon whether his holding it accords with some sort of pattern. Nozick's particular version of a historical principle is what he calls the entitlement theory of justice, which consists of three principles:

1. A person who acquires a holding in accordance with the principle of justice in acquisition is entitled to that holding.
2. A person who acquires a holding in accordance with the principle of justice in transfer from someone entitled to the holding is entitled to the holding.
3. No one is entitled to a holding except by (repeated) applications of (1) and (2).

In addition to these principles, Nozick also endorses a principle of rectification, which would provide for the redress of past injustices (involving violations of the principle of justice in acquisition or the principle of justice in transfer).

Note that this conception of justice essentially entails the defense of the free market and the capitalist system—that is, a system of trading, contracts, and disposal of goods by individuals and firms unfettered by state action where there is private property and private ownership of the means of production. However, it is *not* a defense of the free market that stresses its economic efficiency or ability to satisfy the welfare of its citizens: Such defenses are really utilitarian in nature, that is, they claim that as a matter of fact because wealth or welfare is maximized by this sort of system, we ought to implement it. In contrast, Nozick's argument is a way of defending the free market insofar as it realizes *justice* by respecting liberty rights of individuals, regardless of its effects on aggregate (or individual) welfare and regardless of its economic implications. So even if the free market were not the most efficient economic structure or the most effective way of securing the welfare of the community, Nozick would still claim that the demands of liberty require its institution.

Nozick assumes that the principle of justice in transfer would involve rules establishing what count as legitimate transfers via contracts, gifts, trades, and so on, and he does not bother to go into details about what such a principle would be like. But he does attempt to fill out the principle of justice in acquisition using highly Lockean ideas. In chapter 5 of the Second Treatise of *Two Treatises of Government*, Locke argues that even if he is in a state of nature and thus not governed by any governmental property laws, a person can rightly be said to acquire a property right in an unowned object if he "mixes his labor" in the object and thereby makes it his own. Locke's idea is that insofar as a person owns himself, he also owns his labor and therefore owns that which he mixes his labor with. Nozick concurs with the Lockean point that labor generates and legitimates initial acquisition, even while puzzling over and finally rejecting Locke's explanation for why this is so. For example, Nozick asks,

> Why isn't mixing what I own with what I don't a way of losing what I own rather than a way of gaining what I don't? If I own a can of tomato juice and spill it in the sea so that its molecules (made radioactive, so I can check this) mingle evenly throughout the sea, do I thereby come to own the sea or have I foolishly dissipated my tomato juice?[42]

So despite his sympathy for and acceptance of the broad outlines of Locke's conception of legitimate acquisition, Nozick is perhaps the best critic of that conception and is not able, despite those sympathies, to figure out how to formulate that conception so as to answer his (or others') criticisms of it.

But ultimately what is most important to Nozick's view (and indeed to any libertarian position) is not the details of the principles of acquisition or transfer (which might be filled out in a number of different ways by different libertarian theorists) but rather the idea that each individual has certain rights and in particular certain property rights that are "absolute" in character in the sense that *no* amount of good accruing to the community generally, or to other individuals, can justify the infringement or overriding of these rights. To put it controversially but in a way that I hope is at least rhetorically illuminating: Whereas utilitarianism might be said to allow individuals to be held hostage to the well-being of the community, libertarianism might be said to allow the community's well-being to be held hostage to the rights, and in particular the property rights, of individuals.

Of course Nozick doesn't put it this pejorative way. It is worth saying a bit more about the libertarian notion of rights, so that readers can appreciate why libertarians are convinced that their notion is defensible. Nozick calls the sort of rights that libertarians grant people "side constraints"; that is, they are claims individuals have regarding their own treatment that may not be legitimately overridden in the pursuit of (even very worthy) goals. Rights so understood are correlated with moral duties that each person owes every other (e.g., the duty not to murder, not to steal from another, not to physically abuse another), and Nozick argues that such rights, including not only the right not to be murdered but also rights to property, are ultimately motivated by a highly Kantian view of morality: "Side constraints upon action reflect the underlying Kantian principle that individuals are ends and not merely means; they may not be sacrificed or used for the achieving of other ends without their consent. Individuals are inviolable."[43]

Readers may well marvel that Nozick would invoke Kant's name in a theory that is in some ways the very opposite of Rawls's view—itself advertised as Kantian! Which one legitimately deserves the name 'Kantian'?

How one answers this question depends upon how one interprets the idea that people should be treated as "ends"; Rawls and Nozick have very different conceptions of what being treated as an end involves. On Nozick's view, once a person gains a property right over an object, either derived from initial acquisition of that object from among the stock of unowned things or derived via legitimate transferring procedures, it is hers absolutely and thus not something that either a person or an institution—including the state—can take, even for some worthy cause. Hence respecting her right to it is required in order to treat her as an end. To allow the state to take it for a good cause of its choice would be to treat the person and her holdings as a means for the pursuit of this cause without this person's consent, in a way that fails to recognize her intrinsic and inviolable value.

But why should we think that a person's right over an object is this strong, such that it cannot be overridden and abridged *for any reason?* Part of Nozick's argument for this conclusion rests on his acceptance of the Lockean idea of a link between property and self-determination. To be able to make effective choices in the world and have effective autonomy in the pursuit of life plans, one must, says Nozick, be able to have total control over objects one owns. And in particular, granting people absolute property rights is a way of ensuring both that they will be protected from arbitrary state power (indeed, this was a major concern of Locke, given the history he and other people in the Britain of his day had with acquisitive rulers who did not respect the private property of their subjects) and that each individual will be treated with respect, as philosophers such as Kant have demanded.

Thus Nozick criticizes Rawls precisely because the Rawlsian conception of justice, in his view, not only fails to protect individuals from intrusive state power but fails to treat individuals as ends who are owed the liberty to determine what they should do with what belongs to them. Moreover, Nozick takes great exception to passages in *A Theory of Justice* that defend state enforcement of the difference principle in ways that Nozick claims fail to respect the liberty of individuals. For example, Nozick quotes the following passage from Rawls's *Theory of Justice*:

> We see then that the difference principle represents, in effect, an agreement to regard the distribution of natural talents as a common asset and to share in the benefits of this distribution whatever it turns out to be. Those who have been favored by nature, whoever they are, may gain from their good fortune only on terms that improve the situation of those who have lost out. The naturally advantaged are not to gain merely because they are more

gifted, but only to cover the costs of training and education and for using their endowments in ways that help the less fortunate as well. No one deserves his greater natural capacity nor merits a more favorable starting place in society. But it does not follow that one should eliminate these distinctions. There is another way to deal with them. The basic structure can be arranged so that these contingencies work for the good of the least fortunate. Thus we are led to the difference principle if we wish to set up the social system so that no one gains or loses from his arbitrary place in the distribution of natural assets or his initial position in society without giving or receiving compensating advantages in return.[44]

But to treat people's talents as collective assets is, claims Nozick, to *use* them, in violation of Kantian moral constraints. Indeed, the idea that people's natural assets must be "dealt with" suggests to Nozick an almost Orwellian way of regarding a person as someone who is made for and supposed to serve collective purposes. Of course Rawls would disagree and contend that he only wants the state to use a person's talent, and not the person. But Nozick is unconvinced by this Rawlsian move, which "presses *very* hard on the distinction between men [*sic*] and their talents, assets, abilities and special traits."[45] Nozick concludes, "Whether any coherent conception of a person remains when the distinction is so pressed is an open question. Why we, thick with particular traits, should be cheered that (only) the thus purified men [*sic*] within us are not regarded as means is also unclear."[46]

Nozick is further troubled by another Rawlsian passage that represents not only talents but also virtues of character as aspects of ourselves for which we cannot take credit and that should therefore be considered "arbitrary from a moral point of view." According to Rawls, it is not only that natural talents and abilities are arbitrary in this way: "The assertion that a man deserves the superior character that enables him to make the effort to cultivate his abilities is equally problematic; for his character depends in large part upon fortunate family and social circumstances for which he can claim no credit."[47] Replies Nozick,

This line of argument can succeed in blocking the introduction of a person's autonomous choices and actions (and their results) only by attributing *everything* noteworthy about the person completely to certain sorts of "external" factors. So denigrating a person's autonomy and prime responsibility for his actions is a risky line to take for a theory that otherwise wishes to buttress the dignity and self-respect of autonomous beings.[48]

Again, Nozick is indirectly claiming that only a system that recognizes individuals' absolute rights over their bodies, their labor, their character and talent development, their choices, and the objects they acquire by virtue of those choices (and the choices of others) will be a system of justice that accords with the Kantian admonition always to treat individual human beings as ends in themselves. In contrast, he insists, a state is "using" people in a Rawlsian system of justice. It might be convenient for the least advantaged to have the more advantaged working for their benefit, but isn't it treating the more advantaged solely as means rather than as ends? It appears to be a way of implicitly precluding them from putting their talents to use so as to substantially benefit themselves (and perhaps indirectly others) whenever the least advantaged can't also benefit from their labor. And why should the least advantaged have the right to a percentage of the proceeds of the labor of others?

This last question is motivated by a subterranean assumption of Nozick's theory: the idea that the choices people make with respect to how they will use their labor and their property are ones for which they should be held responsible. The idea is that if people do not work hard and invest poorly, they should be held responsible for those choices and not be "bailed out" by an egalitarian regime. And if they work hard and invest well, they should also be held responsible for those choices and allowed to reap the benefits of their labor. Ultimately, one might wonder whether the ground of Nozick's conception of absolute rights is not only a conception of liberty but also a conception of moral responsibility that is, at least arguably, closely associated to our notion of liberty.

There have been many criticisms of libertarian views in general and Nozick's version of libertarianism in particular—some of them passionate.[49] The most obvious and popular criticism has been of the libertarian notion of rights: For why should we think that morality demands that we accord people such absolute rights? How could rights be thought to trump so decisively *all* considerations of others' welfare in the community? Would Nozick really have us resist "overriding" rights even if their respect would effect disaster to the community at large? Moreover, what if the economy would flourish better if the state interfered in the market economy (and thus in individuals' transferring activity via contracts, etc.), for example, through antitrust legislation? Libertarians would still not allow it, and yet most citizens and firms might actually want it and even demand it, insofar as they believe they will be better off with such governmental interference. That such "interference" would be precluded by the libertarian notion of "rights" shows not only how strong but also how implausible that notion seems to many. Moreover, libertarians have thus far been able to rely on little more than intuition to try to make their views compelling to their critics, although recently interesting attempts have been made to provide a more reason-based and structured defense of the view.[50]

There are signs that even Nozick is unable to stomach his own absolute conception of rights. In the process of defending his very Lockean view of property rights, Nozick tells us that he also accepts what is called the "Lockean proviso" on property acquisition and transfer. Locke says that individuals who obtain a property right over unowned objects in which they "mix their labor" do so only so long as there is "enough and as good left in common for others."[51] Generations of political theorists have puzzled over exactly what this phrase means and how strong a constraint on acquisition it is. But Locke's general idea is clear: He wants to disallow some acquisitions whenever they severely prejudice the interests or well-being of others. I will not go into various controversies about how this proviso should be understood, but suffice it to say here that one important reason Locke believes it is necessary to recognize such a proviso is because he believes that all of us are under a moral obligation to further, and thus not to endanger, the survival of others as well as ourselves (Locke calls this the "Fundamental Law of Nature," and we discussed it in Chapter 2). Locke appreciates that such endangerment can occur not only through overt action but also through appropriation of objects, and when it occurs, he takes such appropriation to be morally precluded.

Nozick's motivation for endorsing the proviso seems somewhat different, having to do with the way that initial acquisition of goods by one person would seem to affect the liberty of everybody else (who can now no longer use that object as they might wish and whose opportunities may be affected as a result). Hence if he is committed to liberty, Nozick must be able to explain when initial acquisitions have a benign and acceptable effect on others' liberty and when they do not. The Lockean proviso is Nozick's attempt to draw a line between liberty-permitting and liberty-denying initial acquisition. As an example of a liberty-denying acquisition that violates this proviso, Nozick himself gives the attempted acquisition by one person of the only water hole in a large desert; were only she to have a right to it, this could adversely affect the interests and welfare of everyone else in the desert (all of whom require water to survive) and thus violate the Lockean proviso.

But if Nozick agrees with the Lockean principle that sometimes a person's property rights give way in the face of others' needs, why doesn't he recognize the way in which other people's welfare can take "moral precedence" over principles of acquisition or transfer, allowing any of them to hold property rights in certain objects? While he might prefer to describe this situation not as one in which welfare is "overriding" property rights but rather as one in which welfare negates the possibility of having property rights, isn't it still the case that he is allowing the welfare of others to "trump" the autonomous (and otherwise rights-creating) choices of individuals? And if this is so, why doesn't this show that even

Nozick admits that morality sometimes allows us to put the well-being of the community first, over the actual (or potential) rights of individuals, in a way that might mandate considerable state action in the distribution—or redistribution—of property?

Indeed, Nozick explicitly says that a Lockean proviso could involve the state in negating certain transfers that although in accord with the rules regulating just transfer, nonetheless result in a distribution of holdings that does not leave as much and as good for others in the community. Nonetheless, he optimistically insists, "I believe that the free operation of a market system will not actually run afoul of the Lockean proviso," even though he does not provide grounds for that optimism.[52] In any case, that he himself has given the state moral license to interfere in property holdings insofar as the state must enforce that proviso is in my view an implicit admission that the state *is* under a moral obligation to enforce a certain "pattern" in its implementation of a system of distributive justice: that is, a pattern of holdings that recognizes and licenses histories of acquisition and transfer that accord with principles governing these things but that also ensures that each person has "enough and as good."

Finally, there is an interesting objection to Nozick's view made by left-wing critics. Suppose we think again about the Wilt Chamberlain example: Nozick suggests that only unreasonable envy would explain why people would not want Wilt to have (far) more wealth than they, in a situation where people are happy to give him that wealth in order to see him play basketball for their city's team. Yet many critics (e.g., G. A. Cohen)[53] have argued that great wealth can be a weapon of considerable power in a society. First, it can give people superior access to political officeholders, enabling their views on issues to have greater influence; second, it can put them in a position where they can more readily secure the satisfaction of their interests; and third, it can allow them to control other people who do not have anything like their share of wealth.

All these ideas were originally suggested in Rousseau's *Discourse on the Origin of Inequality*, and many subsequent philosophers have endorsed them. For example, John Stuart Mill remarks that even if the poor are "no longer enslaved or made dependent by force of law," most people are still enslaved

> by force of poverty; they are still chained to a place, to an occupation, and to conformity with the will of an employer, and debarred by accident of birth both from the enjoyments, and from the mental and moral advantages, which others inherit without exertion and independently of desert. That this is an evil equal to almost any of those against which mankind have hitherto struggled, the poor are not wrong in believing.[54]

As I discuss later in this chapter, this is also a theme of Aristotle, explaining why he commends a relatively equal distribution of society's resources, so that some do not take themselves (wrongly) to be "masters" of the poor. Perhaps most famous, it is the basis for much of Marx's condemnation of the capitalist economic system.

Rousseau, Mill, Aristotle, and Marx would all wonder why Nozick and other libertarians, who are so keen to protect individual liberty from intrusion by the state, would "forget" to protect it from intrusions by the rich or by firms with far greater assets than the individual. Just as political power can be used to threaten, coerce, and (as we discussed in Chapter 3) master people in a society, so, too, can superior wealth. Libertarians who are truly interested in liberty and equality should, it seems, be just as interested in stopping wealth-based interference in the liberty of the citizens and wealth-based treatment of people as mere means as they are in stopping political interference and political use of citizenry as means. Arguably, Nozick's own reluctant support for the Lockean proviso is an admission that the former interest is morally required.

So it seems that we can completely agree with Nozick that the values of liberty and equality are fundamental to any just regime but still deny that his libertarian conception, which attempts to make property rights supreme, adequately captures or implements either of these political values (which even Nozick may subtly admit in his support of the Lockean proviso). Can a more left-wing conception of justice better capture and implement them?

Egalitarianism

Many political theorists have endorsed some form of egalitarian theory of distributive justice, and it is an idea that is frequently associated with "socialism" (although it is not, as we'll see, an idea that Karl Marx endorsed).

But it is also an old idea. For example, Aristotle suggests it in *The Politics*. As I discussed in Chapter 1, Aristotle believes that the best kind of state is what he calls a "polity," which mixes elements of democratic and aristocratic rule. But for him one of the most important features of a polity is the way that it distributes wealth relatively equally among the citizenry. Only by doing this, says Aristotle, does one secure a genuine "partnership" among all the citizenry in the state,[55] because only when wealth is spread equally does one prevent people from using greater wealth to try to secure mastery over others. In a state where wealth is unequal,

> the result is a state not of free men but of slaves and masters, the former full of envy, the latter of contempt. Nothing could be farther removed from friendship or from partnership in a state. Sharing is a token of friendship;

one does not want to share even a journey with one's enemies. The state aims to consist as far as possible of those who are like and equal, a condition found chiefly among the middle people.[56]

So equality of means produces, in Aristotle's view, the right kind of *relationship* among the citizenry—that is, a friendship among equals—and thereby encourages not only the right kind of political community but also a secure and stable political regime.

There is, as I argue later in this chapter, perhaps no better argument for distributive equality than this, but contemporary political theorists have sought to mount other, more complicated arguments for this distributive conclusion as a way of trying to say not only that distributive equality is a good idea given its good consequences but also an idea required by the concept of justice.

One of the first questions that any egalitarian must answer is, Equality of *what?* (which is also the title of a well-known essay by Amartya Sen).[57] That is, precisely what is it that the state is supposed to make equal? There are two prominent answers in modern egalitarian theories: equality of *welfare* and equality of *resources*.

Welfare egalitarianism is popular among those who are attracted to utilitarianism's view that human welfare is ultimately the most important morally relevant feature of a community to which a state must pay attention yet who want to chart a way for the state to pursue welfare not in an "aggregated" way but in a way more responsive to the distinctiveness of individuals. However, there are some serious problems with this way of formulating an egalitarian view. Consider that one person might be harder to make happy than another because her tastes are more difficult and more expensive to satisfy. Someone who loves sailing and high-quality champagne will require more resources to make happy than someone who loves in-line skating and jug wine. To "equalize their welfare" it would seem we would have to give far more to the would-be sailor than to the would-be skater. But why should we be rewarding some people for their expensive tastes and penalizing other people for their inexpensive tastes? Shouldn't each of them take responsibility for her tastes and not be allowed to demand that no matter what tastes she develops, society has a role to play in helping her satisfy these tastes? To cater to such demands is potentially to allow the state to be held hostage to the unreasonable whims of some, to the detriment of everyone else.

Part of the problem here is that we have no clear sense of what a person's "welfare" is (as we discussed earlier in the section on utilitarianism). If welfare simply means the experience of pleasure, then any whim that could produce pleasure must be taken seriously, no matter how much doing so violates our intuitions. But if welfare is a certain kind of pleasure or something that can come about only if certain preferences a person might have are not heeded (e.g., immoral preferences), then egalitarians must develop and defend this conception of welfare prior to directing a state to equalize it. This is, obviously, a difficult thing to do, especially since it seems to rely heavily on intuitions, whose status and reliability we might have reason to doubt. Things are little better if we try to rely on a conception of welfare as preference satisfaction. For if the well-being of some depends upon satisfying preferences that are morally problematic or inauthentic, how can the state defensibly pursue welfare so defined and remain just?

Finally, no matter how welfare is defined, equalizing welfare will be impossible or extraordinarily expensive and difficult if (as is overwhelmingly likely) there are some people in the society who suffer from natural disadvantages (e.g., illnesses, mood disorders, disabilities) that negatively affect their well-being (on any conception of what human well-being is) and precipitate great unhappiness, and who would require enormous resources even to approach the happiness and well-being of those who are not so disadvantaged. While many people would endorse the idea that society has a responsibility (perhaps a considerable one) toward those who are ill, handicapped, and so on, they would balk at the idea of giving enormous amounts to a few at the expense of the many in what might well be a vain attempt to make everyone equal in well-being, especially when those healthy, nondisadvantaged people who produce most of these resources through their labor are precluded from enjoying very many of them.

Hence many egalitarians have followed Ronald Dworkin in espousing "resource egalitarianism," which would have the state equalize resources (perhaps defined along the lines of something like Rawls's primary goods), not welfare.[58] But Dworkin argues that it is interestingly difficult to distribute resources "equally" in a way that is genuinely fair. It is not as simple as giving the same amount of resources to each person and using the state to monitor transfers to ensure that they remain the same. Instead, what Dworkin wants to advocate is a way to distribute resources that while not resulting in everyone's having *exactly* the same amount, nonetheless leaves each person both content with her lot and able to take responsibility for how her tastes will be satisfied and her welfare secured.

To clarify his conception of equality, Dworkin proposes a thought experiment similar to a contractarian approach to defining justice. Imagine, he says, that a group of people are shipwrecked on an island and that they have to decide how to divide up the resources on the island. Knowing who they are, their tastes, and so on, they decide to follow an "auction" procedure. Each of them is given an equal amount of purchasing power, the units of which we'll call "clam shells."

Each distinct item on the island (not including the immigrants themselves) is listed as a lot to be sold, unless someone notifies the auctioneer . . . of his or her desire to bid for some part of an item, including part, for example, of some piece of land, in which case that part becomes itself a distinct lot. The auctioneer then proposes a set of prices for each lot and discovers whether that set of prices clears the markets, that is, whether there is only one purchaser at that price and all lots are sold. If not, then the auctioneer adjusts his prices until he reaches a set that does clear the markets. But the process does not stop then, because each of the immigrants remains free to change his bids even when an initially market-clearing set of prices is reached, or even to propose different lots. But let us suppose that in time even this leisurely process comes to an end, everyone declares himself satisfied, and goods are distributed accordingly.[59]

Now, says Dworkin, we have equality. Of course, everyone doesn't have the same things, nor would they value one another's allotments in the same way. Their different tastes will convince them that some of them have done better than others. But the important point is that all of them will have had the same chance as the others, with the same initial resources, to secure the satisfaction of their desires as best they can and thus to be responsible for how they have done so. Most important, each will be satisfied with what he or she has received from this process. As a result, no one will envy anyone else's share, which is a sign that the distribution is both equal and fair. Note that Dworkin's thought experiment makes use of an auction, which is a *market device:* That device, he says, highlights the idea that "the true measure of the social resources devoted to the life of one person is fixed by asking how important, in fact, that resource is for others. It insists that the cost, measured in that way, figure in each person's sense of what is rightly his and in each person's judgement of what life he should lead, given that command of justice."[60]

How does this thought experiment translate into political practice? Dworkin's idea is that through a variety of means, including taxation policy, the state can try to arrange the environment (and probably also rely on markets) so as to duplicate the results of this auction, giving people roughly equal (but not exactly equal) shares of resources to spend so as to enable them to pursue their life plans.

But things are not so simple: What if some members of our island were handicapped or ill? Mightn't the resources they were able to secure be insufficient to allow them to live the sort of life they want, leaving them dissatisfied and envious? Dworkin admits that the problem of the naturally disadvantaged is not addressed by his auction. He suggests that some of the island's resources might be given to such people prior to the auction to enable them to get a leg up before the rest of the resources are distributed. But if their disadvantages are severe, this may result in so many of the resources' being given away to them that everyone else gets little or nothing—a result that will strike the rest as unfair. Hence Dworkin proposes that we add to the auction the possibility of buying insurance: That is, suppose we modify our auction slightly so that each person does not know whether or not he or she suffers from some form of severe natural disadvantage. In that situation, Dworkin argues, each will want to purchase "insurance" paying them a certain amount if it turns out that they are blind, infirm, subject to some debilitating disease, or otherwise handicapped. In real-life political practice, this would translate into a system of compensating naturally disadvantaged people but not at a rate that severely affects the amount of resources available to other people. That is, we could say to people: Think of these compensating payments as insurance payments against being naturally disadvantaged that each of us would have bought had we been in a hypothetical "auction" situation as described by Dworkin. That we would have wanted such insurance is a morally revealing fact about how we should think about the state's role in ameliorating the problems of the naturally disadvantaged.

But things are more complicated still: What if some people are naturally *more* advantaged to a rather extreme degree? How do we handle such advantages, given that they may quickly result in a person's producing and trading her way into a situation where she has a much larger share of resources than her fellows? Dworkin puzzles over this: Perhaps, he proposes, we shouldn't "handle" this situation at all and simply allow the more talented to keep the larger number of resources they get through their greater talents, particularly if they have worked hard and used great industry to do so. Not to allow them to keep the fruits of their labors seems to violate the idea that the state should let people take responsibility for their choices— an idea to which Dworkin is just as committed as Nozick. Yet to the extent that their greater productivity is a result of raw (genetic) luck, why should they be allowed to benefit more than others from it, any more than the naturally disadvantaged should be allowed to suffer more than others because of their bad luck in the natural lottery? So maybe we should design a system that lets people keep the larger share of resources they get because of their ambition and hard work but not because of their raw biologically based talents. The main problem with this suggestion, however, is figuring out how to distinguish between raw talent and effort or ambition. Our labor is really a combination of both—indeed, talents don't get created without a lot of effort, so the very fact of having a (developed) talent involves that person's choice to work at developing it.

In the end Dworkin does not clearly answer any of these questions, and his discussion of them is sufficiently complicated that I will not pursue it further here. Note, however, that his discussion shows just how difficult it is to generate an adequate account of what distributive equality actually *is.* Should it be concerned with welfare or resources (or both)? How should it respond to good luck and bad luck in personal fortunes, natural talents, and so on? How should it involve personal responsibility and equal concern? Even committed egalitarians can disagree with one another about what the ingredients of a genuinely "equal" state are.[61]

Perhaps all these questions would be easier to answer if we knew *why* equality was so important in the pursuit of distributive justice. Many contemporary philosophers tend to take it for granted that equality is simply part of our conception of what a "just" distribution is. But note that Aristotle does not take this for granted; Aristotle believes that it is both possible and necessary to defend the linkage between equal distributions and justice via a moral argument. On his view, distributive justice is a moral concept whose content we *derive* rather than discover, and we do so by understanding the way in which some distributions promote certain moral or social values better than others. So Aristotle first asks, What kind of society do we want? And after answering that question, he asks, What kind of distribution of goods promotes this kind of society?

His answer to the first question is reminiscent of Kant: We want, he says, a society in which people treat each other as equals (no one should be allowed to be master of another or the slave of another) and in which these equals treat each other as partners—or "civic friends." The way to get that is to pursue not exact equality of resources but sufficient equality to ensure that no one is able to use his greater wealth to gain political advantage over others in a way that damages their partnership. So Aristotle sees distribution as a means to an end—the end of a morally sound community. He does not require strict equality and thus leaves scope for some to have more than others depending upon how they choose to live their lives, develop their natural talents, and so on. So he does not recommend that we try to equalize *everything*, but we need enough equality to pursue a sound human community. His remarks, in my view, connect nicely with the premisses of a consent-based theory of political authority, which I discussed in Chapter 3, requiring that a genuine state eschew mastery and involve every citizen in the process of maintaining the state.

For my money, this Aristotelian approach to justice is the most promising and the one that I am ready to back. Still, Aristotle's ideas are not precisely stated, and we have yet to see them worked out in concrete terms. Contemporary democratic societies, which endorse Aristotle's concern for a community of equals, are clearly divided about how to construct a system of distribution that fits with such a community. Some might even argue that it should be a distribution that fits much more with Nozick's theory than with Dworkin's, insofar as, on their view, "equal treatment" in a democratic society requires respect for liberty that only a lightly regulated free market society can give. Moreover, the Aristotelian view under-

stands a just (i.e., roughly equal) distribution as a means to the end of political equality and friendship, and some might insist that justice should
not be defined as a *means* to something but rather as a concept that makes
its own intrinsic demands, regardless of how it might promote other political values.

Neither I nor anyone else has a convincing and decisive argument determining the right answers to these (terribly difficult) issues about how
to pursue equal treatment in democratic societies; hence I must conclude
this section without proposing any remedies for the controversies surrounding the issue. There is, in my view, no issue so "live" in political
philosophy today as the issue of the nature of distributive justice.

Are We Too Late?

There have been a number of philosophers who have lamented the preoc-
cupation of contemporary political theory with the issue of distributive
justice. I want to close this chapter by reviewing three positions taken by
philosophers who hold this view. This will help us set the stage for our
discussions in the next chapter, where we take up other aspects of justice.

The Communitarians

Recently, some philosophers, called communitarians, have questioned
the unrelenting emphasis on the individual in the theories of distributive
justice we have reviewed, both left-wing and right-wing, because, these
critics say, the appropriate locus of concern for a political society must be
what is good for the *community*, not what any particular individual
should get. Only utilitarianism comes close to having this locus of concern, but even utilitarianism, on this view, fails to incorporate what might
be called the "values of community," focusing instead on the aggregate
welfare of individuals conceived as separate and distinct beings, not
united by any common bonds of culture or society. But community is
highly important to us, and why shouldn't its importance have implications for how we distribute resources, in ways that none of these theories
takes seriously? Of all the philosophical accounts we have reviewed,
probably only Aristotle's has been sensitive to the connection between
community and distributive justice. In the next chapter, we explore more
fully the communitarian position to see how far it is correct in trying to
reorient the focus of political theory.

The Marxists

Marxists also criticize those who emphasize distributive justice but for
reasons quite different from those of the communitarians. Karl Marx
(1818–1883) argued that any distribution of resources in a society is in-

evitably generated by the economic form of organization in that society. In our time that form of organization is capitalism, and Marx argues that capitalism operates to generate great inequalities of wealth (and welfare) because of the way markets and capitalist firms operate to advantage owners and disadvantage workers. In *Das Kapital* Marx even puts forward an economic theory based on the "labor theory of value" (popular in the nineteenth century but now largely rejected by economists) to try to show how the exploitation of the worker in this system is inevitable. In particular, Marx argues that a worker will always be paid in wages for his labor but that wage will always be less than the value that his labor creates. The capitalist will pocket this surplus value, leading eventually to the impoverishment of the worker and the enrichment of the capitalist for whom he labors. Marx was also sensitive to forms of domination that are made possible both by inequalities in wealth and by private ownership of the means of production (so that he would oppose Nozick's claim that there is "nothing wrong" with Wilt Chamberlain's having considerably more money than his fellows).

Many of Marx's economic theories have not proved successful, and his argument for the inherently exploitative nature of capitalism has been heavily criticized (although there have been theorists sympathetic with the conclusion of that argument who have tried to argue for it more effectively). Moreover, his theory about the kind of economic system that should replace it has been hard to define with any precision and hard to implement. Marx argues for the creation of a full "communist" regime in which there is no private property and in which goods are commonly owned by everyone. Agreeing with Aristotle that the ideal society is one in which everyone relates to one another as a friend, Marx believes that we get such a society not by creating a world in which everyone has the same amount of private property as everyone else but by destroying the idea of private property altogether so as to create a new society with a new economic system, in which there is only collective ownership of almost everything—particularly the means of production. His view is summarized in his famous phrase: "From each according to his ability, to each according to his needs."

One striking feature of this ideal society is that it is not governed by a state. Marx's vision is ultimately anarchist: We won't need a state when private property is transcended, he says, because people won't be competing against one another or see each other as rivals to be defeated or put down in the struggle to get ahead. Such attitudes of competition and violence are a product of capitalism, and when they do not exist and a communist economic system is put in its place, people will develop the kind of benevolence to help one another and work together to remedy conflicts that precludes both the need for justice and for a state to implement it. Recall that limited benevolence was one of the "circumstances of justice"; Marx argues that communism can enlarge human beneficence so that there is no longer a need for justice.

Unfortunately, Marx did not chart the way to attain such an ideal society, and some of his followers have used his ideas to create (sometimes dreadful) authoritarian regimes that generally did the workers very little good and created considerable economic and political inequality between the rulers and the ruled. But is the failure of Marxist-style states in recent times a failure of Marxism itself or only a failure of Marxists to understand that vision well enough to know how to pursue it?

While Marxists tend to blame their fellow Marxists for failing to implement Marx's ideal correctly, many political theorists believe that the problem is with the theory of Marxism itself. Consider, as we discussed in Chapters 1 and 2, that those who argue for the necessity of the state tend to have a rather "misanthropic" view of human beings;[62] that is, they tend to see human beings as by nature limited in their generosity and fellow-feeling, prone to behave cruelly, attracted to the idea of domination, prone to use violence to resolve conflict, and so forth. For these philosophers, the "circumstances of justice" that we reviewed earlier—which are the circumstances that make necessary a theory of justice and a legal system to enforce it—involve a limitation in benevolence that cannot be remedied in human beings, no matter how hard we try. Hence they believe we need a system of justice to adjudicate and resolve conflicts and a political system to authoritatively command and enforce those resolutions. On this view, there is no way we can transcend the need for a theory of justice or for a state to implement it and probably no way to design an effective theory of justice for a political society that does not to some extent involve private property and markets. For them, Marx's dream of a perfect community of friends lovingly related to one another is not possible among real human beings and is thus an illusion. Moreover, these critics believe that the Marxist naivete about the capacity for any human to be cruel and exploitative if put in a position of power can lead to the construction of Marxist regimes that fail to plan for and develop institutions to contain such evil and therefore end up becoming horribly unjust.

Who is right in this debate? Is it Marx, who says we can design a society using a new and better economic system that will directly and indirectly structure social life and social institutions so that people don't desire to be cruel to one another? Or is our cruelty a fact of our human natures that cannot be overcome, so that we will always need a state not only to secure the solution to various coordination problems but also to insist on "justice" in the face of people's trying to use, abuse, and dominate one another?

For my money, it is the critics of Marxism who are right, where this judgment is based as much on my observations of my fellow human beings as it is on any psychological or biological theory of human nature. I leave it to you to reflect on where you stand on this issue. But even if Marx's ideas turn out to be hopelessly utopian and thus impossible to implement, his belief that problems of distribution can be understood as *systemic* problems that must be remedied via wholesale construction of new social or political institutions has been, as we'll see in the next chapter, enormously influential in our time. Moreover, his appreciation of the fact that cruelty can be wielded not only by political leaders but also by those of great wealth and economic capital has generated political movements and ultimately legislation designed to limit inequalities in economic power, even in noncommunist countries. We will discuss both these Marxian ideas further in the next chapter.

The Feminists

Finally, there are feminist critics of political theory's focus on distributive justice.[63] Some feminists believe that social or political systems of domination, such as that of men over women, can distort society so severely that none of the theories of justice we have reviewed will prove acceptable unless these systems of oppression are overturned. For example, if women live in a society where they are not allowed to hold certain forms of property or to vote or to engage in various occupations, then merely distributing resources in some kind of "equal" fashion will not be enough to secure justice. Greater resources do not solve or ameliorate the fact that in such a society women are partially mastered.

Or consider the way a theory of justice that tries to equalize welfare or tries to maximize total welfare will fail to address forms of oppression if it does not ask *why* people have the preferences they do. If people's preferences are partly created by an unjust system of domination, then a theory of distributive justice that simply satisfies those preferences without assessing them or seeking to correct the oppressive forces generating them is also morally unsatisfactory. So, for example, if a society precludes women from getting higher education or working outside the home after marriage, the attempt to make them happy when they express a desire to lead a happy life in the home (where else are they allowed to lead it?) fails to address the fact that their opportunities, and thus their desires, have been severely and unfairly constrained.

Similarly, a libertarian system that refrains from involving itself in the market choices of its citizens can allow people to satisfy their desires in ways that can severely discriminate against people of certain racial or ethnic groups or against women. If, for example, women or members of certain racial minorities are persistently refused the opportunity to be hired for certain jobs, then that fact can have an impact not only on their resources but also on their opportunities, life prospects, and chances for happiness. How can a theory of distributive justice that fails to address such discrimination really capture the nature of justice?

Even egalitarians cannot escape the feminists' criticism. For *who* is it that is supposed to get the resources on the egalitarian view? Each person, whether male or female? Or only the "head" of the family, where in patriarchal societies this will likely be a male? One feminist notes that almost all prominent studies of resource distribution in the social sciences use as their unit of analysis "the individual." But they then define that individual in ways that show the researcher's assumption that this individual is likely a male head of household and measure such things as class, income, and status in ways that treat the average adult female as invisible.[64] And even if each person (whether male or female) is given equal resources, this may be insufficient to cure systemic discrimination, social practices that deny women opportunities, or forms of socialization that constrain the formation of preferences in women.

Because Rawls explicitly mandates equalizing each citizen's opportunities and liberties and securing for every citizen the grounds for self-respect, his theory might be able to address at least some feminist concerns. Susan Moller Okin has explored the extent to which a Rawlsian theory of justice might be interpreted, revised, and implemented in a way that would end the oppression of women.[65] In my own work, I have argued that (something like) his "contractarian" method is a promising way to begin an attack on forms of oppression, because a social contract thought experiment can be designed to test for the presence of domination in any relationship, whether it is political or personal.[66]

Consider that our ties to friends or spouses or fellow citizens, when they are to people who are able to reciprocate what we give to them (as opposed to victims of serious diseases, impoverished people, infants), are morally acceptable only insofar as they do not involve, on either side, the infliction of costs or the confiscation of benefits over a significant period of time that implicitly reveal disregard rather than respect for that person. Someone who persistently takes more from you than you get from this person is using you by treating you as a source of benefits for which he or she need not reciprocate, as if you were some kind of servant. So it is not merely that the allocation of costs and benefits in such a relationship is unequal, it is that in the sort of situation I am describing this unequal allocation reveals the presence of disrespect. And it is this disrespect that I believe (along with Kant and Aristotle) is at the heart of injustice and that can kill off the relationship altogether if it is allowed to persist. It can end marriages and friendships, and it can also destroy political societies, as people who have been persistently relied upon to play important roles in that society but who receive very little in return get fed up with these unequal terms and rebel against the political forces that do not sufficiently acknowledge their contributions.

So by using a thought experiment in which you consider whether you and your partner(s) in a relationship (either a personal relationship between you and another person or a political relationship between you and every other member of your state) would be able to agree on the current distribution of costs and benefits, you are testing for implicit disrespect in that relationship. Note that an acceptable distribution needn't be strictly equal. Exploitation doesn't loom every time a person gets a present from a friend but then forgets her friend's birthday or when some people make more money in wages than other people. Instead, it occurs when there is persistent and serious lopsidedness in the distributions among those in the relationship, which the person who benefits from the lopsidedness fails (persistently) to correct. The contract test, on this view, is a device that if used in the right circumstances will call to mind the fundamental Kantian idea that all people are equal and deserving of equal regard, in a way that will enable us to diagnose successfully the presence of injustice in a relationship. In the end, I would argue, this is also the way Rawls tries to use his original position procedure (although it is, as I noted above, controversial whether or not he succeeds).

These remarks are meant to suggest that creating a just state is ultimately more than simply a matter of distributing goods in a certain way but also a matter of securing each citizen's *equal worth* in that society such that it cannot be denied or threatened by those with political or economic power. It is my own view that until and unless such equal worth for all can be assured, all schemes of distributive justice will end up hurting rather than helping those who are being dominated.

Further Reading

To learn about the foundations of classical utilitarianism, see Jeremy Bentham, *An Introduction to the Principles of Morals and Legislation,* and John Stuart Mill, *Utilitarianism, Liberty and Representative Government.* For a selection of essays setting out different forms of utilitarianism, see Jonathan Glover, ed., *Utilitarianism and Its Critics.*

The contractarian position is represented by John Rawls, *A Theory of Justice,* and David Gauthier, *Morals by Agreement.* For essays setting out John Harsanyi's views, see his *Essays on Ethics, Social Behavior and Scientific Explanation.* A useful collection of essays on Rawls is Norman Daniels, ed., *Reading Rawls.* A collection of essays that explore, among other things, the debate between contractarians and utilitarians is Amartya Sen and Bernard Williams, eds., *Utilitarianism and Beyond.* A feminist perspective on Rawls's work can be found in Susan Moller Okin, "Justice and Gender," *Philosophy and Public Affairs* 16, 1 (1987): 42–72.

Nozick's statement of libertarianism can be found in *Anarchy, State and Utopia*. For a collection of essays on Nozick's work, see Jeffrey Paul, ed., *Reading Nozick*. A probing critical look at Nozick's arguments from the left is given by Gerald A. Cohen, "Robert Nozick and Wilt Chamberlain: How Patterns Preserve Liberty," in John Arthur and William H. Shaw, eds., *Justice and Economic Distribution*. For a more recent defense of libertarianism, see Loren Lomasky, *Persons, Rights and the Moral Community*.

Amartya Sen's influential discussion of egalitarianism is his "Equality of What?" in Sterling McMurrin, ed., *The Tanner Lectures on Human Values*. Ronald Dworkin's egalitarian views are spelled out in two articles, "What Is Equality? Part I: Equality of Welfare" and "What Is Equality? Part II: Equality of Resources," *Philosophy and Public Affairs* 10, 3 and 4 (1981): 185–246 and 283–345. An interesting egalitarian proposal can be found in Richard Arneson, "Equality and Equal Opportunity for Welfare," *Philosophical Studies* 56 (1989): 77–93. See also Gerald A. Cohen, *Self-Ownership, Freedom, and Equality*.

Three books on Marx that introduce readers both to the historical Marx and contemporary Marxist ideas are John Roemer, *Free to Lose: An Introduction to Marxist Economic Philosophy;* Gerald A. Cohen, *Karl Marx's Theory of History: A Defence;* and Jon Elster, *Making Sense of Marx*. For readings on feminism and communitarianism, see those listed at the end of Chapter 5.

Notes

1. Jeremy Bentham, "Anarchical Fallacies," in *Collected Works of Jeremy Bentham,* vol. 2, eds. James H. Burns, John R. Dinwiddy, and Frederick Rosen (Oxford: Oxford University Press and London: Athlone Press, 1983), p. 500.

2. But he does not explain what he means by a "community." Why should it mean only the members of existing political units? Why shouldn't political societies be concerned with the welfare of those human beings outside their borders? Indeed, why should they be concerned only with *human* welfare? And what about including the welfare of those human beings who have yet to be born? For more discussion of issues surrounding this last question, see Derek Parfit, *Reasons and Persons* (Oxford: Oxford University Press, 1984), and his "Overpopulation and the Quality of Life," in Jonathan Glover, ed., *Utilitarianism and Its Critics* (New York: Macmillan, 1990).

3. Jeremy Bentham, *An Introduction to the Principles of Morals and Legislation,* eds. J. H. Burns and H.L.A. Hart (London: Athlone Press, 1970), chap. 1, sec. 3, p. 12.

4. Ibid., sec. 7, p. 14.

5. For example, this term is used by John Rawls in *A Theory of Justice* (Cambridge: Harvard University Press, 1971).

6. John Stuart Mill, *Utilitarianism,* in Mill, *Utilitarianism, Liberty and Representative Government,* ed. H. B. Acton (New York: E. P. Dutton, 1972), p. 7.

7. Ibid., p. 7.

8. Ibid., p. 9.

9. See Oskar Morgenstern and John von Neumann, *Theory of Games and Economic Behavior* (Princeton: Princeton University Press, 1953), and Leonard Savage, *The Foundations of Statistics* (New York: Dover, 1972).

10. See R. Duncan Luce and Howard Raiffa, *Games and Decisions* (New York: John Wiley and Sons, 1957).

11. See articles exploring this idea in Jon Elster and John Roemer, eds., *Interpersonal Comparisons of Wellbeing* (New York: Cambridge University Press, 1991).

12. Amartya Sen is particularly critical of John Harsanyi's use of the expected utility theory as a foundation for utilitarianism. For a discussion of their debate, see John Weymark, "A Reconsideration of the Harsanyi-Sen Debate on Utilitarianism," in ibid., pp. 255–320.

13. I pursue them in Hampton, "The Failure of Expected Utility Theory as a Theory of Reason," *Economics and Philosophy* 10, 2 (October 1994): 195–242.

14. See Kenneth Arrow, *Social Choice and Individual Values* (New York: John Wiley and Sons, 1951).

15. Rawls, *Theory of Justice.*

16. However, Rawls tries to tie his argument to Locke as well as to Rousseau and Kant (but not Hobbes); see *Theory of Justice,* p. 11. My argument to follow is that his inclusion of Locke in his list of philosophical antecedents is a mistake.

17. See Epicurus, fragments 31 and 33, translated and discussed in Julia Annas, *The Morality of Happiness* (Oxford: Oxford University Press, 1993), p. 294; and see generally pp. 293–302.

18. Immanuel Kant, "On the Common Saying: 'This May Be True in Theory, but It Doesn't Apply in Practice,'" in *Kant's Political Writings,* ed. Hans Reiss (Cambridge: Cambridge University Press, 1970), p. 79; emphasis in the original.

19. Thomas Scanlon suggests this idea in his "Contractualism and Utilitarianism," in Amartya Sen and Bernard Williams, eds., *Utilitarianism and Beyond* (Cambridge: Cambridge University Press, 1982).

20. See Immanuel Kant, *Groundwork of the Metaphysics of Morals,* trans. H. J. Paton (London: Harper Torchbooks, 1964), chap. 2.

21. Rawls, *Theory of Justice,* p. 29.

22. Hence Rawls attacks the idea of an "impartial sympathetic spectator" sometimes used by advocates of utilitarianism to explicate and defend the utilitarian reasoning procedure. See ibid., p. 29, and chap. 30.

23. See ibid., chaps. 27 and 28.

24. From ibid., p. 60; the complete and most specified version of the two principles is on pp. 302–303. For a detailed discussion of the way in which Rawls believes that benefiting the least advantaged will invariably redound to the advantage of everyone else, see sec. 13, esp. p. 80. The second principle precludes inequalities that advantage people who are better off but not the least advantaged.

25. Rawls discusses "good" and "bad" forms of envy in ibid., secs. 80–81, pp. 530–541.

26. Rawls, *Theory of Justice*, pp. 18–19.

27. See ibid., secs. 3 and 4.

28. The circumstances of justice were first articulated by David Hume in his *Treatise of Human Nature*, ed. L. A. Selby-Bigge, rev. P. H. Nidditch (Oxford: Clarendon Press, 1978), book III, part ii, sec. ii, pp. 486–488.

29. I discuss this representation of the reasoning procedure in the original position at some length in Jean Hampton, "Contracts and Choices: Does Rawls Have a Social Contract Theory?" *Journal of Philosophy* 77, 6 (June 1980): 315–338.

30. Rawls, *Theory of Justice*, p. 102.

31. At one point in *A Theory of Justice*, Rawls claims that the knowledge that the parties will have to contract with one another in the original position introduces "strains of commitment," which play a role in their decision to select the two principles of justice (see sec. 29, esp. pp. 76 ff.). But these "strains" are unimportant in that decision, insofar as the grounds for that choice are already established through other constraints (e.g., the finality constraint, one of the constraints of the concept of right, which Rawls says requires the parties to choose a conception of justice that will be the final court of appeal in their society) and because a contract isn't nearly as constraining as Rawls suggests (and needs for his argument): Agreements can be made, and they can also be remade if some parties are dissatisfied with their operation.

32. Rawls, *Theory of Justice*, p. 139.

33. In Hampton, "Contracts and Choices."

34. Consider that Kant also had different formulations of his moral reasoning procedure. Why, then, can't there be different formulations of a political reasoning procedure designed to elicit the nature of justice? I discuss this possible connection in "Contracts and Choices" and in "Two Faces of Contractarian Thought," in Peter Vallentyne, ed., *Contractarianism and Rational Choice: Essays on Gauthier* (Cambridge: Cambridge University Press, 1990), pp. 31–55.

35. Scanlon suggests this in "Contractualism and Utilitarianism."

36. See John Harsanyi, "Can the Maximin Principle Serve as a Basis for Morality? A Critique of Rawls's Theory," *American Political Science Review* 69 (1975): 594–606. For Harsanyi's more positive views, see his *Essays on Ethics, Social Behavior and Scientific Explanation* (Dordrecht: D. Reidel, 1976).

37. See Rawls, *Theory of Justice*, pp. 153–156. The crux of the problem is this: Rawls claims that the maximin rule is appropriate in this situation because each person in the original position "cares very little, if anything, for what he might gain above the minimum stipend that he can, in fact, be sure of by following the maximin rule" (p. 154). But this contradicts Rawls's early stipulation that each original position party wants as many primary goods as possible.

38. David Gauthier, *Morals by Agreement* (Oxford: Oxford University Press, 1986).

39. Robert Nozick, *Anarchy, State and Utopia* (New York: Basic Books, 1974).

40. See ibid., chap. 7.

41. Ibid., p. 163.

42. Ibid., pp. 174–175.

43. Ibid., p. 31.

44. Rawls, *Theory of Justice*, p. 102; quoted in ibid., p. 228.

45. Nozick, *Anarchy*, p. 228.

46. Ibid.

47. Rawls, *Theory of Justice*, p. 104.

48. Nozick, *Anarchy*, p. 214.

49. For example, see Thomas Nagel's review of Nozick's book, entitled "Libertarianism Without Foundations," in Jeffrey Paul, ed., *Reading Nozick* (Totowa, N.J.: Rowman and Littlefield, 1981).

50. See Loren Lomasky, *Persons, Rights and the Moral Community* (New York: Oxford University Press, 1987).

51. Locke, *Two Treatises of Government*, ed. Peter Laslett (Cambridge: Cambridge University Press, 1988), Second Treatise, chap. 5, sec. 27, p. 288.

52. Nozick, *Anarchy*, p. 182.

53. G. A. Cohen, "Robert Nozick and Wilt Chamberlain: How Patterns Preserve Liberty," in John Arthur and William H. Shaw, eds., *Justice and Economic Distribution* (Englewood Cliffs, N.J.: Prentice-Hall, 1981), pp. 246–262.

54. John Stuart Mill, "Chapters on Socialism," in *Collected Works*, vol. 5 (Toronto: University of Toronto Press, 1967), p. 710; quoted in Will Kymlicka, *Contemporary Political Philosophy: An Introduction* (Oxford: Clarendon Press, 1990), p. 121.

55. Aristotle, *The Politics*, trans. T. A. Sinclair, rev. Trevor J. Saunders (Harmondsworth: Penguin, 1992), 1295b28, p. 267.

56. Ibid., 1295b20–27, p. 267.

57. Amartya Sen, "Equality of What?" in Sterling McMurrin, ed., *The Tanner Lectures on Human Values* (Salt Lake City: University of Utah Press, 1980).

58. Dworkin's views are spelled out in two articles, "What Is Equality? Part I: Equality of Welfare" and "What Is Equality? Part II: Equality of Resources," *Philosophy and Public Affairs* 10, 3 and 4 (1981): 185–246 and 283–345.

59. Dworkin, "What Is Equality? Part II," pp. 286–287.

60. Ibid., p. 289.

61. One interesting suggestion to try to capture the nature of equality has been made by Richard Arneson: He proposes that an egalitarian state should pursue "equality of opportunity for welfare." See Arneson, "Equality and Equal Opportunity for Welfare," *Philosophical Studies*, 56 (1989): 77–93.

62. See Judith Shklar, *Ordinary Vices* (Cambridge: Harvard University Press, 1984).

63. See especially Iris Young, "Impartiality and the Civic Public," in Seyla Benhabib and Drucilla Cornell, eds., *Feminism as Critique* (Minneapolis: University of Minnesota Press, 1987). And see Young's *Justice and the Politics of Difference* (Princeton: Princeton University Press, 1990).

64. See Judith Hicks Stiehm, "The Unit of Political Analysis: Our Aristotelian Hangover," in Sandra Harding and Merrill Hintikka, eds., *Discovering Reality* (Dordrecht: D. Reidel, 1983).

65. Susan Moller Okin, "Justice and Gender," *Philosophy and Public Affairs* 16, 1 (1987): 42–72.

66. Jean Hampton, "Feminist Contractarianism," in Louise Anthony and Charlotte Witt, eds., *A Mind of One's Own* (Boulder: Westview Press, 1993), pp. 227–255.

5

Liberalism, Communitarianism, and Postliberal Theory

Justice is a complicated topic, and distributive fairness is only one aspect of it. Political theorists who have reflected on the nature of justice have proposed a variety of characteristics that a just state would have besides distributive justice, some of which we will pursue in this chapter. By doing so, we will be exploring theories of the nature and extent of the state's authority when it is *justly* exercised—theories that purport to tell citizens how their state ought to use its authority such that it is morally legitimate and worthy of its citizens' strong consent. We do so by attempting to answer the following question: Should the ideally just state be constructed from the standpoint of how to realize an ideal *community*, or should it be constructed from the standpoint of how to foster the well-being of *individuals* in that society? Most (albeit not all) of Western political theory has been highly individualistic in character: Hobbes and Locke begin their theories from individuals existing in prepolitical and (in Hobbes's case) presocial states of nature. Modern consent-based theories of authority derive political authority from the actions of individuals—and notice how this is true of the theory that I put forward in Chapter 3, where the leadership convention is generated by the private actions of particular people seeking what is best for each of them.

Moreover, theories of distributive justice are normally driven by what is best for individuals conceived independently of the communities of which they are a part; this is true of all the theories of distributive justice reviewed in the previous chapter (indeed, think of Rawls's original position procedure, which asks us to imagine people abstracted from their particular social positions). Such individualistic theories are examples of a genus of political theory called liberalism. When philosophers use this term, it generally does not refer to any particular political position but rather to a historically important approach to political theory shared by a wide variety of political theorists, from Rawls to the libertarians. In this chapter I define what liberalism is and what liberal theorists agree about, even when they disagree (sometimes radically) about the nature of distributive justice or the characteristics of just government.

Since the 1980s liberal political theories have been opposed by (what are called) communitarian political theories. Such theories are put forward by people who advocate a democratic polity for a liberal state (unlike, say, Platonic perfectionists) but who reject the individualism of the liberal approach and who believe (like Plato) that the best locus of philosophical concern in reflecting on the ideal state is the community, not the individual. Communitarians also come in many different varieties: In this chapter I discuss a number of these forms. However, liberals have good responses to their communitarian critics, and they have raised powerful objections to all forms of communitarianism, which I also review. Their objections challenge those who advocate the communitarian approach to develop that approach more successfully than it has been thus far.

Still, this chapter ends on a note that is not terribly favorable to the liberals. I review what I take to be a new and (in certain respects) nonliberal way of thinking about how to structure the ideal society, pioneered by Marxists, civil rights thinkers, and feminist critics of liberal society. This new view shares with liberalism the commitment to freedom and equality but has a quite different conception of the role and nature of the state. I call this postliberalism, and I argue that it is a promising (but still incompletely developed) alternative to both liberal and communitarian ways of thinking about the ideal state.

Liberalism

So what is liberalism? As I understand this question, it asks us to focus on how liberalism has been understood in the philosophical tradition in the modern world and does not ask about how the term has been used in the political life of various countries over the years. Clearly, from the definition of the word liberals believe in liberty, prompting one philosopher to refer to liberals as "philosophers of freedom."[1] The phrase is felicitous, and yet those who are held to be in this tradition have had strikingly different conceptions of what freedom is. We can distinguish two prominent types of liberalism in terms of how they conceive of liberty: The first conceives of it in ways initially suggested by Locke, the second in ways initially suggested by Rousseau.[2]

The Lockeans focus on the danger to liberty coming from the power of the state and thus advocate minimal government and certain liberties (or rights) of subjects (such as habeas corpus and the right of bail); such Lockeans include Baron de Montesquieu, Benjamin Constant, Wilhelm von Humboldt, and many of the American Revolutionaries. Hence modern philosophers such as Joel Feinberg also work within this tradition when they insist that a liberal society can only allow criminal laws sanctioned by the "harm principle," which requires that the state only interfere with behavior that harms people other than the person interfered with.[3] Any broader role for the state, on this view, threatens people's freedom by allowing the state too great a say in what people's life choices should be.

Particularly in the nineteenth century and particularly in England, Lockean liberals tended to endorse the economic doctrine of laissez-faire; today Locke's descendants are invariably committed to markets and market-based solutions, both because of their economic efficiency and because, these Lockeans say, markets best realize freedom. As we saw in Chapter 4, this style of liberalism has inspired libertarianism and other "right-wing" political parties and movements.[4]

However, the term 'liberal' is slippery, and particularly in North America it is often used in political contexts to refer to the "left-wing" opponents of the Lockeans, whose concerns and forms of thinking have their source in ideas first put forward by Rousseau. These philosophers, including Rawls and egalitarians such as Ronald Dworkin, focus on the danger to liberty that comes from a society that is distributively unjust and unequal. Those oppressed by poverty, on this view, cannot be said to be free; nor can those suffering from a social system that favors and ranks some over others. Nor does it make sense, on this view, to design a political system that tries to implement freedom by uncritically trying to maximize the satisfaction of preferences, since preferences are affected by social structures and can be corrupt, distorted, and damaging to the realization of an individual's autonomy, properly understood. The remedy, according to these liberals, is not a limited but an active state, one that reflects and implements the will of the people who own it, that strives to end poverty and secure equal opportunities for all, that attempts to ensure that the people who develop within it have authentic preferences whose satisfaction will realize their autonomy, and that attempts to create not only a democratic polity but also a democratic social culture. Such liberals include certain American and French Revolutionaries, certain English thinkers such as T. H. Green and Matthew Arnold, and in contemporary times "left-wing" thinkers such as Rawls and Dworkin.

Whereas the Lockeans emphasize ideas such as freedom of conscience and toleration and tend to think in individualistic terms, the Rousseauian liberals tend to emphasize equality. Sometimes they are also more collectivist in outlook. However, Rousseauians remain committed to the individual as the basic unit of political justification. Indeed, Rousseau himself was so concerned about the importance of ensuring each individual's voluntary participation in his political society that he argued against any form of representative government.[5]

Some liberals are noted for wanting to unify both strands of liberal thought. For example, in *Utilitarianism* Mill emphasizes the well-being of the community and the role of the state in securing it, whereas in *On Liberty* he emphasizes the liberty of the individual and the need for the state to stay out of private concerns, claiming that individual liberty is socially advantageous. But philosophers have been persistently troubled about whether Mill's two books are mutually consistent, reflecting the fact that it is not at all obvious that Lockean and Rousseauian ideas can be consistently fit together in one position. In *A Theory of Justice*, Rawls tries to join them by repudiating Millian utilitarianism and, as we discussed in Chapter 4, puts forward two principles that together constitute his conception of justice. The first of these requires each individual to enjoy "the most extensive total system of equal basic liberties compatible with a similar system of liberty for all," and the second requires that social and economic inequalities be arranged so that they are to the greatest benefit of the least advantaged and attached to offices and positions open to all under conditions of equal opportunity.[6] However, as we noted, the union of these principles has struck some critics as optimistic.[7] Rawls insists that the first principle is prior to the second, but he says little in *A Theory of Justice* about the tensions and conflicts that many are convinced must exist between policies that pursue certain basic individual liberties (which he lists as the right to vote, the right to run for public office, the right to freedom of speech and assembly, the right to hold personal property, the right to freedom of conscience, and the right to freedom from arbitrary arrest),[8] as the first principle commands, and policies that pursue economic equality in the way the second principle requires. And a common libertarian reaction to Rawls's conception of justice is that if the first principle really is prior to the second, the second has no force, because the implementation of the first principle precludes legislation or policies that would be required to implement the second.[9] Rawls clearly has a conception of what the first principle requires that differs from a libertarian conception, such that its implementation does not jeopardize the pursuit of economic equality, a conception that Rawls's followers have subsequently attempted to make precise.

These differences in their conceptions of freedom and equality affect how various liberals conceive of justice: Although all of them agree that a political society should be just and that the notion of justice must be explicated in terms of the freedom and equality of the citizenry, because they have disagreed extensively about how the notions of freedom and equality are to be understood, they have put forward very different conceptions of justice. It is also worth pointing out that their commitments to these ideals generally have not stopped them from acquiescing in and sometimes even arguing for the subordination of some kinds of persons to others, in particular the subordination of women to men. (Mill is a notable exception in this regard.[10]) We have more to say about this phenomenon later in the chapter.

Liberal thinking also tends to differ along national lines. For example, the American experience of religious pluralism has produced the doctrine of the separation of church and state as a hallmark of American liberalism, and yet no European democracy has accepted the idea that church and state should be completely separated. What institutions are required to realize the creation of a liberal state is controversial and connected to the very different historical experiences of Western democracies.

Disagreements among liberals over the meaning of freedom and equality are also associated with differences in the philosophical arguments they have used to defend their views. Some liberals are utilitarian, and some are contractarian. Some are committed to the centrality and priority of the notion of individual rights, and some believe that the idea of natural, nonderivative rights is nonsense (recall Bentham's characterization of rights as "nonsense on stilts"), necessitating a different moral foundation for their liberal views.

One general area of agreement among liberals is that the government should be committed to tolerating the views and cultures of its people and, in general, committed to staying out of individuals' decisions regarding the best way to lead their lives. But they have differed, sometimes dramatically, in how they have defended this commitment to toleration and a limited governmental role. For example, Rawls has recently defended a form of liberalism he calls "political liberalism," which is so thoroughly committed to toleration that it eschews any kind of metaphysical, moral, or religious foundation for basic liberal principles, lest such a defense strike some members of contemporary states (in which there is no agreement on metaphysical, moral, or religious ideas) as sectarian.[11] As we saw in Chapter 4, Rawls accepts that freedom and equality are the two ruling concepts in a liberal political regime. Nonetheless, Rawls says he now wants to affirm them merely as "political" values and avoid endorsing them as part of some kind of metaphysical, moral, or religious theory, or what Rawls calls a "comprehensive" or "partially comprehensive" view. They are supposed to be "free-standing" values that are implicit in the political culture of the liberal society.

Perhaps most important, Rawls says that a liberal society's commitment to these values should *not* be a function of this society's belief that it has in hand a moral or religious argument establishing them as *true*.

While these values are supported by what Rawls terms "public reason" in a liberal society, this reason is not understood as the discloser of universal moral truth or the vehicle through which citizens of a liberal society seek to get access to the moral values that should animate it.[12] Instead, public reason is something common to all members of the society because it is constructed out of commonly accepted values. Public reason involves appeal to fully public *reasons* that all citizens use in their political arguments and that are concerned with the good of the public.[13] The implication of Rawls's discussion is that such reasons are commonly accepted because no matter how they differ, all (reasonable) members of the state accept that these reasons count in their society. Or to put it in Rawlsian terms, the members of the state have constructed "an overlapping consensus" on them. Such reasons are supposed to be at the intersection of their differing comprehensive views.

Whereas (as we further discuss shortly) the position of traditional liberals is that the reasons to which people appeal in political argumentation are commonly accepted because reasoning has shown them to be "right," Rawls says that the reasons to which people appeal in a liberal society come from "a conception of justice that may be shared by citizens as a basis of a reasoned, informed, and willing political agreement."[14] Not surprisingly, he argues that his own two principles of justice turn out to be the conception that at least in the United States is shared by all reasonable Americans. In any case, Rawls insists that such a conception, once constructed, "expresses their shared and public political reason."[15]

So on Rawls's view, liberals are not supposed to say to one another, "It is a moral fact that *x*; therefore we must have policy *y*." Instead, they are supposed to work together as reasonable people to develop an overlapping consensus, accepting that reasoning yields plural results and looking for political values and policies that all of them, despite their different starting points and moral views, can accept. Moreover, even though public reason is constructed out of the beliefs of the citizenry, this public reason is supposed to be vigorously nonpartisan:

> To attain such a shared reason, the conception of justice should be, as far as possible, independent of the opposing and conflicting philosophical and religious doctrines that citizens affirm. In formulating such a conception, political liberalism applies the principle of toleration to philosophy itself. The religious doctrines that in previous centuries were the professed basis of society have gradually given way to principles of constitutional government that all citizens, whatever their religious view, can endorse.[16]

Such nonpartisanship makes a liberal state governed by this public reason tolerant and respectful of the competing moral views of all its citizenry.

However, there are other forms of liberalism that are just as committed to toleration as Rawls's political liberalism but whose foundations are deliberately intended *not* to be neutral. For example, Kant, like most traditional liberals, justified liberal political theory by first putting forward a moral theory stressing the equal worth and moral autonomy of all human beings and then using this theory to justify a political society that recognizes rights of autonomy and equality. I call this sort of liberal theory "rights-based liberalism";[17] it invokes the moral idea of rights in order to define and legitimate political authority and power. There have been a number of different theories of rights upon which liberalism has been founded (as our discussion of distributive justice in the previous chapter demonstrates).[18] All such theories, however, see rights as theoretical vehicles for expressing and requiring respect for each individual's freedom and equality; Dworkin's felicitous way of putting it is that rights are "moral trumps."[19] Hence this form of liberalism is unafraid of explicitly incorporating moral ideas in its foundations and indeed welcomes the idea that the liberal state has a certain kind of moral role to play in the community, insofar as it must respect, and in certain cases promote, individual rights. But despite this particular appeal to controversial moral foundations, this kind of liberalism is generally vigorously committed to toleration. Indeed, proponents of such liberalism argue that the rights-based moral foundation they endorse *demands* such a commitment, so that even if a member of the regime attacks that foundation, the state is committed to allowing that person to be heard insofar as it is committed to recognizing that person's right to his own opinion and, more generally, to freedom of conscience.

This nonneutral conception of liberalism, with its rights-based defense of toleration, has influenced even those theorists such as Feinberg who are leery of relying on controversial moral theories to ground liberal theory, by bequeathing to them both a commitment to rights (to which all members of a liberal society are supposed to be committed no matter their religious or moral views) and a commitment to the idea that the state plays (and must play) a moral role in enforcing these rights. For example, Feinberg presents his harm principle as (merely) a middle-level theory,[20] one that describes the extent of state interference in the life of the citizenry but does not take a stand on deep foundational questions regarding the source of justification in political theory. Nonetheless, he still believes he must ground the tolerant, nonpaternalist liberal state he advocates with a certain kind of moral theory, one that makes use of the notion of rights. Starting with the distinction between the general justifying aim of an institution and the rules of fair procedure governing its actions, Feinberg maintains that when we apply this distinction to the criminal law we find that

it is a misrepresentation of the liberal position (at least as I have tried to formulate it) to say that it ascribes an entirely nonmoral justifying aim to the
criminal law. There is a clear respect in which the liberal's liberty-limiting
principle *is* a moral one. The justifying aim of the system of criminal law, on
his view, is not merely to minimize harms, in the sense of setback interests,
all round. If that is what he advocated he would have no quarrel with the
legal paternalist. In fact, his principle permits prohibitory statutes only when
necessary to prevent those harms (and offenses) that are also *wrongs:* those
that are unconsented to, involuntarily suffered, and neither justified nor ex-
cused. The criminal law, he insists, must serve a profoundly moral purpose,
namely the protection of individual's [sic] moral *rights.*"[21]

Whereas a Rawlsian political liberal has to attribute to any modern pluralist liberal state a nonpartisan understanding not only of the state's punishment actions but also of the offenders' acts that warrant it, Feinberg appreciates that a rights-based liberal is free to appropriate partisan moral
language to characterize criminal actions not merely as harms but as
wrongs, insofar as these acts are taken to be violations of rights. Hence
Feinberg's liberal state is unabashedly taking (perhaps controversial) ethical positions: Some conceptions of right and wrong are rejected out of
hand, and lawbreakers who perform criminal actions that demonstrate that
they subscribe to what this state determines to be false moral views are told
by Feinberg's state, via punishment, that both their views and their actions
following from these views are unacceptable by virtue of the moral theory
that grounds that state's actions. As Feinberg puts it, "Even a penal code
based exclusively on the harm principle (and any penal code will be *largely*
based on that principle) is meant to do more than merely prevent harm. In
so protecting people, it also means to vindicate the morality of preventing
harm and respecting autonomy."[22] Again, to quote Feinberg:

> The liberal . . . can and must concede that the criminal *process* in its very con-
> ception is inherently moral (as opposed to non-moral)—a great moral ma-
> chine, stamping stigmata on its products, painfully "rubbing in" moral judg-
> ments on the persons who had entered at one end as "suspects" and
> emerged from the other end as condemned prisoners. The question the lib-
> eral raises about this moral machine is: "which actions should cause their
> doers to be fed into it?", and his answer is: "only those actions that violate
> the rights of others." There is no doubt in his mind that the law may "enforce
> morality." The question is *"which* morality (or which sector of morality) may
> it properly enforce?", and he restricts the criminal law to the enforcement of
> "grievance morality."[23]

So whereas Rawls's liberal state attempts to bind together people of
disparate views via shared political conceptions and public ways of reasoning that even if they are moral, are not meant to be generated by any
particular partisan moral theory, Feinberg's liberal state is a "moral ma-

chine" animated by a particular kind of moral theory, which unifies disparate people by insisting on a common commitment to (what it takes to be) universal moral values (and particularly the idea of universal rights).

Another form of liberalism that explicitly relies on a moral theory is Raz's "perfectionist liberalism."[24] Like rights-based liberalism, perfectionist liberalism understands the liberal state to have a moral foundation and a moral role but does not start from the idea that the liberal state must enforce rights. On this view, the liberal state has a duty to engage in policies that aim in certain ways to improve the moral quality of the lives of its citizenry. In that sense, the perfectionist liberal agrees with Plato about the role of the state. But unlike Plato, this kind of liberal believes that human perfection is fundamentally concerned with autonomy (so it is a position that mixes Kantian and Platonic ideas). Raz disputes the idea that autonomy requires that governments refrain from encouraging a "good life" for its citizens, and he rejects the idea that the pluralism in modern society can be protected only by a government that substantially limits its political action. Instead, Raz believes that human autonomy requires a certain kind of community life, the creation of which is the central task of liberal government. That life must be one that allows and promotes what Raz calls "value pluralism," so that the citizenry have plenty of options and opportunities to choose from in creating their lives. Most important for our purposes, it must also be one that incorporates and promotes moral behavior: "Governments should promote the moral quality of the life of those whose lives and actions they can affect."[25] This is because, on Raz's view, the moral quality of a person's life is intrinsically related to that person's nature as an autonomous being. So an essential element of the good life, on Raz's view, is personal autonomy. Any government committed to autonomy is also committed (contra claims of Rawlsian political liberals or Feinbergian rights-based liberals) to promoting the good life of its citizenry. However, Raz thinks that one way a state can promote the moral quality of its citizens' lives is to legislate according to Feinberg's harm principle:

> The argument of this book . . . [is that] it is the function of governments to promote morality. That means that governments should promote the moral quality of the life of those whose lives and actions they can affect. Does not this concession amount to a rejection of the harm principle? It does according to the common conception which regards the aim and function of the principle as being to curtail the freedom of governments to enforce morality. I wish to propose a different understanding of it, according to which it is a principle about the proper way to enforce morality. In other words I would suggest that the principle is derivable from a morality which regards personal autonomy as an essential ingredient of the good life, and regards the principle of

autonomy, which imposes duties on people to secure all the conditions of autonomy, as one of the most important moral principles.[26]

Raz's position still preserves a limited and attenuated commitment to the idea that the liberal state stays out of its citizens' conception of the good, because in a Razian liberal state the government will not presume to dictate how a citizen chooses to define her conception of the good; however, that is because, ironically, it is concerned to promote each citizen's good! That is, a Razian government believes that letting each person work out what she believes to be the best life for her is the way to ensure her autonomy, which is, in Raz's view, an "essential ingredient" of her leading a good life. So *because it is concerned to promote her good, the Razian liberal state refuses to tell her what her good is.*

In its use of the harm principle to develop criminal legislation, the perfectionist liberal state is treating the harm principle, and the idea of autonomy from which Raz insists it is derived, as perfectionist ideas to which the state is responsive: "If the government has a duty to promote the autonomy of people the harm principle allows it to use coercion both in order to stop people from actions which would diminish people's autonomy and in order to force them to take actions which are required to improve people's options and opportunities."[27] Moreover, on Raz's view the harm principle is consistent with the government's undertaking a variety of tasks that it regards as promotive of individual autonomy (e.g., providing educational and artistic opportunities). Whether in the end Raz's liberal state can genuinely promote the good by "leaving people alone" in something like the way liberalism has traditionally advocated is certainly debatable. Some liberals regard Raz as giving away too much by even admitting that the moral quality of its citizens' lives could be a concern of a liberal state. Other, nonliberal critics doubt that a state that is genuinely concerned with the moral quality of its citizens' lives would be able to pursue that concern adequately by relying primarily on the harm principle to guide its legislation. Nonetheless, Raz's distinctive form of liberalism raises interesting challenges for traditional liberals and nonliberals alike.

This review of the variety of liberal theories developed in the past few hundred years shows that the term 'liberalism' is really a kind of umbrella that can include a variety of particular liberal philosophies. One might distinguish between the various and competing liberal conceptions of our political life and the liberal "movement" in political philosophy. Or alternatively, we might call traditional liberalism a kind of overarching "secular political faith" consisting of many rival denominations.[28]

So any account of philosophical liberalism must be formulated so as to be able to accommodate the diversity of views denoted by this label. Some liberals have been reluctant to deal with that diversity, arguing that all forms of (so-called) liberalism that are substantially at odds with their view don't count as "liberal" properly speaking. I call these disowning arguments. If we are to characterize effectively both the diversity and the commonality of the liberal movement, we should try as far as possible to avoid such arguments and instead seek to determine the common characteristics of all theories whose authors embrace the "liberal" description. These common characteristics must be stated in a highly general, imprecise form, in order to take account of the variety of ways in which that form has been concretized in theory. To use Rawls's terminology, liberalism must be stated in terms of "concepts" rather than "conceptions": Liberals are, I argue, largely united on the issue of what concepts a liberal society should affirm, but they have different conceptions of these concepts.

With these caveats, let me propose that all theories that are properly considered "liberal" share the following five fundamental commitments:

1. *A commitment to the idea that people in a political society must be free.* As I have already noted, the concept of freedom can be understood in a variety of ways, some highly individualistic, others more collectivist.
2. *A commitment to equality of the people in the political society.* Again, the concept of equality can be understood in a number of ways, ranging from the mere denial of natural subordination to the affirmation of pure procedural equality for all people to the insistence on substantive economic equality.
3. *A commitment to the idea that the state's role must be defined such that it enhances freedom and equality (as defined by that theory).* As we have seen, different liberals disagree quite severely about how the state can best enhance freedom and equality—some maintaining that it can do so only by taking a very minimal role in the society, others maintaining that it must take a very extensive role. This disagreement relates in part to different understandings of what freedom and equality are. Despite this disagreement, all liberals tend to agree on the following three general theses about the state's role and structure.
3a. *The state has the best chance of securing the freedom and equality of its citizenry when it is organized as a democracy.* The idea that democracy is central to the construction of a liberal polity has been largely unchallenged in recent times. And although this commitment to democracy tends to go along with a commitment to certain procedures that a liberal state must follow in its legislative and judicial processes, such as habeas corpus, in general liberals in different liberal societies have disagreed about what procedures and practices best implement the democratic ideal.
3b. *The state can ensure freedom only by pursuing policies that implement toleration and freedom of conscience for all citizens.* As we shall see, for theorists such as Rawls this is a particularly important feature of liberalism. But again, how toleration and freedom of conscience are best

implemented is the subject of controversy (e.g., consider the debate over the best construction of freedom of speech laws).

3c. *The state must stay out of the individual's construction of his own life plans—his "conception of the good."* As we have seen, however, the agreement on this last thesis is matched by controversy over its interpretation: Some liberals believe that when they say this, they are committing the state to a minimal role; others insist that the state's neutrality with respect to life plans may well require rather extensive state involvement in the life of the community, for example, in assuring the economic equality necessary for individuals to have a free and equal chance to pursue their own conception of the good. And liberals such as Raz claim that the best way of justifying tenet 3c is to appeal to the state's appropriate concern that its citizens live a good and morally successful life.

The fourth tenet of liberalism focuses on the importance of individual consent in the legitimating of a political society:

4. *Any political society must be justified to the individuals who live within it, if that society is to be legitimate.*[29] Or in other words, individuals are the ultimate units of normative political analysis, so that political policies, institutions, and large-scale conceptions of justice must always be legitimated on the basis of how each person in that society would be affected by them.

To use the terminology of Chapter 3, the liberal state must not only receive the convention consent of the people, which merely makes it authoritative in that territory, but also their endorsement consent, which makes it not just a state but a legitimate state. Presumably, their strong consent is connected to their belief that their state is operating justly, so that this consent is a marker for the justice of the state. It cannot, however, be considered an infallible marker, since people can consent (mistakenly) to that which is not just. However, controversy surrounds this fourth tenet: How do we understand the individuals to whom the justification is made? Are they real individuals in the society, or should they be appropriately cleansed of bias, irrationality, and bad reasoning in order for the justification to be morally compelling? What form does the justification take? Does it have to be contractarian in nature, or can a utilitarian argument be responsive to individuals in the right way? And does the justification require that individuals respond with their actual consent, or does the hypothetical consent of their fully rational counterparts suffice? Different liberals have given a variety of answers to these questions.

But all of them construct their answers in such a way that they take them to be justified by reason. The birth of liberalism in the Enlightenment points up this "common faith" in reason that liberals have had:

5. Reason is the tool by which the liberal state governs. Whatever the religious, moral, or metaphysical views of the people, they are expected to deal with one another in the political arena through rational argument and reasonable attitudes, and the legitimating arguments directed at individuals in order to procure their consent must be based on reason.

Implicit in this commitment is the idea that reason is common to all human beings—indeed definitive of what it is to be a human being. But liberals differ on the nature of reason: Some have a Kantian conception, others a utilitarian conception, others a rational choice conception. Rawls's political liberalism relies on a conception of the "reasonable" that is deliberately meant to provide a certain measure of substantive neutrality toward competing political views, even while ruling out views that should not be part of any overlapping consensus in a society that attempts to realize justice. These different conceptions of reason are associated with different conceptions of how morality and thus liberal values are "based on" reason, some of which support moral objectivism and some of which do not. So liberals hold a great variety of positions on moral metaphysics. And that means there is a variety of liberal positions on how we should understand the "truth" of normative prescriptions about our political life. But although liberals disagree about what that rational capacity is and what it reveals, the idea *that we can improve our society through reasoning*, enabling us to construct a legitimate and well-functioning political society, has been a fundamental liberal belief.

It is this commitment to reason that makes all traditional liberal theories (including Rawls's theory) descendants of the Enlightenment.[30] But having said this, I want to be careful to distinguish liberals' general commitment to the idea that reason can reveal politically relevant truth from any particular conception of how reason informs us of political truth. For example, some liberals have been committed to reason as *superior* to religious belief or revelation and held the view that religion is mere superstition that good reasoning enables us to overcome. This particular view about reason has not been universally held among liberals; Thomas Jefferson, for example, specifically rejects it.[31] By "Enlightenment liberalism" I do not mean a theory that would embrace such a particular view but rather a theory that holds there is a faculty of reasoning "common to the typical theist and the typical atheist" that suffices for working out how our political societies ought to be structured.[32] This latter view is compatible with a host of positions on religion and religious revelation, both hostile and friendly. And it is this latter view, and not any particular stand on the relation between reason and religion, that has been the hallmark of all liberal theory.

Note that there is a connection between the liberals' commitment to reason and their commitment to human beings as free and equal. To maintain that public policy is to be pursued via the use of reason is to be committed to the use of rational argument in the setting of public policy. When you argue with an opponent as opposed to, say, fighting with him, you seek to win him over to your side not by coercing him but by asking him to *choose* to accept your position in view of its rational superiority. Thus you are respecting his autonomy and rejecting the idea that his views make him inferior to you and thus subject to coercion by you or by those who hold your views. To be committed to persuading by rational argument is therefore to be committed to respecting the individual, not necessarily as a virtuous person or as a smart person or as a person satisfying some normative ideal, but as a human being who, like you, can and should choose what he believes in his life.[33]

Communitarianism

Since the 1980s some political theorists have criticized not just particular liberal views but the entire liberal family of theories, claiming they are too focused on the individual, too focused on the importance of individual liberty, and insufficiently appreciative of the way in which human beings require a place in a well-functioning community in order to flourish. One might say that whereas liberals encourage each person to define and seek her own "good" within a political structure that defines and enforces what is "right," communitarians believe that a political structure has an important role to play in defining both the right and the good and in helping those people in that political structure to seek the good. This is because like Plato, communitarians believe human beings can achieve a good life only if they live within a well-functioning society that government must help to create (although, as I noted, communitarians are, unlike Plato, generally committed to democratic forms of government).

As their name suggests, communitarians are first and foremost concerned with *community:* They insist that each of us, as an individual, develops an identity, talents, and pursuits in life only in the context of a community. Political life, then, must start with a concern for the community (not the individual), since the community is what determines and shapes individuals' natures. One communitarian, Alasdair MacIntyre, ridicules the liberals' "autonomous moral agent" operating disconnected from any social context and argues that individuals flourish only within the context of what he calls "practices," through which individuals develop and perfect virtues. For MacIntyre, a practice is

> any coherent and complex form of socially established cooperative human activity through which goods internal to that form of activity are realized in the course of trying to achieve those standards of excellence which are appropriate to, and partially definitive of, that form of activity, with the result

that human powers to achieve excellence, and human conceptions of the ends and goods involved, are systematically extended.[34]

So on this view, the state's role is to help develop and protect practices that encourage the development of human excellence. Were the state to let individuals loose to realize their "autonomy" (as liberals seem to wish), treating them as if they were socially disconnected beings who are concerned with their "rights," MacIntyre and other communitarians believe that the result would be social disintegration and moral disaster. Indeed, they argue that such disintegration and degeneration have already started to occur in modern liberal states, given the prevalence of crime and violence, the breakdown of the family, and drug abuse in these societies.[35]

MacIntyre's criticisms have been echoed by Charles Taylor, who attacks the plausibility of the liberals' "atomistic" conception of human beings as autonomous choosers, arguing that it treats the human being as primarily a "will" and does not acknowledge the complexities of the human personality and the fact that it is (and must be) situated in a society in order to develop.[36] These same themes have been echoed by some feminists: As Jean Bethke Elshtain has put it, "There is no way to create real communities out of an aggregate of 'freely choosing' adults."[37] Such sentiments are usually attended by dissatisfaction with the morality of rights upon which many (albeit not all) liberal theories are based.[38] Finally, certain religious thinkers have argued that liberals' reliance on individualism and reason are in reality hostile to religious belief and religious community life.[39]

Another communitarian critic of liberalism is Michael Sandel, whose work focuses on the form of liberalism exemplified by Rawls in *A Theory of Justice*. Sandel is struck by the disconnected, disembodied nature of the people in Rawls's original position. That Rawls could even conceive of people in this way shows, according to Sandel, the extent to which he and many other liberals in the past few hundred years try to understand human beings independently of all activities, desires, ideas, roles, and pursuits that characterize human lives in an actual society. But why should we think there is anything left of the person when we subtract all of this? Isn't the Rawlsian (and for that matter any liberal) view of the person woefully impoverished? Writes Sandel:

> We cannot regard ourselves as independent in this way without great cost to those loyalties and convictions whose moral force consists partly in the fact that living by them is inseparable from understanding ourselves as the particular persons we are—as members of this family or community or nation or people, as bearers of this history, as sons and daughters of that revolution, as citizens of this republic. Allegiances such as these are more than values I happen to have or aims I "espouse at any given time." They go beyond the obligations I voluntarily incur and the "natural duties" I owe to human beings as such. They allow that to some I owe more than justice requires or even permits, not by reason of agreements I have made but instead in virtue

of those more or less enduring attachments and commitments which taken together partly define the person that I am.[40]

So Sandel is saying that liberal theories fail to come to grips with the nature of our "embeddedness" in a particular time, place, and culture. Not only is this embeddedness a fact, it is also a fact that a political theory must recognize if it is going to generate laws, institutions, and practices that are genuinely good for us and constitutive of an ideal and fully just society. He calls for us to pursue justice not by working out ways that independent and separately conceived selves might profitably relate to one another (e.g., in markets or in political institutions) but by thinking about how people with attachments that partially constitute their identities can come to know and relate to one another as friends.[41] Only in this way, says Sandel, can we create a "deeper commonality" than benevolence allows, one of "shared self-understanding" as well as affection.[42]

Communitarians have also taken issue with the liberal penchant for freedom and autonomy. Communitarians insist that many adult human beings (because of illness, personality, mental impairment, or immaturity) are simply not capable of the kind of autonomous choice of life plan that liberals believe a state must respect, and they point out that even highly mature and intelligent people frequently use their freedom to make bad (sometimes dreadfully bad) choices. Does a state respect its citizens if it tries to pretend that the residual "childishness" in all of our natures simply isn't there? Does it respect people when it permits them to make choices that will clearly preclude their own future happiness (and indirectly affect the happiness of those who are connected to them)? And finally, why think that autonomy is one of the most important political values that a society must respect? (Wouldn't Plato be profoundly puzzled by the liberal penchant for liberty as a primary political value?) Aren't there other values a government must implement that are at least as important as—and maybe more important than—autonomy, such as stability, the preservation of social bonds, the preservation of culture, and the safety of its citizens?[43]

To summarize the communitarians' position, we can contrast their views to the views of liberals expressed in the five liberal tenets I presented in the previous section. Whereas liberals believe that the most important political values are freedom and equality (tenets 1 and 2), communitarians regard other values to be as important, and perhaps more important—in particular, what might be called the "values of community life," as I have just articulated them above. Moreover, whereas liberals are committed to the idea that the state's role must be defined such that it enhances the freedom and equality of the people, meaning that it should be democratically organized, pursue policies that implement toleration and freedom of conscience for all citizens, and stay out of the individual's construction of his own life plans and "conception of the good" (tenet 3 of the liberal view), communitarians believe the state's primary role is to ensure the health and well-being of the community life that makes possible all human flourishing and all human good. They are particularly adamant in rejecting the idea that in order to ensure human liberty the state must refrain from articulating a conception of the good to which all people must conform. Communitarians regard as a ridiculous illusion the liberal idea that we can autonomously pursue the good as individuals independent of cultural traditions and social roles; instead, they believe, in order to ensure that its citizens flourish, the ideal state must use its power and authority to encourage the continuation and health of the cultural traditions and roles through which each person must find her good life.

In addition, whereas liberals are committed to tenet 4 above, maintaining that any political society must be justified to the individuals who live within it if that society is to be legitimate, communitarians see the state as responsive not to individual citizens but to the *society* of which these individual citizens are a part. I do not say very much in this chapter about this particular communitarian tenet but spend a great deal of time discussing it in Chapter 6.

Finally, communitarians dismiss the liberal acceptance of tenet 5, committing them to reason as the tool by which the liberal state governs. The problem with the liberals' reliance on reason, say the communitarians, is that their conception of reason is disconnected from social traditions, operating in a vacuum (think of the reasoning in Rawls's original position) and hence unconnected to the real concerns, assumptions, goals, aspirations, and belief systems that real, socially embedded people actually have. In contrast, communitarians insist that the way to social harmony and health is through discourse that is informed by the culture of the community. We can achieve the ideal state only by engaging in discourse that is tied to the social practices that constitute and define the goals of the culture of the community.

The Liberals Strike Back

The communitarian challenge has generated considerable response by liberals, the outlines of which I review and evaluate here. The first response liberals have made to the communitarians is: We care about communities, too! Whereas Hobbes (as we saw) was inclined to think that people were radically asocial, other liberals, including Locke, Rousseau, Kant, and, in modern times, Rawls, Gauthier, and Feinberg, have insisted on the social nature of human beings.[44] To quote Feinberg:

Whatever else a human being is "by nature", he is essentially a social product. He is born into a family, itself part of a tribe or clan and a larger political community, each with its ongoing record or history, his first concepts shaped by a language provided for him by the larger group of which he is a member, his roles and status assigned by social custom and practice, his membership and sense of belonging imprinted from the start. He finds himself, as Alasdair MacIntyre puts it, "embedded" in a human culture not of his own original design or "contractual agreement," but one that is simply given.[45]

Such remarks endorse all sorts of communitarian ideas, yet they are made by a liberal who obviously feels that an enthusiastic endorsement of human sociality in no way threatens liberal political theory. Indeed, much of the liberal interest in allowing individuals to pursue their own conception of the good comes from their view that individuals should be able (and need to be able) to develop or pursue social connections—especially of a religious nature—that they take to be vital to their well-being and identity without being in any way impeded by government.

So both groups care about communities and acknowledge the sociality of human nature. What really differentiates them is their different views of state power: Whereas communitarians want the state to use its power to protect and encourage the development of communities and community values, liberals want the state to stay out of community life, so as not to harm, threaten, or limit those who are participating in it. This way of putting their disagreement shows that liberals and communitarians have very different views of the dangers, advantages, and consequences of state power. Whereas communitarians "seem to assume that whatever is properly social must become the province of the political,"[46] liberals want to limit the state's role in this province since they distrust it, fear its effects, and have faith in the ability of social groups to flourish without its help.

There are at least two reasons for the liberals' concern to limit the state's responsiveness to and interference in community life. The first reason has to do with the liberal commitment to the value of human autonomy. It is really this value that is driving the liberals' concern for the individual, and not some sort of implausible theory of the person as a socially naked atom. Again, to quote Feinberg: "The liberal can give up the excesses of individualism, acknowledge the social nature of man, and still hold on to what is essential in his normative theory, the doctrine of the human right of autonomous self-government within the private sphere."[47] The liberal is convinced that the best way to ensure that an individual can flourish within her community is to give her the freedom she needs to live (what will surely be) a highly social life in the way that she chooses.

The second reason arises from the liberals' deep distrust of state power and authority. Judith Shklar has argued that this distrust was born in the early modern period, in the midst of Calvinist proclamations of the innate sinfulness of the human soul, misanthropic writings of men of letters such as Michel de Montaigne, and grim experiences with the abusiveness and cruelty of state power and authority.[48] The lesson learned by the early moderns, whose thinking provides (as we have seen) the foundation for modern liberals, is that no human being can be counted upon to be "good enough" not to abuse extensive state power and authority. (As the saying goes, power corrupts and absolute power corrupts absolutely. Compare these liberal concerns with our discussion in Chapter 3 of the way political power can be used to create the conditions for mastery.) Hence in order to ensure that individuals will not be harmed in their pursuits— pursuits that (particularly when they concern religion) are generally highly social—liberals have insisted on constraining state power and authority in order to protect those subject to it from being abused by it.

Communitarians, in contrast, have been influenced by different thinkers and different historical experiences in ways that have given them a far more benign view of state power. They tend to agree, for example, with the nineteenth-century German philosopher G.W.F. Hegel, who considered the state "the actuality of the ethical Idea"[49]—that is, that aspect of society which articulates and maintains the conditions for moral life in a society, drawing from the social traditions that compose it. They are also influenced by the way in which many modern states appear to have successfully taken on all sorts of moral roles, including the provision of education, health care, and art (supporting dramatic arts, fine arts, literature, music); the responsibility for caring for the poor; even the moral improvement of the citizenry (through programs designed to improve their mental health and social functioning). Those liberals who reject these Hegelian sentiments are either hostile to many of the moral roles Hegelians would have the state play or are concerned to limit them, lest the state's power and authority get out of control and compromise the liberty of the people.

Liberals and communitarians, however, disagree not only about the benignity of state authority and power but also about the benignity of culture. Consider that the communitarian sees the state as playing a moral role that is responsive to and at least partly defined by the traditions and moral views of the cultural traditions of the society it governs. But in many ways liberals have been just as suspicious of cultures as they have been of governments—and with good reason. For example, the American cultural experience has been sexist, racist, and antihomosexual. It has also been strongly influenced by a variety of philosophical traditions, ethnic groups, and religions. Were a U.S. government to rule in a way that was responsive to any one of these elements in American cultural life, many other groups would be subject to state power that enforced ideas they would regard as discordant with or antithetical to their beliefs and interests. So if communitarians would have the state respond to "social roles" and "community values," how can they ensure that when it does so, it will not, say, compromise religious liberty or enact laws that reflect the prejudices of a majority against a minority? Why couldn't either use of state power and authority endanger not only the liberty and equality of certain people but also their very well-being? As one liberal critic of communitarianism puts it:

> The communitarian critics [of liberalism] want us to live in Salem, but not to believe in witches. Or human rights. Perhaps the Moral Majority would cease to be a threat were the United States a communitarian society; benevolence and fraternity might take the place of justice. Almost anything is possible, but it does not make moral sense to leave liberal politics behind on the strength of such speculation.[50]

Such worries show that to persuade the liberal opposition, communitarians can't simply hope for the best. They need to develop their theory so that it can show us how we can take a morally critical attitude toward community, even while recognizing the importance of community. Otherwise, their theory gives them no critical moral distance from existing social practices, which means that it could be used to license any abuse, injustice, and cruelty implicit in the community's culture.

Liberals influenced by those early modern thinkers who were impressed by the human capacity for cruelty have been very willing to recognize the way in which human beings and human social institutions can be morally corrupted and abusive. It is, I believe, for this reason that in their argumentation liberals start from the individual. By insisting that the individual is the focus of moral concern, the liberal gets the critical moral distance from community and the government that the communitarian lacks. In particular, by requiring that social arrangements are to work to the benefit of each person, the liberal has a way of recommending political policies that are not indebted to potentially cruel or unjust cultural practices of that community. This means liberal arguments start from the individual, not because they deny the sociality of human beings but because they require that *all* social arrangements, to be morally acceptable, must be morally acceptable from the individual standpoint.

Hence liberalism has implicit within it a kind of critical facility for judging cultures that communitarianism appears to be lacking. Perhaps the best example of this is Rawls's original position procedure: That procedure, contra some communitarians, doesn't deny human sociality. Instead, quite the opposite is true—it affirms the extent to which our lives are influenced by a variety of social structures. The point of the original position procedure is to give us a way of *morally evaluating those social structures* or, in other words, a moral vantage point from which to reliably assess and evaluate social structures (what Rawls calls an "Archimedian point").[51] The original position is a moral standpoint from which we attempt to assess the effects of a social practice on *every* member of society by freeing ourselves of beliefs, biases, and traditions that can prejudice that assessment. A social practice is easy to affirm if one uses the ideas generated by that practice to do so; the trick is to figure out a way of freeing oneself of the effects of a practice (which might be racist or sexist or in some other way unjust) so that one can come up with an effective moral assessment of it.

Indeed, this sort of "freeing" is what Rawls's original position procedure aims to do. Communitarians have attacked that procedure, as we saw, contending that it implicitly denies our thoroughly social natures. But is each of us *entirely* a product of the confluence of social forces on her biological nature? Can none of us critically assess the social forces to which we have been subject, because each of us is so completely a product of those forces that anything we would use to assess those forces would itself be generated by them? To say yes to this question is to raise an interesting (and chilling) possibility: If such complete social definition of human beings were possible, could not a government learn to control these social forces so effectively that it could design a society in which some individuals were socially constructed so as to be contented subordinates (happy "socialized" slaves), while other individuals were socially constructed to be fully comfortable in their role as superiors (happy "socialized" masters)?

If one answers no to this last question, one is postulating that there is something in individuals that will inevitably object to and fight social "definition" that attempts to oppress and subordinate them. It is this "something" that Rawls attempts to isolate in his original position procedure: The veil of ignorance, he says, tries to isolate each individual's "moral conception"—that is, that aspect of our personhood that is the source of our moral evaluations not only of individuals (including ourselves) but also of societies, cultures, and governments. Whether or not Rawls succeeds in defining this moral component of individuals is arguable, but it would seem that communitarians must recognize such a component if they are to construct a way of morally assessing cultures. And doing so would seem to require them to take individuals, rather than social groups, as the foundational moral concern of all well-ordered societies, because social groups can be as much the source of the abuse of individuals as they are the source of roles that contribute to their happiness.

Still, communitarians can insist that even if they have trouble formulating a critical stance toward the community, liberalism has trouble formulating a way to respect and use (what might be called) the "moral wisdom" implicit in that community. If one's political theorizing is too individualistic and fails to focus on the community, it can fail to acknowledge that all sorts of social structures in our society, including our legal institutions, family structures, and systems of educating the young, have been worked out by generations of people responding to a variety of

problems in ways that are complicated, nuanced, and often highly successful. One argument in favor of communitarianism (linking up to some
of the sentiments expressed by MacIntyre above) is that it encourages us
to respect the moral wisdom implicit in these social structures and not to
adopt the hubristic attitude that any one of us could do better by reasoning about these social structures by ourselves. This argument for communitarianism therefore links it with philosophical conservatism, a position
associated with the writings of Edmund Burke (1729–1797).[52] An important political figure and member of the British Parliament, Burke argued
that a society is ill advised to try to govern itself by relying on abstract
reasoning, because such reasoning cannot compete with the accumulated
wisdom of generations of people struggling with highly complicated issues in various areas. How can a single individual, for example, generate
an adequate code of criminal conduct simply by using her reason? Moreover, Burke argued that custom, human sentiments, and the lessons we
learn from experience are as important as reason in giving us the tools to
construct a well-functioning political society. (These themes are also present in the novels of George Eliot, who criticized certain zealous attempts
at reform in the nineteenth century by people who had no respect for the
moral life of the community.[53])

As we have seen, liberals such as Feinberg have also been persuaded of
the importance of respect for custom and community life and have
sought to incorporate such respect in their theories. Still, these liberals are
committed to assessing these commitments by reference to a reason-
based theory of what is good for, or owed to, individuals. Such liberals
will surely want to know how communitarians can assess and criticize
the status quo in their society unless they rely upon some such reason-
based, individualistic theory. Thus far, communitarians have not yet developed a way of supplementing their respect for custom and culture
with a fully worked out theory of how we are to critically assess custom
and culture.

Liberals have other arguments against the communitarian position.
For example, they can object to the way such a position seems to license
a paternalistic attitude toward the citizenry. That is, rather than respecting individual pursuits of the good, the communitarian state seems to be
licensed to dismiss them as "wrong" in the way that a parent may dismiss a child's pursuits as wrong. They can also contend that communitarianism rests on the wildly implausible idea that governmental officials know better than those whom they rule what counts as the good in
life. Unless a group of Platonic guardians turns up among us, liberals
would insist that state officials as a group are no wiser about what ought
to be pursued in life than any other group of human beings and thus
should not be allowed to use the state's power to insist that *their* view of

the good be accepted. Such sentiments may also be related to the liberals' commitment to the Jeffersonian idea that truth is something each individual must seek for herself if she is to be rightly related to it and effectively incorporate it into her own life, so that it cannot be foisted upon her by culture or society.[54]

These liberal responses to communitarianism, while compelling, do not refute the communitarian view completely, but they do show that communitarians have more work to do in order to develop their theory effectively: In particular, they must defend their trust of government power to pursue the good, and they must develop a way of achieving critical moral distance from the communities they would have the government respect, so that this "respect" does not end up encouraging any oppression, subordination, and abuse that has been part of that culture's traditions.

However, in the next section I argue that the successes of the liberal response to the communitarian challenge are not sufficient to vindicate fully the liberal approach to understanding and constructing an ideal political community.

The Attempt to Construct a New "Postliberal" Political Theory

There is an important problem with liberalism: On the liberal view, the government is supposed to be designed to protect the individual from state power; thus it is supposed to be responsive to a moral code that is deliberately not meant to be an implementation of any particular culture (which might be corrupt) but rather a code that somehow implements the idea that people should be treated as "free" and "equal"—where, as we have seen, these concepts can be filled out in a variety of ways, producing a variety of forms of liberalisms with different political codes.

However, there is a sense in which this blueprint for pursuing the ideal society does fail to recognize the effects of sociality, just as the communitarians say—but not for the reasons the communitarians give. Liberals try to design political societies so as to protect the individual from the coercive power of the state and preserve the conditions for individual freedom and equality, allowing each person to pursue social connections as she sees fit. But how effective will the liberal state be in ensuring the conditions of freedom and equality if the *culture* of the society operates so as to benefit some kinds of human beings and oppress others? In that situation no *individual* is doing anything wrong; hence the criminal or tort laws of the liberal state are not particularly effective in preventing such harms or correcting such oppression. Instead, that harm or oppression is coming from systemic effects of certain kinds of social institutions in which individuals find themselves and in which they operate. These social forms are such that individuals, despite any good intentions they might have, are forced to act and react in ways that result in considerable damage to some people. If the liberal state is committed to maximizing "autonomous self-government," concerning itself only with individual acts of harm, it will fail to be responsive to restrictions on freedom and equality that are socially generated, with the result that subordination, loss of freedom, and abuse (generated by social rather than political forces) will actually flourish, to the great harm of many individuals within that society.

In fact the history of modern liberal states shows that this is exactly what has happened. The first person to notice this phenomenon was Marx, whose brilliant analysis of the devastating effects of the capitalist economic structure as it operated in his day on the lives of workers (adults and children) went hand in hand with his recognition that the capitalists themselves often did not intend these effects. The capitalist uses his capital to create means of production, over which he has control; because he needs labor in order for these means of production to work, he hires workers to use their labor. As they work, their production of goods is what Marx calls an "alienating" experience: They lose control over their labor, control over their working conditions, and control over that which they produce, and as more and more workers are pulled into the competitive capitalist system, each of them tumbles into impoverishment and a life of suffering. Yet the capitalist doesn't intend these effects: He simply plays a role in a system permitting private ownership of the means of production that inevitably produces them. Hence Marx asks: "Do not the bourgeois assert that present-day distribution is 'fair'? And is it not, in fact, the only 'fair' distribution on the basis of the present-day mode of production? Are economic relations regulated by legal concepts or do not, on the contrary, legal relations arise from economic ones?"[55]

The solution, for Marx, is not to preach at the capitalist or try in some piecemeal fashion to improve the working conditions in his factories: Such efforts are futile in the face of an enormously powerful economic mode of organization pressing the capitalist to behave as he does. Instead, says Marx, one must change that economic mode of organization so that people interact in new and more successful ways.

Most theorists have come to reject Marx's prescriptions for a cure for the oppressive nature of capitalism, as I discussed in the foregoing chapter. But his view that evils in a human community can come from certain systemic social disorders has been (deservedly) enormously influential. Even in societies such as the United States that have tended to be very hostile toward Marxist ideas, the systemic problems he identified were recognized and addressed (albeit not through the political means Marx himself advocated) through the introduction of labor unions, laws regulating safety in the workplace and working hours, the banning of child labor, and antitrust legislation. Whether these remedies are sufficient to cure the systemic abuse of workers is arguable, but liberal societies have certainly come to realize that this socially generated abuse is real and requires redress.

That realization was not, however, easy: Those who benefited from the systemic abuse of workers blocked the development of labor unions and opposed laws regulating labor practices by protesting that government support for these things amounted to unjust interference in their rights as property owners. Relying on liberal arguments meant to limit the potentially abusive nature of state power, these opponents of labor legislation argued that liberal governments were too limited in authority and power to constrain them justifiably in their private activities. This argument has been largely rejected in modern liberal states, but the fact that it could be made is instructive: It shows that liberalism has usually been conceived as a theory addressing how to deal with the abusiveness of state authority and power and has not been developed so as to recognize or deal with abusiveness generated by other social institutions.

Another example of the failure of liberal society to anticipate or include theoretical structures for remedying socially caused (but not politically caused) oppression and injustice comes from the American experience. When the United States was founded, it was not a true liberal society precisely because it tolerated slavery. But even after the legal toleration of slavery ended, the oppression of African Americans did not. Various forms of abuse that were legally permitted, even enforced, when slavery was legal continued in new forms after it was abolished, supported by social structures, practices, roles, and beliefs that the state not only did not challenge but even at times encouraged (for example, through Jim Crow laws, restrictions on voting, etc.). Although the U.S. Constitution provided a remedy for discrimination by federal, state, and local governments, it did not provide a cure for *social* practices of discrimination because it was designed to ensure individual freedom by protecting the individual from the evils of unconstrained state power. Its provisions, particularly the Bill of Rights and the Fourteenth Amendment, were meant to guarantee that individual liberty is not compromised by state action (through laws or court decisions) that take away the individual's right to lead her life as she sees fit, consistent with the rights of others to do the same. (The Fourteenth Amendment provides that "no state shall make or enforce any law which shall abridge the privileges or immunities of citizens of the United States; nor shall any state deprive any person of life, liberty, or property, without due process of law, nor deny to any person within its jurisdiction the equal protection of the laws.") However, in the face of certain systemic denials of the freedom of certain groups coming from *social* rather than governmental practices, the document could do little.

The framers of the Constitution (and its amendments) were concerned with combating government denials of freedom, not social denials of freedom.[56] Hence that document only prohibits government from interfering with certain activities (speech, religion, etc.) or from denying due process or compromising equality under the law; it does not prohibit any nongovernmental institution from liberty-denying or equality-denying activities. Although it may well be a violation of local, state, or federal statutes to deny someone admission to your restaurant or store or private club because he is of a race you happen not to like, it is not a violation of the U.S. Constitution to do so.[57]

But if members of a particular group are *systematically* denied access to most or all restaurants, stores, or clubs or find that when they travel they are unable to locate a place to stay or when they seek higher education few colleges will admit them or when they seek employment few people will employ them—all because they are a member of a race, sex, religious group, or ethnicity that the majority in that country wants to exclude—then even if the law of the land provides these people with the same *legal* rights as the majority, the social behavior of the majority severely restricts their freedom and opportunities and their social equality. Moreover, note that their share of this society's resources will inevitably be low—vindicating the Marxist point that the social structures of a society are vitally important in determining the allocation of resources to individuals, no matter what the official ideology of distributive justice in this society happens to be.

So in this kind of society, even if there is no *legal* mastery (as I defined it in Chapter 3) of any population, there is still "social mastery" perpetrated through social forms that the liberal state seems helpless to stop insofar as its design is meant merely to protect individuals from government. Indeed, the ideology of the liberal state has actually been helpful to those who wished to sustain oppression of certain groups, in that it has enabled them to argue that laws prohibiting, say, whom they admit to their businesses or clubs or colleges or whom they could employ are unjustified governmental intrusions into their freedom. So the liberal interest in protecting individuals from the state can and indeed has been put to use to preserve forms of social organization that severely disadvantage and/or discriminate against certain members of that society.

Beginning in the 1960s, the undeniable fact of the severe constraints on the freedom and equality of African Americans that were socially rather than politically generated prompted the creation of legislation at the state and federal levels outlawing discrimination in employment, educational opportunities, access to public facilities (restaurants, stores, clubs), and so forth. (Thus at the federal level title 7 prohibits employment discrimination, and title 8 prohibits discrimination in housing.) Such legislation was meant to address a problem that the U.S. Constitution was relatively helpless to solve—the oppression of a minority not by government but by powerful social groups. This necessity for legislation highlights the failure of advocates of the traditional liberal state to consider the way in which the state could become (perhaps inadvertently) a threat to rather than an ally of the cause of liberty if it resisted opposing various discriminatory social practices out of concern not to compromise individual autonomy. However, such legislation not only redefines the state's role (giving it an active part to play in assuring that social roles and practices are not defined so as to deny liberty or equality) but also redefines what it means to be concerned with individual autonomy (giving that phrase a substantive meaning of the sort that, as we discussed in the previous section, Raz endorses). Not only current antidiscrimination legislation but also affirmative action laws are indicative of many modern governments' assumption of this new role.

Despite this history, oppressed groups in the United States are still fighting the traditional liberal idea that the state's role should be limited in order to protect individual autonomy. This is particularly evident in the case of women, who now enjoy to a considerable extent what is called "formal equality" in the United States but who still suffer restrictions on their equality and liberty in virtue of pervasive sexist practices.

The achievements of those liberals who have fought to combat sexism in modern political societies are important: All sorts of statutes prohibiting discrimination in hiring, educational admission, and access to medical care, as well as all sorts of court battles, including battles that have resulted in the legalization of abortion, have been waged in many political societies by women and men determined to ensure that their governments grant equal legal rights to men and women. This approach to sexual equality has enjoyed considerable success. (The author of this book wouldn't be in a position to write it and many of its readers wouldn't be in a position to understand it had not this approach succeeded in winning women access to higher education and university positions.)

It is worth noting, in passing, that advocates of this legislation have had some trouble getting its form right. In the mid-1970s the insistence on formal equality resulted in cases (e.g., *Geduldig v. Aiello* and *Gilbert, General Electric Company v. U.S.*)[58] in which the U.S. Supreme Court ruled that excluding pregnancy from insurance coverage was not a violation of the Civil Rights Act insofar as "there is no risk from which men are protected and women are not." Recoiling from this implausible result (doesn't it imply that insurance need not cover prostate surgery for the same reason?), Congress passed legislation that required such coverage, recognizing that sexual equality does not need to deny relevant differences between the sexes. This "difference thesis" (as Catharine MacKinnon calls it)[59] has been attached to the pursuit of formal equality; it says there are differences between the sexes that can be legitimately taken into account by laws that nonetheless recognize sexual equality (so that both pregnancy and prostate surgery can be covered by insurance and bathrooms and certain sports activities segregated by sex). But where sexual differences are irrelevant in employment, access to educational institutions, access to political office, and so on, this doctrine insists that the law allow no differential treatment according to gender and enforce equal opportunities for men and women.

Yet after many years of such battles, much remains unchanged with respect to the status of women in liberal societies. Consider, for example, the extent to which women still suffer from violence directed at them both outside and inside the home; indeed, statistics grimly point out that violence of men against women, in the form of rape, battery, and assault, is actually increasing, not decreasing.[60] Moreover, women's wages continue to lag behind those of men (in part because they are underrepresented in jobs that are high paying and powerful), and statistics show that in Western societies women rather than men still assume the majority of childcare and housework, are far more likely to care for elderly relatives, and are far more likely to give up full employment (dropping back to part-time work or giving up employment entirely) in order to care for small children.[61] Such facts make it clear that in societies strongly influenced by feminist ideals men and women still play roles (and experience problems associated with those roles) within family and within society that are not as far from traditional gendered roles (and traditional problems with those roles) as some feminists might have hoped.

There are two conflicting explanations of why change in these societies has not been more radical. One explanation insists that the nature of men and women is biologically influenced to a much greater degree than many feminists intent on believing in the "social construction of gender" like to admit. Being male, on this view, naturally leads to certain forms of behavior (sometimes highly violent) and certain kinds of roles (in particular leadership roles in the family). Being female, on this view, naturally leads to other forms of behavior (passivity, emotionalism, nurturing attitudes toward children), leading to victimization in certain situations (and the inability to combat male violence) and a willingness to take on certain caring roles (e.g., primary care for children within the family). According to those who believe in these natural differences between males and females,[62] the sorts of social practices and gendered roles that have persisted in liberal societies despite feminist pressure to equalize the legal rights of males and females are no surprise: These practices and roles reflect, they say, our biological nature. This explanation is quite old; it was even used by Locke in the first of his *Two Treatises of Government*.[63]

The second explanation of the persistence of these roles and practices denies that they are biologically inevitable and blames certain cultural and social traditions for creating and perpetuating them. The reasons behind the social construction of these practices cry out for analysis and have been the subject of much feminist debate.[64] However, for our purposes, what is important is that social practices oppressive to women have been supported by the legal systems of liberal societies. On this view, certain equality-denying and liberty-limiting social practices (such as rape or persistent spousal abuse or unequal allocations of childcare and household duties) have actually received the support of the law, making them particularly robust (where otherwise they might have collapsed) and difficult for those who are victimized by them to combat.

For example, consider the case of domestic abuse. In the medieval and early modern period, many important political and religious figures actually *approved* of wife-beating—if done in moderation. For example, Friar Cherubino of Siena, who compiled the *Rules of Marriage* between 1450 and 1481, counsels husbands:

> When you see your wife commit an offense, don't rush at her with insults and violent blows. . . . Scold her sharply, bully and terrify her. And if this still doesn't work .'. . take up a stick and beat her soundly, for it is better to punish the body and correct the soul than to damage the soul and spare the body. . . . Then readily beat her, not in rage but out of charity and concern for her soul, so that the beating will redound to your merit and her good.[65]

A few centuries later, in his famous *Commentaries on the Law of England,* William Blackstone declared that the early common law allowed wife-beating as long as the husband does not exceed the reasonable bounds of "due governance and correction":[66] "For, as [the husband] is to answer for her misbehavior, the law thought it reasonable to intrust him with this power of chastisement, in the same moderation that a man is allowed to correct his apprentices or children."[67] Note that Blackstone justifies this practice by assuming that women lose their separate identities once they marry, meaning that their husbands are responsible for their acts (in the way that a father is answerable for the acts of his children), so that a husband must sometimes administer physical "chastisement" lest his wife act in unacceptable ways.

Blackstone's influence on the American legal system in the eighteenth and early nineteenth centuries was enormous, and various states enacted legislation that accorded with his principles of "appropriate" wife-beating. For example, in 1824 the Mississippi Supreme Court in *Bradley v. State* voiced approval of the idea that the husband is the disclipinarian of his wife: "Let the husband be permitted to exercise the right of moderate chastisement, in cases of great emergency, and use salutary restraints in every case of misbehavior, without being subjected to vexacious prosecutions, resulting in the mutual discredit and shame of all parties concerned."[68]

Other U.S. cases[69] endorse the idea that (in the words of the court in *State v. Black*) "the law permits [the husband] to use towards his wife such force, as is necessary to control an unruly temper, and make her behave herself." Some decisions cite what they call the "old law": that a husband has the right to whip his wife provided that he use a switch no wider than his thumb.[70] Such legal rulings in a self-described "liberal" state show the way that law in such societies has supported conceptions of the family and of the roles of men and women within a marriage that give the husband the right to "rule" the wife, allowing him to carry out "moderate" physical punishment as part of that rule.

One explanation of these legal practices is the persistence—even in liberal societies supposedly committed to human equality—of the idea that women are naturally subordinate to men. (It is worth pointing out that until the twentieth century virtually all liberal societies were reluctant to grant women the right to vote and participate in the convention-generating activity of modern democracies.) The Supreme Court of Georgia, in *Warren v. State*,[71] reviews the way in which three traditional views of the subordinate status of women contributed to the reluctance of liberal courts in the United States to recognize the concept of spousal rape: first, the view that when she marries a woman implicitly consents to having intercourse with her husband under any circumstances; second, the view that a woman is the property or chattel of her husband; and third, the view that in marriage the woman's person is subsumed by that of the man's, so that in a marriage there is only one legal person—the husband, meaning that the wife has no legal standing to object to an act of abuse against her. All three views are expressions of the idea that women are naturally subordinate to men, and they articulate the (slavelike) terms of that subordination in the context of marriage.

However, as I have discussed, liberalism itself denies any doctrine of natural subordination. So why haven't we seen more hostility to subordinating practices in liberal states? The answer, I believe, is that liberal reasoning and liberal reluctance to involve the state in personal relations has played an important role in allowing practices subordinating women to men not only to continue but even to flourish. Consider a nineteenth-century U.S. court's decision in *State v. A. B. Rhodes*, in which it refused to allow a woman to file a claim against her husband, who had beaten her. The court reasoned that to allow such a claim would mean involving the state in the private affairs of its citizens:

> Our conclusion is that family government is recognized by law as being as complete in itself as the State government is in itself, and yet subordinate to it;

and that we will not interfere with or attempt to control it, in favor of either husband or wife, unless in cases where permanent or malicious injury is inflicted or threatened, or the condition of the party is intolerable. For, however great are the evils of ill temper, quarrels, and even personal conflicts inflicting only temporary pain, they are not comparable with the evils which would result from raising the curtain, and exposing to public curiosity, the nursery and the bed chamber. Every household has and must have, a government of its own, modelled to suit the temper, disposition and condition of its inmates.

The effect of such a legal policy, however, is to let stand abusive practices that are endemic in these little family kingdoms. Aware that some might charge them with prejudice against women, the court in this case insisted that the basis of its decision was respect for autonomy, not bias toward men:

> It will be observed that the ground upon which we have put this decision, is not, that the husband has the *right* to whip his wife much or little; but that we will not interfere with family government in trifling cases. We will no more interfere where the husband whips the wife, than where the wife whips the husband; and yet we would hardly be supposed to hold, that a wife has a *right* to whip her husband.[72]

The problem with this argument, however, is that when the whipping is virtually always of the wife by the husband, in a culture that implicitly approves or at least does not disapprove of the husband's doing so by virtue of the fact that he is the rightful "king" of the family "kingdom," then a legal system that refuses to stop those whippings is essentially licensing women's subordination, abuse, and loss of liberty. Hence in the name of autonomy, the liberal court in *State v. Rhodes* denied women the possibility of freedom and confirmed their mastered status. Although a later case overturned *Rhodes*,[73] the residual effects of this way of thinking persist to the present-day; for example, in many states in the United States spousal rape is considered a less severe felony than stranger rape (and is very difficult to prosecute successfully).

Compare these social facts to the facts of racial discrimination in a highly racist liberal society: Just as the racists who hold power in such societies used liberal rhetoric to justify legal policies that permitted or supported their racist practices ("It's my house, so I can sell it only to whites if I like" or "It's my business, so I can hire whom I like, and I don't like hiring blacks"), so, too, have those enamored of patriarchal family structures used liberal rhetoric to justify (and even formulate) legal policies that permitted or supported those structures even when they resulted in violence ("Family life is private, and government should stay out of the private affairs of people, so as a husband I can do what I like with my wife, because she's mine").

Again, by the mid–twentieth century, reformers began to succeed in getting laws requiring certain forms of behavior *within* the family, such as laws against spousal battery and spousal rape. Such laws were meant to change family practices that had disadvantaged women (in just the way that laws proscribing employment discrimination were meant to change social practices that had disadvantaged people of certain races). However, note that liberalism has generated not only rhetoric but also forms of argument that (as I noted above) have actually been used to block such legislation.

Nor has the interest in blocking this legislation ended. In the United States, the Federal Crime Bill, enacted in the fall of 1994, contains the Violence Against Women Act (VAWA), which allows women (or, for that matter, men) to sue in civil court if they are attacked because of their gender.[74] Interestingly, the American Civil Liberties Union, which prides itself on defending (what it takes to be) the values of liberalism implicit in freedom of speech, freedom of assembly, and freedom of religion, testified against the VAWA, in part because it said the act is not necessary: If we already have laws against assault and battery and murder and rape, why add to these laws that already provide a remedy in criminal court for such violence another law allowing civil suits when such violence is motivated by gender animus?

Note, however, that this last question presumes that the VAWA is unnecessary because the state has already successfully fulfilled its role by developing criminal legislation that protects women from violent actions directed against them by other individuals; it does not recognize that the state may have a role to play in combating social practices that are the source of persistent and systemic forms of abuse against some members within that society. And what is interesting about VAWA is that it tries to involve the government in fighting the social sources of violence against women in two ways:[75] First, by allowing a woman to sue in civil court if she has been a victim of a violent felony that involves her gender, it gives her the ability to go after her attacker without having to convince (sometimes reluctant) prosecutors to take the case to criminal court. And second, it has symbolic value: It recognizes that women are the subject of so much violence in our society (from rape to spousal abuse to muggings) in part because they are *women* and hence in the view of their attackers less worthy of respect than men—and indeed the sort of person for whom significant disrespect is permissible.[76] Whether their denigration occurs through violent rape, spousal beatings, sexual harassment, systematic denial of employment, or denigration of their roles as mothers or wives, it attempts to establish them as worth less than men. VAWA's symbolic repudiation of that idea makes it legislation that directly involves the state in actually combating social practices and social understandings of the nature and importance of gender. In that sense, it is akin to legislation combating racial discrimination or abusive labor practices: All laws of this sort are directed at social institutions or practices that result in the denial of freedom and equality to some of the society's citizenry.

Another example of the failure of liberalism to respond to social denials of these values has occurred in the area of employment. In *Sears, Roebuck and Company v. Equal Employment Opportunities Commission*,[77] Sears successfully argued that it had not discriminated against women even though few of them were represented in its relatively high paying sales commission jobs. According to Sears, women's greater devotion to their families and in particular their greater interest in caring for their children made them less interested in these sales positions and less likely to remain in them. There is good reason to question Sears's evidence purporting to establish that fact.[78] But even leaving aside the issue of the genuineness of their claim that women were less interested in these jobs than were men, there is the issue of whether social practices in this society are such that women are *forced* to be less interested in these jobs, for if women live in a society structured around the assumption that they will be the primary childcare providers, it is hardly surprising that such women will find it difficult to seek or maintain jobs that make that role difficult. As one feminist puts it,

> If a group is kept out of something for long enough, it is overwhelmingly likely that activities of that sort will develop in a way unsuited to the excluded group. We know for certain that women have been kept out of many kinds of work, and this means that the work is quite likely to be unsuited to them. The most obvious example of this is the incompatibility of most work with the bearing and rearing of children; I am firmly convinced that if women had been fully involved in the running of society from the start they would have *found* a way of arranging work and children to fit each other. Men have had no such motivation, and we can see the results.[79]

There are many other examples that could be used to make the same point. The opposition of feminists such as MacKinnon and Andrea Dworkin to pornography and the liberal use of the idea of freedom of speech laws to oppose them is another example of the clash between, on the one hand, liberal theory attempting to combat threats to the liberty and equality of the individual by restricting governmental power and, on the other hand, feminists attempting to combat threats to individual liberty and equality that come not from government but from cultures or social forms.[80] MacKinnon also recites the variety of ways in which the sexist culture in the United States has encouraged social practices advantaging men over women, which have not only been permitted but also supported by law:

> Men's physiology defines most sports, their needs define auto and health insurance coverage, their socially designed biographies define workplace expectations and successful career patterns, their perspectives and concerns define quality in scholarship, their experiences and obsessions define merit, their objectification of life defines art, their military service defines citizenship, their presence defines family, their inability to get along with each other—their wars and rulerships—defines history, their image defines god, and their genitals define sex. For each of these differences from women, what amounts to an affirmative action plan is in effect, otherwise known as the structure and values of American society.[81]

What is most interesting for our purposes is that the liberal state has reinforced this "affirmative action" favoring men because its conception of the state has given men, who are advantaged by sexist social practices, a powerful conceptual tool to prevent the state from interfering with these advantageous practices, namely, the idea that the state should stay out of the private affairs of individuals (e.g., in families, clubs, or businesses) so as not to compromise autonomy. So at the deepest level, feminists are challenging liberals to rethink what is "political" and what is "private," that is, where the jurisdiction of government ends and where the private and personal decisions of each autonomous individual begin.[82] Feminists are fond of criticizing the distinction between public and private in liberal theories; my argument here is stressing the extent to which their concerns also raise a rather different issue: the distinction between the private and the political. I am arguing that it is because liberalism has persisted in thinking of large areas of public life as immune from political intervention that various forms of abuse and subordination have persisted.

But do those theorists who espouse feminist, Marxist, or civil rights views count as critics of liberalism, or are they really liberals after all, in virtue of the fact that they are all animated by liberal values? Consider the following passage from a work by Andrea Dworkin: "The refusal to demand . . . one absolute standard of human dignity is the greatest triumph of antifeminism over the will to liberation. . . . A universal standard of human dignity is the only principle that completely repudiates sex-class exploitation and also propels us into a future where the fundamental political question is the quality of life for all human beings."[83] Note that in this passage Dworkin *accepts* rather than repudiates liberal values and the universalism that goes along with a commitment to these values (that is, a commitment to the idea that no matter the culture, the place, or the time, these values are right and should be endorsed by a well-operating political community). Indeed, she expresses ideas that should be very congenial to any Rawlsian, insofar as she presumes there is an aspect of each human being—namely, her dignity—that is conceptually prior to her socialization, so that no matter what form socialization might take, it cannot remove, destroy, or lessen that dignity.

Moreover, Dworkin expresses the idea that this dignity is something that all cultures are morally required to respect, no matter their traditions and practices, and it provides us with the foundations for assessing the morality of any social or political practice. So are feminists such as MacKinnon or Dworkin, as well as advocates of legislation that attempts to combat racist social practices or abusive market structures, really liberals after all, by virtue of the fact that they are driven by the same values as traditional liberals?

Yes and no: I would argue that even though many of these reformers accept tenets 1 and 2 of liberalism, committing them to the values of freedom and equality (which they interpret in particular ways), and even though many (albeit not all) accept tenet 5, committing them to using reason as the primary tool for achieving social order and justice, as well as tenet 4, requiring that the legitimacy of a regime be justified to the individual members of that regime, nonetheless they reject the conventional liberal understanding of tenet 3, requiring that a government implement liberal values by putting constraints on governmental policy, promoting toleration, and allowing the good to be defined by each individual. To the extent that tenet 3 is accepted, social practices denying freedom and equality cannot be addressed or remedied, and indeed (as we have seen) tenet 3 is actually an aid and comfort to those doing the oppressing, insofar as they can insist that it requires that the liberal government refrain from interfering in these oppressive social practices, lest it unjustly constrain individual liberty.

So "postliberals" (as I call them, for lack of a better name) are attempting to create a more sophisticated way of ensuring the freedom and equality of *all* citizenry in the face not only of governmental threats to these values but also oppressive social practices that persist despite the government's moral commitment to freedom and equality for all.[84] What should the details of this more sophisticated approach be?

This is a fascinating and difficult question, because this new form of political theory is still being developed.[85] Some ways of formulating it, however, clearly have not worked. For example, heavy reliance on the state to correct oppression generated by social forms has not been successful, as the failure of Marxist regimes around the world attests. A government with the authority to interfere in all social practices to correct oppression is generally going to be a government whose power is so substantial that it can (and likely will) use it to abuse and constrain the liberty of its citizens. Liberals are surely right that freedom and equality require constraining government power. So if that is correct, how can abusive social practices be stopped in liberal states?

I would suggest that governments have an important role to play in ending oppressive social practices but that recent political history shows governments are effective in doing so only when there are nongovernmental social structures that lead the attack. Consider, for example, the importance of labor unions in changing abusive working conditions in the workplace. Of course labor unions were possible only because of government legal support (which unions initially found very difficult to win). But progress in labor relations was not something purchased solely by the state; it was a partnership of the state and a social movement that aimed at changing an oppressive social system. The same appears to be true with respect to combating racism and sexism; governments cannot legislate away racist or sexist attitudes. What governments can do, however, is to align themselves in a variety of ways (sometimes using something other than the criminal law, as the civil provisions of the VAWA illustrate) with forces committed to opposing these attitudes, thus encouraging the evolution of societal forms that give every human being the chance to live freely and equally.

Moreover, a government may attack abusive social structures not by using its coercive power but by using its authority to encourage, upbraid, preach, and reward (e.g., with certain kinds of tax policies). So even if a postliberal reluctantly comes to the conclusion that the harm principle must animate the state's criminal legislation, she may still believe that the state has a role in successfully combating social denials of freedom and equality by using all the nonpunitive measures that its considerable authority makes possible.

This requires that governments take seriously the liberal rhetoric that has animated their legislation. As I have noted, this is the same rhetoric that Andrea Dworkin uses to animate her feminist principles in the quotation above, but she and other feminists are interested in applying it to the monitoring of not only individual behavior but also cultural practices. (And mightn't Rawls's original position procedure be a useful conceptual tool for carrying out that monitoring? That is, can't postliberals use it to ask about the extent to which people behind the veil of ignorance could agree to certain social structures as well as certain political structures?[86])

But here we hit upon a profound problem: If governments do interfere in cultural practices that they take to be abusive, won't that be a violation of the principle of tolerance? And can't such violations lead to infringement of religious practices, traditions of family structure, and social lifestyles? If that is so, doesn't this show that the postliberal theorists I have described are actually advocating governmental policies that are liberty-limiting rather than liberty-creating? Now as a matter of historical record, it is worth pointing out that liberal societies have always been prepared to interfere with religious practices when they took them to be harmful to individuals (think of the U.S. legislation against bigamy, directed against the Mormons). But is such legislation right? Would laws that, say, banned clitoridectomy of adolescent females (of the sort practiced by some Muslim communities) be a violation of religious liberty, or would it protect the liberty and equality of girls who would otherwise be subject to it? And are feminist-inspired prohibitions of pornography indirectly dangerous to the cause of all feminist reformers—including those such as MacKinnon and Dworkin, who advocate such prohibitions—insofar as they open the door to governmental restrictions of speech that the reformers themselves might come to regret?

Indeed, the success in Canada of antipornography laws of the sort advocated by MacKinnon and Dworkin has explicitly raised this issue. In February 1992 the Canadian Supreme Court decided in *Butler v. Her Majesty the Queen* that the nation's criminal obscenity law covers pornographic material that degrades or demeans women. In the opinion of the court, "If true equality between male and female persons is to be achieved, we cannot ignore the threat to equality resulting from exposure to audiences of certain types of violent and degrading material. Materials portraying women as a class of objects for sexual exploitation and abuse have a negative impact on the individual's sense of self-worth and acceptance."[87] However, since that decision, bookstores in Canada have complained that Canadian customs have been emboldened to seize or delay importation of a great deal of sexually explicit literature—including gay and lesbian literature and even some feminist literature, causing some to argue that the Butler decision and the climate of opinion generated by MacKinnon's arguments have encouraged censorship that is harmful even to feminist and homosexual reformers. Ironically, two of the books seized (but later released) by Canadian customs were Andrea Dworkin's *Womenhating* and *Pornography: Men Possessing Women.*[88] The conclusion of some Canadians is that despite the subordinating nature of pornography, the feminist cause is better off without antipornography laws. Here we see the way in which liberal and postliberal feminists are quarreling over the means by which to attack the social sources of subordination of women and, in particular, disagreeing over whether or not reliance on governmental laws to make this attack is helpful or harmful to the cause. (That is to say, they are quarreling over the legitimacy of what I have called tenet 3c of liberalism.)

Some liberals may insist such events show that even though postliberal reformers may long to use the state to aid them in their fight against unjust social structures, doing so is too dangerous not only to the society but also to *them* to make it the right course of action. Moreover, these liberals might say, reformers should have faith in the power of their reform movements to change the structure of society to their liking without the help of government. If the cause is just, shouldn't we be optimistic about its ultimate success in effecting social change, even without the government's help? The reformers can reply, however, that the law in liberal societies has been (and continues to be) at least indirectly supportive of the social practices they wish to change, as the preceding discussion shows. (Nor should this be surprising: Haven't people who enjoy social advantages always tried to use their state's power to help them keep it?) So how can these practices be changed unless the law "changes sides"? In the view of the reformers, the abstract quality of liberal reasoning (which the communitarians also dislike) blinds liberals to the way in which existing legal structures in liberal societies—including family law, criminal law, and employment law—have worked to the advantage of those who hold cultural power in virtue of the racist or sexist social traditions in that culture.

What sort of theory of distributive justice fits with a postliberal outlook? Advocates of any of the theories of justice we reviewed in Chapter 4 might believe that their favorite theory can simply be appended to a postliberal perspective to produce a multifaceted theory of justice. But it isn't as easy as that. Characteristic of a postliberal perspective is the idea that the distribution of resources is the result of certain systemic features of the society (e.g., capitalism, racism, sexism), so that it is a mistake to try to impose what one takes to be a "fair" pattern of distribution on a society without realizing that these systemic forces are going to be propelling the society toward a certain (unfair) distribution anyway. Hence the postliberal wants her society to develop the right kind of social institutions— ones that do not encourage the abuse or oppression of any of society's members—lest some of those members, because they are abused or oppressed, end up being unfairly deprived of resources. Of the theories of justice we reviewed in Chapter 4, two suggest how we might think critically about social institutions such that they will be well ordered. One of them is Rawls's theory, which proposes a method of evaluating social institutions from the standpoint of each person in the society: Whether or not one likes Rawls's particular conception of justice, his interest in finding a way to evaluate and critically assess social institutions is an interest that postliberals ought to share, given their commitment to the idea that social institutions in their own societies have encouraged injustice. Second, there is Aristotle's theory, which asks us to arrange the distribution of resources so as to encourage the right kind of relationship between and among members of a polity. I am a partisan of this Aristotelian idea because of the way it gives us a standard to use both in assessing social institutions and in changing them. Part of the task of developing this Aristotelian idea will be specifying the kind of relationship that is characteristic of an ideal polity and then working out how that relationship affects not only the society's distribution of resources but also its criminal justice system, mode of economic organization, family structure, and so forth. The idea suggested by some communitarians that this relationship should be analogous to a friendship seems to me to be dubious. (Do any of us really want to be friends with *every* person in our society?) And yet the relationship many liberals commend, which is extremely weak and attenuated (analogous to a relationship among strangers who have resolved not to interfere with one another), seems too frail upon which to build an ideal and robustly fair community. However, one feature of the ideal relationship among citizenry to which a postliberal is surely committed is its absolute *equality,* so that no matter whether one is an employer or an employee and no matter one's race, gender, or religion, one will be acknowledged as the equal of every other member of that society. What equal acknowledgment means, how social institutions must be designed so as to encourage and require it, and how the distribution of resources must be managed so as to ensure it—these are the questions that postliberals will need to answer.

There is one more interesting issue involved in the development of postliberalism. In the course of setting out this position, I have spoken of "systemic" forces. Traditionally, "leftist" thinking has been associated with the idea that certain phenomena in our society are the products of such systemic forces, whereas "rightist" thinking (e.g., libertarian thinking of the sort exemplified by Nozick) has insisted that what happens in society is the result of the personal decisions of individuals, who must take and be granted responsibility for those decisions (and either rewarded or punished for them, depending upon whether those decisions are good or bad). Many postliberals will align themselves with "leftist" thinking and tend to downplay the idea of personal responsibility. But others of them embrace the idea of personal responsibility. There are Marxists, civil rights activists, and feminists whose writings show an interest in acknowledging both the power of systemic forces and also the fact of personal responsibility in the face of those forces. For example, John Roemer, a Marxist, is interested in developing Marxist ideas in a way that acknowledges (what he takes to be) the legitimate role that different effort should play in the distribution of resources, even while proposing a new egalitarian social structure (which Roemer calls "market socialism") for the distribution of resources.[89] Moreover, there are many feminists who believe that even though sexism is systemic in many societies, individual men and women should nonetheless be held responsible for their sexist beliefs.[90] Finally, consider the way in which Cornel West, an African American scholar, criticizes both the left and the right in their attitudes toward race:

> [Liberals] relieve their guilty consciences by supporting public funds directed at "the problems"; but at the same time, [because they are] reluctant to exercise principled criticism of black people, liberals deny them the freedom to err. Similarly, conservatives blame the "problems" on black people themselves—and thereby render black social misery invisible or unworthy of public attention.[91]

West wants us to see how white America has systematically (and systemically) failed to recognize the equal humanity of black Americans, even while he insists that this humanity involves the recognition that blacks must be held responsible for their actions (good or bad). This combination of ideas is, I would argue, characteristic of a postliberal perspective.

It is not clear, however, how we put together the idea that people do things because of the way that social institutions affect them, with the idea that people's decisions are ones for which they are responsible. If I do something because society has influenced me to do it, isn't society responsible for what I do? To give an example: If I am a sexist male, raised in a society whose institutions encourage and even mandate such sexism, can I really be held responsible for my sexist actions? The postliberal who insists that I can be held responsible must believe that I somehow have access to the fact that such sexist actions are wrong, even if my society is encouraging me to perform them. The ability to critically evaluate social institutions, which is the hallmark of the postliberal position, is an ability that postliberals who believe in personal responsibility must believe we all have, such that we can be blamed for our participation in institutions that we have the ability to criticize as unjust. Note that this ability presupposes the idea that there are moral facts (e.g., that racism and sexism are wrong) that are still accessible even in oppressive societies that try to obscure them.

If this form of postliberalism can be successfully developed, is it a "right" or a "left" political theory? It seems to be neither. If it can successfully incorporate both the idea of personal responsibility and the belief in the power of systemic forces, it is a political theory that collapses together the appreciation of the power of social institutions characteristic of the left and the interest in personal accountability characteristic of the right. Moreover, given that such a theory would want to promote both the ideal of equality and the ideal of a "just relationship" among society's members, that theory puts together characteristically left-wing egalitarian thinking with characteristically right-wing community-based thinking (although what postliberals take to be the hallmarks of an ideal community tend to be different from the hallmarks recognized by many conservatives, insofar as postliberals focus on equal treatment and dignity rather than on the conservatives' "traditional values"—particularly because some of these values strike postliberals as values that actually promote sexist, racist, or classist social structures). In any case, I believe one of the most interesting aspects of postliberal thinking is the way that it (deliberately) tries to destroy the old dichotomy between the right and the left.

The debate between liberals and their critics cannot be resolved here and will continue for some years to come, as those who challenge liberalism try to develop theories and institutional structures that attempt to benefit people better than liberalism (itself a highly successful reform movement in the history of political theory) has thus far been able to do. In a way, liberals and communitarians are at two ends of the debate, with postliberals somewhere in the middle, accepting the communitarians' view that government has a role to play in the maintenance of social and cultural institutions but also insisting that it must be committed to the liberals' values of freedom and equality as it plays this role. All three theories, as I've noted, are attempting to define the nature of (nondistributive) justice in an ideal society and, in particular, attempting to define and circumscribe the role of the state in that society. In this way, all three theories offer accounts of the state's legitimate authority and thus tell citizens how the state ought to behave such that it deserves their endorsement consent. I have argued that the most promising but least developed of the three theories is the postliberal conception, and in the years ahead we should expect to see that theory developed and more controversy generated by proponents of all three views. The readers of this book will inevitably participate in the debate among these three views as they involve themselves in the political processes of their societies.

Further Reading

Three classic statements of liberalism are Joel Feinberg, *The Moral Limits of the Criminal Law*, in four volumes: *Harm to Others, Offense to Others, Harm to Self*, and *Harmless Wrongdoing;* John Rawls, *Political Liberalism;* and Joseph Raz, *The Morality of Freedom.*

Two classic communitarian works are Alasdair MacIntyre, *After Virtue,* and Michael J. Sandel, *Liberalism and the Limits of Justice.* For an accessible introduction to communitarian ideas, see Charles Taylor, *The Malaise of Modernity.*

For a fascinating discussion of race in America, see Cornel West, *Race Matters.* For a collection of classic essays on racism (e.g., by W.E.B. Du Bois, Marcus Garvey, and Frederick Douglass), see Howard Brotz, ed., *Negro Social and Political Thought, 1850–1920.* For an introduction to the thinking of Martin Luther King Jr., the architect of the civil rights movement in the United States, see a collection of his essays and sermons, *A Testament of Hope,* ed. James Melvin Washington.

For a review of feminist literature, see Rosemarie Tong, *Feminist Thought,* and Alison Jagger, *Feminist Politics and Human Nature.* For what I have called a "postliberal" perspective on feminism, see Catharine Mac-Kinnon, *Feminism Unmodified,* and Joan Williams, "Deconstructing Gender," in Patricia Smith, ed., *Feminist Jurisprudence.*

For a list of Marxist literature, see the Further Reading section of Chapter 4. A selection of Marx's own writing is available in *Karl Marx: Selected Writings,* ed. David McLellan.

Notes

1. Maurice Cranston, "Liberalism," in Paul Edwards, ed., *Encyclopedia of Philosophy* (New York: Macmillan and London: Collier, 1967).

2. I borrow these terms from Cranston; ibid.

3. To be precise, Feinberg's harm principle is "state interference with a citizen's behavior tends to be morally justified when it is reasonably necessary (that is, when there are reasonable grounds for taking it to be necessary as well as effective) to prevent harm or the unreasonable risk of harm to parties other than the person interfered with"; *Harm to Others,* vol. 1 of *The Moral Limits of the Criminal Law* (Oxford: Oxford University Press, 1984), p. 11. Feinberg also permits some criminal law to be generated by the offense principle, which sanctions state interference in a citizen's behavior when that behavior gives offense to others in the society (see ibid., p. 13). Feinberg then defines liberalism "as the view that the harm and offense principles, duly clarified and qualified, between them exhaust the class of morally relevant reasons for criminal prohibitions"; ibid., pp. 14–15.

4. However, some of these have evolved in ways that make them more appropriate exemplars of a kind of conservatism that fits better with communitarian concerns than with Lockean liberalism; I discuss this later in this chapter.

5. See Rousseau's *Social Contract,* trans. G.D.H. Cole (London: J.M. Dent, 1968), esp. book 3, chaps. 11–15, pp. 73–80. For discussions of voluntarism in modern liberal theory, see Patrick Riley, *Will and Political Legitimacy* (Cambridge: Harvard University Press, 1982).

6. See John Rawls, *A Theory of Justice* (Cambridge: Harvard University Press, 1971), p. 302.

7. See H.L.A. Hart, "Rawls on Liberty and Its Priority," in Norman Daniels, ed., *Reading Rawls* (New York: Basic Books, 1974), pp. 230–253; and Robert Nozick's criticisms of Rawls in *Anarchy, State and Utopia* (New York: Basic Books, 1974), discussed in Chapter 4.

8. See Rawls, *A Theory of Justice,* p. 60.

9. For example, see Nozick, *Anarchy, State and Utopia,* part 2.

10. See Mill's *Subjection of Women* (1869), in *Essays on Sex Equality by J. S. Mill and Harriet Taylor Mill,* ed. Alice Rossi (Chicago: University of Chicago Press, 1970).

11. See Rawls's *Political Liberalism* (New York: Columbia University Press, 1993).

12. For a discussion of this conception of reason, see Richard Rorty, "The Priority of Democracy to Philosophy," in Merrill Peterson and Robert Vaughan, eds., *The Virginia Statute for Religious Freedom* (New York: Cambridge University Press, 1988), see esp. pp. 262 and 268.

13. Rawls, *Political Liberalism,* p. 213.

14. Ibid., p. 9.

15. Ibid.

16. Ibid., pp. 9–10.

17. For a recent example of such a view, see Joel Feinberg, "Some Unswept Debris from the Hart-Devlin Debate," *Synthese* 72 (1987): 249–275.

18. For example, see Nozick, *Anarchy;* Joel Feinberg, *Rights, Justice and the Bounds of Liberty* (Princeton: Princeton University Press, 1980); Ronald Dworkin, *Taking Rights Seriously* (Cambridge: Harvard University Press, 1977). For a discussion of the history of the development of the idea of rights, see Richard Tuck, *Natural Rights Theories: Their Origin and Development* (Cambridge: Cambridge University Press, 1979). For a sample of contemporary rights theories, see Jeremy Waldron, ed., *Theories of Rights* (Oxford: Clarendon Press, 1984).

19. Dworkin, *Taking Rights Seriously,* see esp. chap. 1.

20. See Hampton, "Liberalism, Retribution and Criminality," in Jules Coleman and Allen Buchanan, eds., *Harm's Way: Essays in Honor of Joel Feinberg* (Cambridge: Cambridge University Press, 1994).

21. Feinberg, "Hart-Devlin," p. 257. See also Feinberg's *Harmless Wrongdoing,* volume 4 of The Moral Limits of the Criminal Law Series (New York: Oxford University Press, 1988), pp. 11–14.

22. Feinberg, *Harmless Wrongdoing,* p. 12.

23. Feinberg, "Hart-Devlin," p. 260.

24. See Joseph Raz, *The Morality of Freedom* (Oxford: Clarendon Press, 1986).

25. Ibid., p. 415.

26. Ibid.

27. Ibid., p. 416.

28. As Jeremy Waldron puts it, "The terms 'socialism', 'conservatism', and 'liberalism' are like surnames and the theories, principles and parties that share one of these names often do not have much more in common with one another than the members of a widely extended family." See Jeremy Waldron, "Theoretical Foundations of Liberalism," *Philosophical Quarterly* 37, 147 (1987): 127–150.

29. Waldron has a very nice discussion of the importance of this idea to the liberal tradition in ibid.

30. Rawls balks at the idea that his is an Enlightenment theory and denies it in *Political Liberalism.* I have argued, however, that his reliance on reason in that book commits him indirectly to the Enlightenment conception of reason's relevance to political theorizing; see Jean Hampton, "The Common Faith of Liberalism," *Pacific Philosophical Quarterly* 75, 3 and 4 (1995): 186–216.

31. Indeed, Jefferson insists that reason and religion are mutually supportive. See his "Query XVII: Religion," in *Notes on the State of Virginia* (Chapel Hill: University of North Carolina Press, 1955), esp. p. 159: "Reason and free enquiry are the only effectual agents against error. Give a loose to them, they will support the true religion, by bringing every false one to their tribunal, to the test of their in-

vestigation." See Rorty, "The Priority of Democracy," p. 257, for a discussion of this point.

32. See Rorty, "The Priority of Democracy," p. 257.

33. I discuss this in Jean Hampton, "Should Political Philosophy Be Done Without Metaphysics?" *Ethics* 99 (1989): 791–814.

34. See Alasdair MacIntyre, *After Virtue* (Notre Dame: University of Notre Dame Press, 1981), p. 187; see also chaps. 5 and 6, where MacIntyre argues for the failure of moral theories of the sort that undergird liberalism.

35. For an argument that uses communitarian ideas to attack the effect of current liberal ideas on university education, see Allan Bloom, *The Closing of the American Mind* (New York: Simon and Schuster, 1987).

36. These views are put forward in a series of essays assembled in Taylor's *Philosophical Papers* (Cambridge: Cambridge University Press, 1985). Note that communitarians such as Taylor and Michael Sandel also object to liberalism because of what they take to be its advocacy of the neutral state; for example, see Sandel's "Morality and the Liberal Ideal," *New Republic,* May 7, 1984, and Taylor's "Alternative Futures: Legitimacy, Identity and Alienation in Late Twentieth Century Canada," in Alan Cairns and Cynthia Williams, eds., *Constitutionalism, Citizenship and Society in Canada* (Toronto: University of Toronto Press, 1986). However, that is to object to only one *form* of liberalism. As my discussion in the previous section shows, there are nonneutral forms of liberalism that advocate a moral role for the liberal state, such as rights-based liberalism and perfectionist liberalism, and neither Sandel's nor Taylor's attack on neutrality refutes these forms of liberal theory.

37. Jean Bethke Elshtain, "Family, Feminism and Community," *Dissent* 29 (Fall 1982): 442. See also Elshtain's *Public Man, Private Woman* (Princeton: Princeton University Press, 1981).

38. See MacIntyre, *After Virtue*, p. 67.

39. For a discussion of whether or not religious life and liberalism are in conflict, see William Galston, *Liberal Purposes: Goods, Virtues and Diversity in the Liberal State* (Cambridge: Cambridge University Press, 1991), chap. 12.

40. Michael J. Sandel, *Liberalism and the Limits of Justice* (Cambridge: Cambridge University Press, 1982), p. 179.

41. Ibid., p. 181.

42. Ibid., p. 182.

43. For a discussion of some of these objections, see Will Kymlicka, *Contemporary Political Philosophy: An Introduction* (Oxford: Clarendon Press, 1990), pp. 199–207. Kymlicka also discusses some communitarians' objections to some liberals' view of the autonomous self as "empty"; see ibid., pp. 208–209.

44. I have already discussed Rawls's insistence on the social construction of human beings as a motivation for constructing the original position procedure, which tries to give us a vantage point from which we can assess that social construction. See the section on Rawls in Chapter 4. Gauthier's commitment to our sociality comes out not only in his book *Morals by Agreement* (Oxford: Oxford University Press, 1986) but also in a very interesting essay, "The Social Contract as Ideology," *Philosophy and Public Affairs* 6, 2 (1977): 130–164. For a discussion of the

way in which liberals are able to accommodate the sociality of persons, see Kymlicka, *Contemporary Political Philosophy*, pp. 216–230.

45. Feinberg, *Harmless Wrongdoing*, p. 83.

46. Kymlicka, *Contemporary Political Philosophy*, p. 222.

47. Feinberg, *Harmless Wrongdoing*, p. 84.

48. See Judith Shklar, *Ordinary Vices* (Cambridge: Harvard University Press, 1984).

49. G.W.F. Hegel, *The Philosophy of Right*, trans. T. M. Knox (London: Oxford University Press, 1976), sec. 257, p. 155.

50. Amy Gutmann, "Communitarian Critics of Liberalism," *Philosophy and Public Affairs* 14, 3 (Summer 1985): 319.

51. Rawls, *A Theory of Justice*, pp. 260–263.

52. Burke's most famous political works include *Reflections on the Revolution in France* (1790) and *A Philosophical Enquiry into the Origin of Our Ideas of the Sublime and the Beautiful*. These and other political works are available in Edmund Burke, *Reflections on the Revolution in France* (Harmondsworth: Penguin, 1969).

53. But Eliot did believe that her society needed reform, and she had respect for those reformers who were not contemptuous of custom. Both respect for and Burkian concern about reformist zeal are present in her masterpiece, *Middlemarch*.

54. Jefferson maintains that one reason there must be freedom of religion in an ideal political society is that coercion is useless in bringing a person to religious truth. "Constraint may make him worse by making him a hypocrite, but it will never make him a truer man." See Jefferson, "Query XVII: Religion," p. 159. Later in the same essay Jefferson makes the very Millian argument that a diversity of opinion in religious matters is good for society and for each individual in it. See ibid., pp. 160 f.

55. Karl Marx, *Critique of the Gotha Programme* in *Selected Writings*, ed. David McLellan (Oxford: Oxford University Press, 1977), p. 566.

56. In *The Federalist Papers*, John Jay, Alexander Hamilton, and James Madison (primarily the last two) defend the Constitution as an instrument for securing human liberty. An excellent edition is J. E. Cooke, ed., *The Federalist Papers* (Middletown, Conn.: Wesleyan University Press, 1961). For a discussion of these arguments and the Constitution as a whole, see Morton White, *Philosophy, the Federalist and the Constitution* (Oxford: Oxford University Press, 1987).

57. There is, however, one interesting exception. The U.S. Supreme Court decided that restrictive covenants that prohibit the selling of houses to certain ethnic groups are unconstitutional to *enforce*, albeit not to make. In *Shelley v. Kramer*, 224 U.S. 1 (1948)—and see also *Barrows v. Jackson*, 346 U.S. 249 (1953)—the court decided that insofar as the enforcement of such covenants requires that the state be the governmental *agent* of those who wish to enforce racist housing policies in their community, the Fourteenth Amendment to the Constitution is applicable. In this case the state is being asked to use governmental power to deny one group access to housing, and hence those individuals who desire such housing can legitimately claim that in such a case the government is acting so as to deprive them of their rights. It is therefore a violation of the U.S. Constitution to enforce such covenants but (remarkably) not a violation to make them. I am indebted to Lynn Baker for discussions of and citations on this point.

58. *Geduldig v. Aiello*, 417 U.S. 484 (1974); *Gilbert, General Electric Co. v. U.S.*, 429 U.S. 125 (1976).

59. See Catharine MacKinnon, *Feminism Unmodified* (Cambridge: Harvard University Press, 1987), pp. 32–45.

60. Statistics compiled for a congressional hearing on violence against women showed that the most serious crimes against women are rising at a significantly higher rate than total crime. For example, rape rates have risen nearly four times as fast as the total crime rate. A woman is ten times more likely to be raped in the United States than to die in a car crash. See Linda Schmittroth, comp., *Statistical Record of Women Worldwide* (Detroit: Gale Research, 1991), pp. 75, 76–87. For a discussion of a cross-cultural study of rape that showed that 44 percent of 95 cultures studied were free of rape, see Myrian Miedzian, *Boys Will Be Boys* (New York: Anchor Books, 1991), p. 74. For a study of domestic violence, see Murray A. Straus, Richard J. Gelles, and Suzanne K. Steinmetz, *Behind Closed Doors: Violence in the American Family* (New York: Anchor Books, 1980). The authors of this book estimate that at the time they did their study, there was violence in almost one of three marriages in the United States; see p. 32.

61. For statistical details, see Schmittroth, *Statistical Record of Women Worldwide:* For household income, see pp. 314–330; for care-giving statistics, see pp. 88–95. Note that in 1991 women employed full time in the United States earned 70 cents for every dollar earned by men, and women with four years of college education earned less on average than men who had not completed high school; reported in the *New York Times*, October 6, 18, and 19, 1992; discussed by James Sterba, *Contemporary Social and Political Philosophy* (Belmont, Calif.: Wadsworth, 1995), p. 68. See also Phyllis Moen, *Women's Two Roles* (New York: Auburn House, 1992).

62. For example, see Michael Levin, *Feminism and Freedom* (New Brunswick, N.J.: Transaction Books, 1987), and Steven Goldberg, *The Inevitability of Patriarchy* (New York: William Morrow, 1973).

63. See John Locke, *Two Treatises of Government*, ed. Peter Laslett (Cambridge: Cambridge University Press, 1988), First Treatise, sec. 47, p. 174. In this passage Locke argues that God did not grant Adam political power over Eve. Nonetheless, he does admit that husbands do have a *kind* of nonpolitical authority over their wives that is "natural" and ordained by God. Citing Genesis 3:16, Locke says the passage "fortels what should be the Womans Lot, how by [God's] Providence he would order it so, that she should be subject to her husband, as we see that generally the Laws of Mankind and customs of Nations have ordered it so; and there is, I grant, a Foundation in Nature for it." The point is reiterated in sec. 48, p. 174.

64. For a review of various psychoanalytic and political explanations of the development of these practices, see Rosemarie Tong, *Feminist Thought* (Boulder: Westview Press, 1989), esp. chaps. 5 and 6.

65. Quoted in Terry Davidson, *Conjugal Crime* (New York: Hawthorn Books, 1978), p. 99.

66. See William Blackstone, *Commentaries on the Law of England*, vol. 1, ed. William Draper Lewis (Philadelphia: Rees Welsh and Company; 1897), p. 444. Linda Hirschman discusses this argument in "Making Safety a Civil Right," *Ms. Magazine*, September-October 1994, p. 45.

67. Blackstone, *Commentaries*, p. 444.

68. *Bradley v. State*, 1 Miss. 156 (1824).

69. Such as *State v. A. B. Rhodes* (61 N.C. 453 [1868]) and *State v. Black* (60 N.C. 262; 1 Win. 266 [1824]).

70. For a discussion of these cases, see Hirschman, "Making Safety a Civil Right," p. 45.

71. *Warren v. State*, 255 Ga. 151; 336 S.E. 2d 221 (1985).

72. *State v. A. B. Rhodes*, 61 N.C. 453 (1868), p. 108. What is particularly nice about the statement of the decision in this case is that it shows the way in which it was animated by liberal doctrine, and not by older, more Aristotelian views of the natural subordination of men to women. Such views certainly played a role in liberal society: Kymlicka discusses the extent to which such views were important in the development of family law in the United States; see his *Contemporary Political Philosophy*, p. 260. See also Stanley Benn and Gerald Gaus, *Public and Private in Social Life* (London: Croom Helm, 1983). However, my argument here emphasizes the way in which liberal courts such as the one in *State v. Rhodes*, even while rejecting any natural subordination theory, were animated by liberal ideology to develop family law in a way that contributed to the persistence of the subordination of women in society.

73. See *State v. Oliver*, 70 N.C. 60, 61–62 (1874).

74. The bill is officially aimed at providing civil remedies for any "crime of violence motivated by gender."

75. For another discussion of the way that VAWA attempts to fight violence directed at women, see Hirschman, "Making Safety a Civil Right."

76. I discuss the way in which abuse of women is associated with the idea that they are worth less (or are of less value) than men in Jean Hampton, "Correcting Harms Versus Righting Wrongs," *UCLA Law Review* 39, 6 (1992): 1659–1702.

77. 628 F. Supp. 126 (N.D. Ill., 1986); affirmed, 839 F. 2d 302 (7th Cir. 1988).

78. For an excellent discussion of this case, see Joan Williams, "Deconstructing Gender," in Patricia Smith, ed., *Feminist Jurisprudence* (New York: Oxford University Press, 1993), pp. 538–542.

79. Janet Radcliffe Richards, *The Sceptical Feminist: A Philosophical Enquiry* (London: Routledge and Kegan Paul, 1980), pp. 113–114; quoted in Kymlicka, *Contemporary Political Philosophy*, p. 242.

80. For feminist arguments favoring restrictions on pornography, see MacKinnon's two books *Feminism Unmodified:* and *Only Words* (Cambridge: Harvard University Press, 1993). For some liberal discussions of this issue, see Joel Feinberg, *Offense to Others*, vol. 2 of *The Moral Limits of the Criminal Law* (Oxford: Oxford University Press, 1985); Ronald Dworkin, "Do We Have a Right to Pornography?" in *A Matter of Principle* (Cambridge: Harvard University Press, 1985); and Frederick Schauer, *Free Speech: A Philosophical Inquiry* (Cambridge: Cambridge University Press, 1982).

81. MacKinnon, *Feminism Unmodified*, p. 36; as if to make MacKinnon's point, Hirschman, "Making Safety a Civil Right," p. 44, cites Jack Greenberg, the former director of the NAACP Legal Defense and Education Fund, telling reporters that while there was a need for something to be done about violence against women, such violence was nonetheless "as American as apple pie."

82. For a discussion of feminist criticisms of the public-private distinction, see Kymlicka, *Contemporary Political Philosophy*, pp. 247–262.

83. From Andrea Dworkin, *Right-wing Women: The Politics of Domesticated Females* (New York: Putnam, 1983); cited by Catharine MacKinnon, "Crimes of War, Crimes of Peace," in Kate Mehuron and Gary Percesepe, eds., *Free Spirits: Feminist Philosophers on Culture* (Englewood Cliffs, N.J.: Prentice-Hall, 1995), p. 388.

84. In his book *Post-liberalism: Studies in Political Thought* (London: Routledge, 1993), John Gray also uses the term 'postliberal' to describe the political theory he believes is emerging out of liberalism. But Gray's theory is far more communitarian than my postliberalism and embued with the sort of Burkean philosophical conservatism that I reject. Hence the type of theory that I am setting out should not be confused with his; that we both use this label demonstrates not agreement but competition over a tag to characterize our opposing theories.

85. Consider, for example, Hegel's remarks that philosophy comes after the creation of new political forms, theorizing about what is already there: "The teaching of the concept, which is also history's inescapable lesson, is that it is only when actuality is mature that the ideal first appears over against the real and that the ideal apprehends this same real world in its substance and builds it up for itself into the shape of an intellectual realm. . . . The owl of Minerva spreads its wings only with the falling of the dusk." *Philosophy of Right*, p. 13 (preface).

86. Susan Moller Okin, *Justice, Gender and the Family* (New York: Basic Books, 1989).

87. For a discussion of the decision, see "Canada Court Says Pornography Harms Women," *New York Times*, February 28, 1992, p. B7.

88. See "Canada Customs a Continuing Problem for Bookstores and Distributors; Trial Postponed," *Publisher's Weekly*, December 20, 1993, p. 12.

89. See John Roemer, *Free to Lose: An Introduction to Marxist Economic Philosophy* (Cambridge: Harvard University Press, 1988).

90. This is certainly my view. See Jean Hampton, "Feminist Contractarianism," in Louise Anthony and Charlotte Witt, eds., *A Mind of Her Own* (Boulder: Westview Press, 1993). This idea also pervades the writings of MacKinnon and Dworkin.

91. Cornel West, *Race Matters* (New York: Vintage Books, 1994), p. 6.

6

Citizenship, Nationalism, and Culture

The controversy about whether states should be focused on individuals or on communities is not some idle, abstract quarrel among philosophers. It also reflects the fact that states as they exist today have different conceptions of what it means to be a "member" of them and what the responsibilities and privileges of membership involve, some of which are community based and some of which are individual based. In this chapter we explore these different conceptions and thus pursue the issue of what I call the "identity" of a political community. This involves in part examining various states' policies on immigration and citizenship, some of which reflect a community-based understanding of political membership and some of which reflect an individualistic conception of political membership. Such policies are a concretized form of the debate between an individualistic and a communitarian conception of the state's role. We will also explore the (recently highly explosive) idea that some states ought to be organized as ethnic nation-states for the good of the ethnic community they aim to serve.

Until fairly recently, the pursuit of issues associated with the idea of political identity was not particularly popular with political philosophers. One prominent philosopher who did take an interest in such issues during the early part of the twentieth century was an American named Horace Kallen, who wrote a number of articles on the topic of immigration and even coined the term 'cultural pluralism' to describe what he took to be the kind of society that would result from the United States' generous immigration policy if Americans sustained their commitment to tolerance and freedom.[1] In our time communitarians (whose views we discussed in the previous chapter) have been intrigued by the development and nature of group identities within political society. Moreover, John Rawls's recent work discussing the kind of liberalism appropriate for a pluralist society such as our own has been indirectly motivated by the way in which large-scale immigration from all over the world has made the United States one of the most heterogeneous of all liberal societies and for that reason a country that might become increasingly difficult to govern unless mutually acceptable and unifying political terms of association can be sustained. However, by and large, the focus of political philosophy since the days of Hobbes and Locke has been elsewhere. Yet how a state responds to outsiders who want to live within its borders raises questions of distributive justice. And more basically, a state's policy on immigration is connected to its sense of the nature and extent of its authority, as well as its view of who and what it exercises its authority *for*. So in this chapter I wish to pursue the connections between citizens' sense of political identity, the immigration and citizenship policies pursued by that society's government, and theories of the role and structure of the just state.

Because philosophers have taken so little interest in this area of political theory, I do not review philosophical theories in this chapter so much as propose new philosophical analyses of the existing conceptions of political membership built into the legislation of contemporary political societies. However, my purpose is not merely to outline these different conceptions of political identity but also to evaluate them from a moral standpoint. Are some conceptions of political membership morally preferable or more just than others? Is it fair, for example, for a society to put out a big welcome mat for immigrants (e.g., for economic reasons, repudiating trade barriers with respect to labor) but nonetheless be chary of granting such people full citizenship insofar as they are not fully of the culture or of the ethnicity that this society takes to define political membership? Is it morally preferable for a country to be strict about admitting immigrants but decidedly less strict about granting citizenship once a person has been admitted? As we shall see, evaluating citizenship and immigration policy involves considering both the economic impact of large-scale foreign immigration and also the extent to which allowing the foreign-born to be admitted or belong to a political society affects its culture and identity. I argue that some policies are more defensible on moral grounds than others and reject most citizenship and immigration policies driven by a strong sense of nationalist identity.[2] I then go on to discuss the way in which individualistic citizenship policies are necessary to the defense of multicultural policies in liberal states. Finally, I conclude by considering when—if at all—secession by one cultural group from a larger political unit can be morally justified.

Although I take a polemical stance throughout much of this chapter by arguing against nationalist conceptions of political membership, my ultimate intention is not so much to convince the reader that I am right as it is to raise questions in this area and encourage the reader to reflect upon them. Philosophers need to pay more attention to the nature of political membership, especially given the extent to which this issue has precipitated war throughout the globe in our time. Whether or not my arguments are right, I aim to help readers to develop philosophical ways of thinking about the issues of nationalism, multiculturalism, immigration and citizenship policy, and secession so as to encourage reasoned ways of solving conflicts (sometimes violent) occasioned by these issues.

Two Conceptions of Belonging

Citizenship and immigration policies articulate a society's conception of what is involved in being a member of that society. In our world there are two prominent and competing conceptions of what it means to be a citizen of a country. I do not mean to suggest that these are the only conceptions of citizenship that exist or could exist, but I do believe these conceptions are particularly prominent and important in our world. First, there is the conception of citizenship as analogous to being a (voluntary) member of a club; second, there is the conception of citizenship as analogous to being one among many organs in a kind of (social) body. At least at first glance, the former might seem to be more congenial to the liberal and the latter more congenial to the communitarian—although we shall see on second glance that this needn't be so. A review of citizenship policies in various states shows that it is much easier to gain citizenship rights in a country that conceives of citizenship in the first way than in a country that conceives of it in the second way.

Consider that up until 1981 Great Britain, while granting its citizens the right to leave the country, nonetheless maintained that (with a few exceptions) they could not lose their British citizenship. For example, a person could not simply renounce her British identity in the course of taking an oath required to assume, for example, U.S. citizenship. Despite this oath, the British government would still regard that person as a British subject, with not only the rights but also the responsibilities of a citizen—including being subject to a draft in time of war.[3] As a result of changes in the 1981 immigration law, the government will now allow someone to renounce his citizenship, but it requires that he must do so by explicit declaration to the secretary of state, who can "deny" the renunciation in certain circumstances (e.g., in time of war).[4] So up until quite recently, British citizenship was regarded by the government as a kind of inalienable feature of anyone born British. The 1981 law doesn't really abandon this conception so much as modify it; that is, it grants that citizenship can be alienated, *but only with the state's permission* (which it will refuse in certain circumstances), so that before 1981 a British citizen was permanently "owned" by his state, whereas now he is "owned" until the state decides to set him free.

This way of conceiving of citizenship is likely derivative from the idea that a ruling lord "owns" his serfs and vassals, and it fits nicely with the claim by many early modern thinkers (e.g., Hobbes in his *Leviathan*) that sovereigns of a nation-state are the "owners" of their people. But what, precisely, is this concept of social "ownership"? We have run across the idea before because, as we discussed in Chapter 2, Locke indirectly invokes it to explain why "members" of a society who have explicitly consented to the state are precluded from emigrating from it. Locke does not mean to convey that the government or head of government has what we today would normally call a property right in the citizenry but is instead trying to point to a special kind of bond that ties the individual and his society together, a bond that cannot be unilaterally relinquished by the individual. In virtue of this bond, the individual holds certain entitlements but will also be required to assume certain responsibilities toward the social group for as long as that group considers him to be a part of it.

Now Locke believed that this bond is consensually created, when the individual explicitly consents to being part of a civil society (which in turn "hires" the rulers of that society). But as we discussed in Chapter 2, a consensual origin for such a bond is incoherent: Whatever reasons (either moral or self-interested) I have for consenting to being part of a political society could, when a political society becomes unjust, become reasons for emigrating from or rebelling against it. And given Locke's moral objections to the idea that the civil society alienates its authority to the ruler when it empowers him, Locke cannot consistently argue that it is morally acceptable for an individual to alienate her authority to the civil society when she explicitly consents to being a member of it.

However, these remarks do not refute the alienation conception of political membership but only a consent-based argument for that conception. As we shall see, there are ways of thinking about a human being's connection with her society that make her bound to it in a way that morally precludes emigration without the society's consent; however, these will not be consent-based ways of thinking. Hence I call this way of thinking about an individual's relationship to her political society the *nonconsensual conception of social membership*. In the end, as I discuss later in this chapter, Britain is not a good example of a society united by this conception of membership. Its liberal tradition, the large number of immigrants recently absorbed into it, and the political agitation of some of its Irish, Scottish, and Welsh populations have been pushing it toward a more voluntaristic conception of social membership, the outlines of which I present below. Instead, I want to suggest that this nonconsensual conception of membership is better realized in countries such as Germany and Japan, explaining why it is very difficult to "become" a German or Japanese citizen if one emigrates to one of these countries.

Although officially Germany's laws are designed to discourage immigration, in fact up until recently outsiders have had easy access to Germany because it has granted admission to any outsider who declared himself a political refugee.[5] Germany's liberality in this regard is connected to its recent history: Many anti-Nazis were able to survive World War II because other European countries allowed them to stay as refugees of political terror.[6] However, the requirements for citizenship in Germany are remarkably stringent and detailed. To review those requirements:[7] All ethnic Germans are granted the right of citizenship regardless of where they are born or presently live. The attribution of citizenship is based solely on parentage, so that a person born of German citizens anywhere in the world is automatically granted German citizenship upon application, and a person with at least one German grandparent has the right to apply and be granted German citizenship (this is called being "naturalized by right"). But a person born on German territory to noncitizens is still a foreigner. The acquisition of citizenship is discretionary and requires that the applicant comply with a number of conditions, including ten years of residence (only five for a spouse of a German national), good moral character, knowledge of the German language and the German political order, and integration into a German way of life. Germany has a very low naturalization rate, most likely because of the difficulty in complying with the requirements and because in the final analysis naturalization is discretionary. Moreover, like Britain, Germany makes the renunciation of citizenship difficult and presumes that it is something that the state must grant, not something that the citizen can insist on as her right.

So the German government is essentially requiring that to be a German citizen, one must have the national identity of a German. This involves two things: First, it means being culturally German, so that one must display a mastery of the language, history, social practices, and beliefs of the German culture. Second, and even more important than the cultural requirement, one must have German "blood." No matter where a person is born and no matter the culture in which he is reared, that person has a right to German citizenship if either of his parents or one of his grandparents is German. Moreover, even if his parents or grandparents previously renounced their German citizenship in order to take up the citizenship of another state, the child can apply and be granted German citizenship solely on the basis of the German nationality of his parents or grandparents.[8] So being German involves in general having a certain genetic connection with other members of the state; I refer to this as the "ethnicity" requirement.

Because Germany regards ethnicity as a more important criterion of membership than culture, German rules on citizenship do not grant citizenship automatically to people born in Germany to non-German parents (unless they would otherwise be stateless—a qualification we discuss later). While the rules allow that those of foreign parentage born in Germany may eventually be granted citizenship if they show evidence of "assimilation," in practice that evidence is hard to furnish if their racial and cultural background is perceived as substantially different from that of the traditional German.[9] As one German descendant in the United States has noted about German citizenship rules:

> This writer, who speaks no German, has never lived there, and whose only connection with Germany is that his paternal grandparents left Baden for the United States a century ago, has a better legal claim on German citizenship than the child of a Turkish worker in Germany, born in Germany, educated there, culturally German, and speaking no other language than German.[10]

So to be a German citizen is to be a member of an ethnic, not a cultural nationality.

Germany is thus an example of a country that conceives of itself as a nation-state and justifies its citizenship policies by reference to what is necessary to preserve the nation politically. I define a *nation-state* as a state that is run by and for members of a particular nation,[11] and I define a *nation* as a group of people that has the following five characteristics:

1. It is typically large and anonymous;
2. it has a common character and a common culture, with a shared history and a shared memory of experiences;
3. it has a system of socializing children so that they share and participate in this culture;
4. it has a conception of membership that makes membership important for each member's self-identity and conceives of membership as a matter of belonging rather than as something one achieves or earns;
5. the members of the group are taken to possess a shared genetic connection, such that most members will regard themselves as genetically similar and/or related to (sometimes very distantly) most other members of the group, where this genetic connection makes them an "ethnic group."[12]

Moreover, using a term of Raz and Avishai Margalit, I call those groups that satisfy only the first four characteristics "encompassing groups."[13] Being "British" is belonging to an encompassing group (because the British comprise many different ethnicities: e.g., Angles, Saxons, Normans, Irish, Welsh, Scots, Indians, Pakistani, Chinese, and various African groups, to name only some), whereas in the eyes of the German state, being "German" is belonging to a nation, insofar as one must satisfy the fifth characteristic, requiring a certain ethnic background. This fifth characteristic is one that recent defenders of nation-states, including Raz and Margalit and Coleman and Harding,[14] have been reluctant to recognize in their characterization of the groups that make up such states. But it has been a very important part of the citizenship policies of many modern political societies.

One can see the ethnicity-driven conception of membership influencing the policies of nation-states in parts of Eastern Europe, many of which were (essentially) colonized by the Soviet Union in the twentieth century or else held under Soviet control through military might. For example, newly independent countries such as Lithuania and Latvia have been attempting to define citizenship so as to exclude Russians, hoping thereby to ensure both that their state has a certain ethnic identity and that those who play a role in running it are not of the same ethnic background as their former imperialist masters.

Another country that exhibits a conception of social membership connected with ethnicity is Japan. Like Germany, Japan grants citizenship on the basis of parentage rather than place of birth: One is automatically granted citizenship if one is a child of Japanese parents, no matter where one is born, whereas a child of non-Japanese parents born in Japan is not an automatic citizen and can only become one through naturalization procedures. The requirements for earning naturalized citizenship *seem* relatively lenient—at least on paper:[15] The would-be citizen must have been continuously domiciled in Japan as a permanent resident for five years, must have upright conduct, and must have sufficient assets not to be a burden on the state. However, the rules also require that making someone a citizen must "accord with the interests of Japan," and that phrase essentially makes the granting of citizenship a largely discretionary matter and in practice remarkably difficult to obtain. Moreover, it turns out that even permanent residency, a necessary condition for citizenship, is granted only at the discretion of the government and is just as difficult to obtain.[16] To become a permanent resident, one must fulfill a vaguely stated assimilation requirement that has been interpreted to involve the taking of a Japanese name (a provision that has offended many of Korean descent in Japan and has been a serious impediment to their becoming citizens). And its interpretation by the Japanese government has been so strict that from 1952 to 1984 only 600,143 people have been granted permanent residence and of that number 577,525 were Korean and 20,000 were Chinese.

So not merely the rules but more important the practice of the Japanese government indicates that to be "one of us" in Japan is not only to have a certain kind of cultural identity, which it would be very difficult for anyone to assume unless he had been raised by parents who were thoroughly part of this culture themselves, but also to have (almost always) a certain kind of genetic connection to others in the group—to have a certain "bloodline." And as in Germany, the cultural requirements are not as important as the genetic background, since no matter where a person is born (and subsequently raised), the Japanese government will grant a right of citizenship to a child born of parents who are Japanese citizens.[17] Japan is therefore another example of a country with a nationalist conception of citizenship.

In contrast to this conception of social membership is the *consensual conception of social membership* held in countries such as the United States and Canada (and to an increasing degree Great Britain), by which membership largely rests on a *voluntary* action on the part of the citizen. Recall our discussion in Chapters 2 and 3 of the idea that membership in a society rests on consent. As we discussed, this idea has been a common theme of social contract theorists such as Locke, Rousseau, and Kant,[18] and it has received a lot of criticism over the years. In Chapter 3 one of our tasks was to figure out how to understand the notion of consent such that it survived Hume's famous criticism of the idea as too contrary to how people actually think about political membership.[19] We isolated two notions of consent that I argued were present in existing political societies: convention consent, given by a person whose behavior supports (or at least does not undermine) the leadership convention in her regime, and endorsement consent, given by people who take a positive attitude toward the political society such that they endorse it and work to ensure its survival and improvement.

However, our review of citizenship policies shows that there is a third notion of consent that is present in some, but not all, political societies extant today: Although consent did not make someone a citizen in the Britain of Hume's day in the eighteenth century and although consent does not make one a citizen of contemporary Germany or Japan, in fact there is a kind of consent that is the foundation of citizenship in countries such as the United States and Canada. If someone is born within the boundaries of these states and/or is born to parents at least one of whom is a citizen, the state will grant that person citizenship, but such a grant is always made with the understanding that this person has the right to *unilaterally* renounce it, if she so chooses, after reaching the age of majority. So it is important that such membership is always understood to be something that a person *can* voluntarily renounce. Hence *it is assumed that if she does not voluntarily and unilaterally renounce it after the age of majority, she has consented to the responsibilities and rights of citizenship.* Let me call this kind of consent by which someone makes herself a member of a society at the age of majority and that she can unilaterally renounce whenever she so chooses in order to join a new political society "membership consent"—it can be either tacitly or expressly given. I understand a citizen to have tacitly consented to membership when she is born into a society that accepts her unilateral right to renounce her membership in it and does not exercise that right after the age of majority. However, this consent is often, sometimes necessarily, expressly given: For example, those who want to become citizens of consensual regimes who have not been born within these countries or born to parents who are already citizens must generally do so by performing a voluntary and *explicit* act of consent and commitment (undertaken in the United States, for example, through a naturalization ceremony).

So the official rules in societies such as the United States and Canada establish that to be a citizen is not to exhibit certain fundamental social or genetic characteristics, nor even to be born within its boundaries, but rather to choose to become a member of the state if given an opportunity to do so, by giving consent, either tacitly (as defined above) or explicitly, to membership. This conception of consent is not sufficient to explain government's creation (only convention consent does that) or to reflect its legitimacy (endorsement consent is connected with legitimacy). Instead, this third form of consent is a necessary condition of *membership* in some—but not all—political societies.[20] So in countries such as Germany or Japan, both convention and endorsement consent exist, and together they explain and legitimate the political society. But neither country recognizes or relies on membership consent (except with a small percentage of naturalized citizens) to establish who belongs to it.

However, in those regimes that rely on consent to establish membership, an individual's giving such consent is a necessary but not a sufficient condition of membership. In these regimes membership also requires that the individual's consent be solicited and *accepted* by the political society. A country such as the United States or Canada grants all who are born within its borders the right to join it if they choose, and outsiders are granted the right to do so as long as certain conditions are met, which include acceptance of certain political beliefs. This is in part because these countries understand the basis of the unity in their society in a political way. They take it that it is because the citizens of these countries have consented to the same political ideals and institutions that they are part of one political society, even if they have different genetic backgrounds, religions, lifestyles, languages, and social customs. Note that one can choose one's political views in a way that one cannot choose the culture in which one has been raised or the genetics of one's family. So in these societies it is possible to assume voluntarily the defining identity of the society simply by embracing its ruling political conceptions (which one will choose to do as long as one's own ideas are in accord with its institutions and ideals). For all citizens of these countries, then, becoming a citizen is a voluntary act based upon giving the political society one's consent to be part of it. Such a political society has a conception of itself as a community—but a community of a very specific sort. It is not a community defined by a genetic connection among the members nor by a common religion or set of social institutions, but by a common political culture to which one commits oneself when one joins the political society.

Membership is not something that can be unilaterally chosen but depends upon the political society's accepting that consent. Hence the citizenship policies in this kind of society depend on the *mutual* consent of both the would-be member and the rest of the political community, which has to decide whether or not to admit her. So the voluntary consent of the would-be member results in membership only if the rest of the community chooses to accept her. In a very real sense this means that such a society rests upon an ongoing "social contract" between that community and each of its members.[21] Clearly, the social contract tradition has affected the way in which the concept of citizenship developed in countries such as the United States and Canada, whose founders knew well the political works of Locke and Hobbes. Contra Hume, the idea that a contract exists between citizens and their state is in a certain sense literally true in these societies, insofar as membership is a function of an agreement between member and state (either explicit, through the naturalization process, or implicit, insofar as the state agrees to the citizenship of the native-born, who have the right of unilateral renunciation and are assumed to consent to these regimes if they do not exercise that right). I would therefore propose that the contractarian argument has had a powerful effect on the historical development of political societies over the past four centuries—encouraging the creation of a type of political society (unknown in Hume's day) united by consent rather than by ethnicity, culture, or conquest.

Moreover, as the contractarians would wish, membership consent in these societies is still connected to the citizens' giving convention consent and endorsement consent, although membership consent is different in that it likely reflects a person's decision that there are mutually advantageous and morally important reasons for working together with other members of this political society and a sense that the terms of cooperation (at least as they are ideally stated, albeit perhaps not always as they are implemented) are fair.[22]

Finally, that this kind of political society is always prepared to grant citizenship to anyone born within its borders or to anyone who is the child of a citizen reflects its responsiveness to a community—defined neither culturally nor ethnically but politically, so that anyone born under its aegis, either through being born in its territory or to a person belonging to this political society, is considered "one of ours." Clearly, however, this sense of community is very attenuated and nothing like the ethnically defined communities of Germany or Japan.

In contrast, a political society such as Germany does not consent to someone's being a member; instead, it *recognizes* the fact of someone's Germanness, after evaluating and tallying up the kind and number of an applicant's characteristics to determine whether they are sufficient for German nationality. Moreover, in societies such as Germany that embrace the nonconsensual, nationalist understanding of citizenship, the nation, defined as above, is conceptually prior both to the individual *and to any political community.* Indeed, this idea was nicely embodied by a 1913 German law (relied upon by West Germany after World War II to establish its laws on citizenship) that states that at bottom the German nation should not be understood as a political entity but rather as an ethnic identity, so that German citizenship was not a purely political matter but an issue that belonged to "the German people." So in Germany the ethnic or national society is understood to be that which defines and authorizes the political society—and surely this idea was one reason so many West and East Germans were eager to unify, despite the profound economic costs to both groups of doing so.

In countries in which political membership is consensually based, the citizenry's genetic backgrounds and cultural identities in matters of custom, dress, religion, or recreation are entirely a function of those who have chosen to constitute it. Hence in social (and nonpolitical) matters the individual member of this type of political society is understood to be conceptually prior to the society itself (so that in general these countries are multicultural in character). If I am a member of such a society, my citizenship does not depend upon whether I have displayed the cultural and genetic characteristics common to the rest of the country's members; instead, the cultural and genetic identity of the country depends upon which individuals (such as myself) have decided to join it.

Although membership in these latter societies does depend upon individuals' choosing to embrace the political identity of the group, which is taken to be a permanent, unifying, and defining feature of these societies, this is the sort of thing individuals *can* voluntarily choose if they wish to do so. Thus actually doing what is necessary to become a citizen is within the rational control of the individual, given the opportunity to do so. Moreover, a country with a consensual conception of membership has a difficult time explaining why certain groups within it cannot, if they choose, secede from the union; if there is individual voluntarism, why not group voluntarism? The United States thus had its Civil War, and contemporary Canada struggles with the separatist issue raised by Quebec. (We discuss the issue of secession and its connection with consensual conceptions of political membership at some length later in the chapter.)

What about states organized around religious beliefs? If a state is dedicated to preserving a certain religious group and welcomes members of any ethnic group or cultural community as long as they accept the religious beliefs of this group, does it understand citizenship consensually or nonconsensually? Consider Israel, which is not really a nation as I have defined it above, not only because non-Jews born in Israel can be citizens but also because anyone can become a citizen of Israel as long as she is a Jew, and being Jewish is not only an ethnic identification but also a religion that can be chosen no matter one's race, sex, or ethnic origin (although what counts as conversion is a controversial subject in Israel). Compare fundamentalist Christian plans for a future America defined as a Christian commonwealth: Advocates of this vision would presumably insist that they are not conceiving of this new America as a nation-state but as a kind of voluntary association, albeit a unireligious one, to which all human beings are invited, no matter their ethnic or cultural heritage. Critics might maintain that religion is so deeply connected with our identity, which is in turn so deeply connected with our membership in groups to which we have not chosen to belong, that it is stretching the truth unduly to say that religious affiliation is under our voluntary control and subject to our consent. Yet it *is* possible to choose to be Jewish or Christian in a way that it is not possible to choose to be, say, an ethnic German. So the issue of how to categorize these sorts of political societies depends upon whether religious affiliation is equated with affiliations one can or cannot choose. I shall not be able to resolve that issue here.

In an important sense, the histories of political societies explain how each of them has come to embrace one of these two very different conceptions of membership. I once had a conversation with a Chinese citizen whose own ancestors were Chinese for hundreds of generations and who could not conceive of what it was like for me to be an American citizen simply because my very recent forebears happened to turn up here. A nation made up of immigrants cannot have the same strong sense of homogeneous cultural identity as a nation with a long cultural tradition and a long tradition of warding off outsiders. Hence an immigrant nation's sense of citizenship as a voluntary affair is as inevitable a consequence of its history as is other countries' perception of citizenship as a nonconsensual, nonvoluntary fact of social identity.

The consent-based conception of citizenship may also explain why in the United States only a citizen may vote. Because a common commitment to its democratic political culture defines American identity, the act of voting is not only a political act but also an act that indicates one's commitment to the nation's defining political identity. Hence the act of voting becomes one of the most important rights withheld until the society is clear that the person seeking membership is genuinely choosing to belong to and participate in the political culture of that society. (It may well be an alarming sign for the polity that the percentage of Americans who do vote is so low relative to the voting rate of many other countries.) In contrast, a country such as Britain, which understands its identity partially in a nonpolitical, cultural way, believes it can afford to grant noncitizens the right to vote, on the grounds that the action of voting is not understood to be an indication of whether or not one can be considered to have a British identity.

The consensual attitude toward citizenship also shows up in the U.S. policy toward dual citizenship. The U.S. Supreme Court has ruled that it is proper for the U.S. government to demand of those who wish to become citizens of this country that they renounce their prior citizenship; as I've noted, such a renunciation assumes that becoming a citizen is a voluntary decision on the part of each individual. However, there are circumstances in which the court will permit dual citizenship, and the way in which it allows this shows that it accepts that there are circumstances in which a person can belong to more than one political society. For example, it allows someone to choose to be both an Israeli and an American citizen.[23] That the United States should even think that this makes sense shows the extent to which it separates a person's religious, cultural, and ethnic identity from her American identity—which is defined in a largely political way. A person can also have dual citizenship if she is born in this country and is the child of a foreign national: She is automatically granted U.S. citizenship (subject to her consent to it at the age of majority) in virtue of her place of birth, and she may also be entitled to citizenship in that foreign country in virtue of her parentage. If the parents on the child's behalf request such foreign citizenship, the child will enjoy citizenship rights in both countries, and the Supreme Court has ruled that the U.S. government cannot, consistent with the Constitution, do anything to make the child renounce that foreign citizenship or make continued U.S. citizenship dependent upon such a renunciation. Hence the ruling means that belonging to the United States involves something like the following: You can have citizenship here if you get it by right of birth and do not reject that right at the age of majority, or if you choose it over your previous political affiliation after having renounced that previous affiliation. But if the former is true, then if some other political society also gives you citizenship rights, that can be no affair of ours. Your citizenship is therefore a function of your consensual relationship between this political community and you and cannot be affected by the independent decisions of a third party. Hence "being American" is *not* manifesting characteristics that are difficult or impossible to assume voluntarily and that mark one out as a lifelong member of a nation; instead, "being American" is belonging to a political "club" (which is perhaps not the only club of which one is a member) after having tacitly or explicitly consented to do so.

Immigration, Nationalism, and Social Identity

Are both the consensual and nonconsensual conceptions of citizenship morally acceptable? Are there moral reasons for rejecting or modifying either of them?

To pursue this question, let us begin by morally evaluating the kinds of immigration policies that societies with one of these conceptions would allow. To welcome immigrants into a political territory is not the same as making them citizens, so a nonconsensual conception of state membership needn't preclude (and hasn't precluded) a generous immigration policy. One of the most important issues to be considered in formulating immigration policy in either a consent-based or non-consent-based society is that of distributive justice—both to those who want to enter and to those who are already in the country. Large-scale impoverishment in a poor country adjacent to a wealthy one can cause many people from the poor country to want to enter the wealthy state, and their poverty is prima facie a reason for allowing them entry. However, allowing large-scale immigration can have an effect on the labor market, and if it depresses wages at the low end of the wage scale, such a policy might be construed as unjust to the poor members of the society who would receive the immigrants. And if such immigration causes a large tax burden for many members of the society, this might also be grounds for objecting to it; such have been the arguments of opponents of large-scale immigration in the United States and Western Europe. Note that such arguments assume that the state should be concerned first and foremost to realize distributive justice *for it own members* and only secondarily for those outside its borders who wish to enter it. The idea that a state is primarily "for" those who are its members is fundamental to both the consensual and nonconsensual conceptions.

To balance these very different considerations of fairness in the setting of immigration policy is difficult; note that none of the theories of distributive justice we reviewed in Chapter 4 will help us to do so, because all of them focus on defining justice only for those already in the political societies. Adjudicating between claims of justice made by those inside a state and those outside a state who want to come in requires a more global theory of justice, which some philosophers have become interested in developing.[24]

However, immigration policy involves not only issues of distributive justice but also issues relating to the social and political identity of a state (which I suspect any adequate global theory of justice will have to accommodate). For example, societies with a nonconsensual conception of membership will want to consider whether immigration, especially on a large scale, that would bring in many people who would not be part of either the culture or the ethnic nationality defining political membership would threaten the ethnic or cultural basis of unity in the state. If it would, it would seem that this would form the basis for an objection to any kind of lenient immigration policy in such a state. Although states with consensual conceptions have a basis for political unity that is unlikely to be threatened by the entry of people of various nationalities or cultures, nonetheless if an immigrant group subscribes to political views that are hostile to the polity or the political philosophy of such a state, the admission of that group might well be a threat to the state's politically defined unity. However, only nonconsensual states will have grounds for thinking that *cultural or ethnic unity* is a concern in setting immigration policy.

But *should* it be a concern? That is, should the mere fact that an immigrant has a different ethnicity or culture from that of the current residents of a state be a reason to deny her admission? To answer this question, we must evaluate the moral legitimacy of a nonconsensual conception of political membership. And we begin with an obvious argument purporting to show that the nonconsensual conception of state membership is morally unacceptable. This argument begins by claiming that a nonconsensual basis for citizenship is inconsistent with the fundamental tenets of democratic societies. If that is correct, then if (as many of us believe) all political societies ought to be democratic in order to instantiate justice, the argument's conclusion is that to be just, all societies ought to embrace a consent-based conception of political membership.

On this argument, to take the attitude that only people of a certain race or religion or culture will be allowed to immigrate into and become citizens of the country is to represent the country as something other than a community defined by democratic political ideals. Such a country conceives of itself as united as much by racial, genetic, and cultural characteristics as by ideals such as tolerance and the respect for individual rights. In its decisions about who will enter or become a member, this kind of state may therefore behave intolerantly toward those people whose skin color or culture are perceived as substantially "different"—and, more than likely, in virtue of that difference also inferior. Such attitudes, on this view, represent a betrayal of the ideal that all human beings are equal and that all human beings have the same basic bundle of fundamental rights. Therefore this argument concludes that we are rightly critical of a country representing itself as a democratic society but doing its best to refuse either entry or citizenship to those people whose ethnic and cultural background is distant from that of the current citizens.

The argument grants that a democratic society can reasonably put restrictions on immigration and citizenship. After all, the arrival of newcomers places costs upon those who are already there (e.g., economic
costs, possible overcrowding of schools, high demand for housing, pressure on health care, etc.); too many newcomers can make these costs extremely high and constitute a legitimate basis for restricting the numbers
who are allowed to enter. But the argument also insists that even while
such restrictions are permitted, they must be formulated in a way that
avoids racial or cultural bias and that citizenship standards should rest in
the main on the immigrants' willingness to consent and remain committed to the democratic ideals of freedom and equality in the nation.

Nonetheless, this argument isn't successful as it stands. The problem
with it is that a society such as Germany, which espouses democratic political beliefs but also insists on a person's meeting strict requirements for
membership in the German nation in order to be a citizen of the German
political society, can plausibly counter that it does not want to be simply a
democratic society but rather an ethnic/cultural society operating according to democratic principles. While those Germans who espouse this
point of view will admit that the ideals of freedom and equality are important, they will also maintain that the social cohesion they value and
aim to protect is not (as in the United States and Canada) created by the
acceptance of those universal ideals but by the bonds of ethnicity and culture. "We want to live under these ideals," members might say, "but we
don't want to give everyone the prima facie right to live under those
ideals *here*. We value our Germanic heritage and wish to see that heritage
preserved and sustained. We can do this only by putting strict requirements on successful citizenship applications."

So to determine the legitimacy of a nonconsensual conception of state
membership, we must confront the issue of the legitimacy of the nation-
state (i.e., a state belonging to a certain nation), since it is the claim of the
moral importance of nations that is the foundation for an argument justifying the nonconsensual conception of political membership. Jules Coleman and Sarah Harding defend nonconsensual citizenship policies on the
grounds that what they call "encompassing groups" have a right to be
preserved.[25] Recall that encompassing groups are just like nations, with
the exception that they do not define themselves using genetic/ethnic criteria. Yet as we've seen, it is the very hallmark of citizenship policies in
states with a nonconsensual conception of membership that ethnicity is
the primary prerequisite for membership. So we should beware not to ask
the wrong question when we evaluate the citizenship policies of nation-
states such as Germany: We should ask *not* whether those policies are legitimate insofar as they enable an encompassing group to protect itself
but whether they are legitimate insofar as they enable a nation (defined in

part as an ethnic entity) to protect itself. After considering how to answer this second question in the rest of this section, in the next section I go on to consider the relationship between (mere) encompassing groups and nonconsensual citizenship policies.

The argument that the nonconsensual policies of nation-states are legitimate goes as follows: If nations have a right to political self-determination in certain circumstances (e.g., when they are prepared to govern justly, when the territory occupied by the nation is viable as a state, and so forth),[26] then, according to this argument, nonconsensual citizenship policies are permitted (and appropriate) once the nation-state is created, insofar as such policies protect the nation—whose state this is.

There are two ways to mount this kind of argument. The first I call *communitarian*. This form of the argument fits most naturally with the rhetoric of Germany's laws—particularly the 1913 law expressing the idea that the state exists to serve the German nation. It starts from the assertion that nations (as defined above) have a right to self-determination (appropriately qualified), and when nations exercise this right, they are nation-states. Note that on this assumption this right is held by *a group*, in this case the nation, and not by individuals in the group. On the basis of this right, the argument goes, nation-states can legitimately limit citizenship to those who are members of the nation. Otherwise the state will no longer be for and under the control of the nation. Or in other words, it will no longer be the *nation's state*. This is particularly true when the state is organized along democratic lines, since allowing people who are not members of the nation into the state will affect legislation, democratically determined. (A communitarian may want to argue that nation-states are obligated, for reasons of justice, to construct a democratic form of government. But even if he does not wish to argue for this conclusion, he can maintain that large numbers of nonnational citizens can affect the policies, influence the legislation, and in general take at least some political control out of the hands of the nationals. Note that this is true only with respect to citizens; it may not be true if the nonnationals are mere residents with only limited rights.)

The second or *liberal* form of argument for the same conclusion also grants a nation the right to self-determination but attributes this right to the *individuals* of the nation, not to the group. On this liberal conception, groups do not have rights; only individuals have rights. Nonetheless, the liberal can maintain that groups are instrumentally valuable to individuals because they are vital to individuals' well-being and central to defining individuals' identities.[27] As Will Kymlicka has recently argued,[28] membership in groups has been an important component of the liberal tradition, providing a "context of choice" in which individuals form identities and formulate projects, plans, and goals based on legitimate expectations regarding the behavior of others.[29] So whereas the communitarian maintains that these groups are intrinsically valuable, Kymlicka argues that for the liberal these groups are instrumentally valuable, insofar as they are important to the well-being of their members.

On this basis, the liberal grants individuals the right to the flourishing of groups of which they are part (assuming, of course, that the groups are not abusive or disruptive of justice)—groups that include nations. The argument continues that nations flourish best when they are organized in states. So individuals have a right to the statehood of their nations, since such political standing will ensure that these groups flourish. Having established the right to self-determination by nations, the liberal concludes in the same way as the communitarian: As long as nation-states are legitimate, it is morally permissible for them to limit citizenship to those who are members of the nation. Otherwise the state will no longer be for and under the control of the nation. That is, it will no longer be the nation's state.

Thus we see that the defenders of a nonconsensual conception of citizenship can employ the terminology of liberalism to justify that conception by saying that this conception's legitimacy ultimately rests on the individual's right to be able to live in a group that she believes is closely connected to her own welfare and personal identity. So understood, it is a right held by each individual in virtue of the instrumental importance of groups to her identity and welfare, and it is not in any way held by or attributable to a group. Whatever other rights liberals recognize, the argument is that liberals must also recognize this right and thus tolerate the restrictions that a society would find necessary to preserve its identity. And note that those restrictions may involve ethnicity and race, insofar as the nation's identity is intimately connected to a certain genetic inheritance.

Therefore, although differences between communitarians and liberals mean they will explain and justify citizenship in nation-states differently, their views will lead them to endorse similar policies. Even though they disagree about where the right protecting the integrity of nations comes from and who holds it, both use this right to establish that it is morally legitimate for a nation to "own" a state. And because the criteria for being a member of a nation are nonconsensual, each view accepts that the criteria for being a member of a nation-state must also be nonconsensual. Now I will admit to having grave reservations about the existence of the right relied upon by both views—and even more serious reservations (which I discuss later) about the assumption underlying this right—that our identity and our well-being are or must be connected with only a *single* culture. But for now I will grant the existence of this right and consider the soundness of these two forms of the argument for the legitimacy of the nonconsensual citizenship policies of nation-states.

Neither the liberal nor the communitarian offers a sound argument for preserving the purity of a nation-state for a number of reasons. The first objection is that, even assuming that a nation has a right to be a state, such a right cannot be sufficiently powerful to trump *all* other rights held by outsiders. The right to the preservation of a group identity is only one right among many in a society and thus one that must be appropriately balanced against other claims that individuals or groups outside the dominant cultural community might make against it. For example, it is plausible to claim that everyone has a right to citizenship in *some* political society.[30] Liberals would tend to agree with this claim. But what is more striking is that because both Germany and Japan grant citizenship to children born within their territories to non-German and non-Japanese parents who would otherwise be stateless, these states also recognize that these children's right to citizenship in some political society trumps other citizens' rights to preserve their group's identity. That is, the right to be a citizen *somewhere* is reasonably understood to be stronger than an individual's right or a group's right to preserve the group's culture and ethnicity. But if this is so, the latter right to preserve a culture or an ethnicity cannot be used to exclude membership to individuals born within the society who nonetheless are from an ethnic and cultural group other than that of the dominant group (e.g., Koreans in Japan, Russians in Lithuania, Turks in Germany) and who do not have citizenship in the country of their ethnic origin. Depending upon how large an ethnic minority is, the effect of acknowledging the power of these children's rights to citizenship could result in the state's becoming a multiethnic society, whether the majority liked it or not. A nation cannot own a state when too many nonnationals born within its territory require political affiliation and only that state can give it to them. (I take it as obvious that it is not morally acceptable for an advocate to reply to this argument that the way to solve the problem of these nonnationals is to engage in some kind of policy of "ethnic cleansing.")

A second objection is that a nation cannot prohibit citizenship to nonnationals when substantial numbers of nonnationals have lived long, productive lives within the territory of the state and require citizenship in order to live on an equal basis with other nationals. If a country persisted in denying rights of citizenship to these nonnationals, it would be allowing a system of different classes of residents in that society, with nonnationals forced to accept unequal treatment and second-class status. The ideals of liberalism would certainly rule out such a policy. So even if liberalism grants that an individual has a right to preserve his group's identity, liberalism also recognizes the right of any long-standing, productive, and law-abiding resident of a country to gain eventual citizenship if he so chooses, even if he cannot meet all of the genetic and cultural requirements that would mark him as a member of the nationality of the dominant group in that country. And this latter right is grounded in the liberal and democratic requirement that all people in a political society should be treated equally and fairly, no matter how much any of them might differ from the majority.

Indeed in nationalist countries such as Germany that have in years past *solicited* foreign immigrants to help augment their own labor force, their subsequent refusal to grant such people citizenship, no matter how law-abiding or productive they have been, on the grounds that they are not (and cannot be) members of the nationality defining the political society violates the right to equal treatment required by liberalism. Such a refusal essentially permits among the society's residents a hierarchy that is not only unjust but also destabilizing, as such a policy engenders anger and resentment among those denied the rights of full citizenship. Communitarians might resist the idea that justice requires this kind of equality, for example, if the nation's culture sanctioned racist or sexist views. If so, I would maintain that a further argument against their position is that equality is morally required no matter the cultural views of the nation.

A third and final objection is that rights associated with distributive justice might also trump rights to group preservation. Consider that not only individuals who are refugees from political terror but also individuals from countries that are desperately poor might be thought to have some kind of right to enter a nearby wealthy society (albeit perhaps only in reasonable numbers, given the costs of their immigration). If this wealthy country had a nonconsensual conception of its identity and refused citizenship rights to all the poor of other societies on the grounds that they did not display the genetic and cultural characteristics that marked them out as members of this society, then depending upon the details of the circumstances of those who wished to enter the society and on how wholeheartedly such a country forbade their entry, we might consider their policies on immigration and citizenship callous and even cruel. Working out when the rights of the desperately poor trump (that is, override) the right to group preservation requires a theory of global justice that has yet to be developed, but it is intuitively plausible to many that sometimes this trumping occurs, in which case a society must compromise its ethnic or cultural purity to satisfy the demands of justice.

Moreover, given the argument above, a wealthy country cannot defensibly admit a reasonable number of poor nonnationals but deny them any chance of eventual citizenship for having exhibited the wrong race or the wrong culture or both; the right to preserve a national identity cannot be outweighed by the rights associated with equal treatment under the law.[31]

On the basis of these three objections, it would seem that even the right to preserve a group identity cannot reasonably be thought to preclude citizenship to *all* who do not meet the nonconsensual cultural or genetic requirements of citizenship in all circumstances. Hence the preceding objections establish that no society appropriately animated by individual rights can have an *exclusively* nonconsensual policy of citizenship.

Nonetheless, this discussion also seems to establish that some kind of nonconsensual policy of citizenship is allowable on both communitarian and liberal conceptions of the state. On either conception, it would seem that a (relatively) homogeneous society could justify the general practice of limiting immigration and citizenship to those who met the nationality test of the dominant group, making certain exceptions to accommodate the rights of (at least some) political refugees, long-term and productive immigrant (nonnational) residents, and (at least some of) the economically destitute. To put it succinctly, the argument concludes that even if the *pure* nation-state is not morally defensible, a state that is nonetheless animated by the principle of preserving a nation is morally legitimate, as long as it makes some exceptions (connected to certain rights of individuals and demands of distributive justice) that grant citizenship to certain individuals who are not members of a nationality.[32] Is this argument sound? In the next section, I argue that it is not.

Liberalism and Community

The argument justifying nonconsensual citizenship policies of nation-states rests on two assumptions, in both its liberal and its communitarian forms.

1. A nonconsensual conception of citizenry is both necessary and morally permissible in order to preserve groups that give their members identity and contribute in a substantial way to their well-being. (The communitarian grants these groups an intrinsic right to exist; the liberal places the right in the hands of the individual members who receive the benefit of group membership.)
2. A nation-state is an effective way to preserve those particular groups, including "nations" and "encompassing groups," that are important to their members' identity and well-being.

In what follows I do not challenge the first assumption.[33] I do, however, present a series of objections to show that the second assumption is often, and maybe even usually, not true.

The first objection challenges the claim that nations, as I have defined them, are worth preserving, even granting that it is morally required to preserve groups (on either liberal or communitarian grounds) that are central to an individual's identity and well-being. The problem with nations is that they are defined in part by reference to race and ethnicity. As I have already noted, philosophers who defend nation-states are happy to talk about preservation of *culture* but omit the fact that in most of the world the concept of nationality is intimately connected to the ethnicity of the members of that society. And there is no reason to think that preserving cultural groups vital to an individual's identity and well-being demands that a government forbid people to join the group unless they are of the same ethnicity or race. To claim that one can be a real member of a culture only if one has a certain genetic background is to assert something false about the role that a genetic background plays in a person's acculturation. And such a falsehood is likely just a cover for the racism of a group that holds its members superior by blood to certain other types of human beings. In any case, because it is simply untrue that someone's mere race or ethnicity is vital to the preservation of a group's identity, and because this idea usually goes hand in hand with racist attitudes, it is indefensible as a foundation for immigration and citizenship policy and indefensible as an argument on behalf of the nation-state.

More fundamental, the idea that there are biologically identifiable races or ethnic groups has no scientific basis. Biologists standardly dismiss it.[34] This shows that particular concepts of race or ethnicity (usually based on visually identifiable characteristics such as skin color or hair color) are nonscientific inventions, and history shows that they have persistently been used by some groups to abuse, oppress, or exclude from their company (sometimes by genocidal means) members of other groups. Hence there is every reason not to grant this pernicious fiction any legitimacy in the setting of immigration and citizenship policy.

This means that even if we grant that maintaining a group's identity is instrumentally valuable to individual members' well-being, we have an excellent reason to reject that this identity can be maintained only as long as the group is "ethnically pure" (whatever that means) and thus good reason to reject citizenship policies in any society that restricts citizenship to those who are of a particular ethnic group.[35] So suppose we reconstruct the liberal and communitarian arguments so that they allow the preservation of groups defined solely in terms of culture, not race or ethnicity, whose nonconsensual citizenship policies don't discriminate on the basis of race or ethnicity and recognize the rights of nonnationals to citizenship in certain instances. Using Raz's term, I refer to groups united only by culture, and not by race or ethnicity, as "encompassing groups"; for convenience I henceforth use the term 'unicultural state' to refer to political societies that are controlled by and for the benefit of a single encompassing group. This would involve our reinterpreting tenet 2 above, so that it now reads as follows:

2′. A unicultural state organized on nonconsensual grounds is an effective way to preserve the encompassing group that is important to its members' identity and well-being.

Note that this reconstructed argument would disallow most of the nonconsensual, genetic-based citizenship policies around the world (including those of Germany and Japan)[36] and would thus be an ineffective defense for nationalistic citizenship policies as we know them today. At best the argument would support citizenship policies that did not restrict (or automatically give) citizenship to people of a certain ethnicity, that required tests of cultural assimilation, and that put restrictions on the rate at which those of other cultures could enter the community. Arguably, such citizenship policies would be more like consent-based policies than non-consent-based policies, insofar as joining the state would be a function of a person's decision to do what was required to meet the criteria for membership as well as the state's consent to have any person as a member. In any case, does the claim that encompassing groups have a right to be preserved establish that these groups have a *right* to political self-determination and thus a right to these kinds of citizenship policies?

No: The most it establishes is that unicultural states can be a good vehicle for preserving these groups, so that for consequentialist reasons we should favor them. But if good consequences are what justify the creation of a unicultural state, then we should be sure that in fact these consequences are indeed good. Now sometimes it seems that they have been good; countries that have formed around a certain group's culture, ethnicity, and history, such as Estonia or Armenia, have been convinced that they are good, and the experience of the people in countries such as these has been that not only their group identity but indeed their very lives were threatened for as long as they were part of a society *not* composed, in the main, of people from their culture. So their longing for a nation-state has been based on a desire to achieve the preservation not only of their culture but also of their people. And it seems reasonable for members of minorities badly persecuted in states dominated by other groups to hold this belief. To be in control of their political destiny seems an effective cure for the persecution they have suffered at the hands of a government run by a group hostile to them. Hence in such circumstances the consequences appear to favor a unicultural state.

But the history of the twentieth century does not show that a unicultural state is always or even usually a highly successful vehicle for the protection of groups of people who are at risk for various reasons. Supporters of the nation-state or the unicultural state, such as Raz and Margalit or Coleman and Harding, are in the grip of a nineteenth-century solution to the problems of conflict among different groups proximate to one another, and at the close of the twentieth century there is good reason to conclude that this solution has generally failed to deliver the protection it was supposed to provide.

In Western Europe many consider the nation-state to have often been a primary *source* of conflict among different cultural groups, not a cure for it. Even though many European states were built upon liberal ideals, strong ethnic and cultural identifications in many of those states have played a role in generating vicious wars, politically sponsored attempts at genocide, and economically damaging trade wars. Group identity is not well preserved through the vehicle of the nation-state or unicultural state when the groups that had previously sought to damage one another inside a state do it instead in wars between states. As this book is being written, the former Yugoslavia is rent by war, as factions that coexisted within a single state now wage war with one another as part of separate states. So the creation of nation-states to "protect" these ethnic groups has been largely unsuccessful. When people want to kill one another, rearranging political boundaries can make things no better and sometimes worse.

Moreover, the nation-state itself can encourage pride-driven aggression and pride-driven reprisals. The behavior of Nazi Germany is instructive and needs no review. So, too, is the history of Sri Lanka: A peaceful society composed of two distinct communities, one Sinhalese-speaking and Buddhist, the other Tamil-speaking and Hindu, was thrown into internecine conflict as a result of a prime minister's 1956 edict to make the religion and language of the Sinhalese majority the official state religion and language. This attempt to harness the state machinery on behalf of the Sri Lankan majority represented an attempt to turn Sri Lanka into a nation-state. The result has been the fury of the Tamil minority, resulting in the murder of two prime ministers, communal riots, civil warfare, and military involvement of another country (i.e., India, whose own prime minister, Rajiv Gandhi, was likely murdered by a Tamil militant). Whatever value the nation-state or unicultural state has had in preserving certain groups, it has also encouraged others to behave in ways that have threatened the rights of members of minority groups living among them.

Indeed, the example of Sri Lanka can be used to show that in many situations creating a nation-state is actually a self-defeating strategy for preserving group identity and culture. When a certain nation is only one of the groups residing in a territory, its insistence that the state controlling that territory must become *its* nation-state will inevitably worry and anger members of minority groups, who fear they will end up residing in a political society that is officially organized for the benefit of a group other than their own. Not only would this mean their rights as individuals would be under threat, but even worse, their group's right to be preserved and to flourish within this territory would be under threat. Hence they will understandably want to fight for the preservation of their group against the majority, provoking dissension and possibly war that can be damaging to all the groups in the territory. The ethnic fighting in the former Yugoslavia offers the most striking and tragic confirmation of this point. Therefore recent history would seem to show that even if a unicultural state sometimes protects cultural units in some parts of the world, it is one of the *worst* vehicles for the preservation of cultures in situations where substantial numbers of people who belong to other groups also reside in the same territory—and that includes most areas of our world today.

The European Community's attempt to weaken national ties and foster political and economic interdependence has been a way of forestalling conflict and encouraging peace among nations emboldened to wage war against one another despite and even because of the fact that some of them became or wanted to become nation-states. Ironically, in contrast to many Americans fearful of the disruptive nature of a highly pluralist society, Europeans have come to perceive homogeneity as a threat to peace rather than a state of affairs that precedes it. (And it is interesting to speculate about how a closer union of European states will affect what will eventually have to become a common immigration policy and how it will affect these states' conceptions of citizenship.) The lesson to be learned from such reflections is that groups may flourish and be best preserved not in separate (and often hostile) nation-states or unicultural states but in other kinds of polity that foster the preservation of cultural identity, protect the members of different cultural groups, and promote a network of economic and political interaction and interdependence, making war and economic competition unacceptable ways of resolving disputes.

In the end both the communitarian and the liberal arguments for nation-states or unicultural states and for a nonconsensual conception of citizenship that links citizenship in these states to national or cultural background are consequentialist in nature: That is, both claim that uninational or unicultural states are justified because they have desirable consequences, particularly with regard to the preservation of nations or cultures. So it is important that the consequences are often otherwise. Of course there may be situations where a uninational or unicultural state *is* an effective vehicle for the preservation of a group. But history shows not only that such a political arrangement often does *not* secure the well-being of the group but also that the idea of such a state has been an incitement to political actions that have encouraged conflict severely damaging to cultural communities.

So if we agree that cultural communities are important to the well-being of the individual and thus worthy of protection, we need to rethink how such protection can be genuinely secured. My argument against nation-states or unicultural states is *not* an argument against the importance of a cultural community but an argument against the idea that political communities should always—or even usually—overlap with ethnic or cultural communities. So what kind of political community should we construct to secure this protection?

I take that to be one of the most open and interesting political questions in the world today. Europe is attempting to shape one answer to this question, and if it can resist the lure of establishing a nation-state, Quebec may well provide another answer by filling out the concept of "sovereignty association" (although to do so it will also have to come to grips with the rights of non-French cultures within it—e.g., native populations such as the Mohawks—to preserve their culture). Finally, the possibility of different groups' getting along even while retaining at least some of their distinctive identities has been demonstrated by the history of immigrant nations such as the United States and Canada. The key to peaceful coexistence may come not from separation and exclusivity but from interdependence and tolerance of diversity in a multicultural society.

Those advocates of the nation-state or unicultural state who believe my argument is wrong must develop a consequentialist defense of these states, in the face of the history of violence generated by nationalism and uniculturalism in the twentieth century. To do so they might try to reinterpret the historical evidence so as to acquit such states of any role in ethnic or national violence in this century. They might also try to develop a conception of the nature and responsibilities of a unicultural state that will be more morally justifiable and more peace-preserving than many of these states appear to have been in the past.

However, any such defense requires that these advocates specify exactly what "preserving" a culture involves, such that a unicultural state can be shown to secure that preservation. Surely "preserving a culture" cannot mean keeping it the same; the introduction of technology, for example, can bring about huge transformations in a culture (think about what the automobile has done to transform our cultures), and yet we do not normally think that its introduction has been antithetical to the preservation of most cultures (although that could be true with respect to some cultures; it may well be antithetical to the preservation of Amish culture). So we await a conceptual analysis of what "preserving" a culture involves.

The defender of the unicultural state must also tell us what a "single culture" is. Even using the definition of 'encompassing groups' given earlier in the chapter, can't we find many groups that meet this definition even in the most homogeneous of political societies? Aren't there, for example, many religious groups in Germany and Japan? Don't "ethnic Russians" still come from a variety of different historical traditions, exemplifying different cultures? Aren't countries such as France made up of a variety of regions whose residents speak different dialects and even different languages (e.g., Basque)? The idea that a country could be responsive to "one culture" is therefore difficult to understand, given that there is no country whose population seems to manifest only *one* cultural tradition. So might not the demand for a unicultural state represent the demand of only one group to get control of the reins of power in a way that might disadvantage members of other groups?[37]

I leave these questions for readers to debate. But let me close this section on a more abstract philosophical note. Because the arguments for and against nation-states or unicultural states that I have reviewed are all consequentialist in nature, they make an assumption about the boundaries of political societies that was originally suggested by Hume:[38] namely, that the territory controlled by a political society is conventionally established and defended on the grounds that a society with this jurisdiction is instrumentally valuable to the individuals and/or groups in this area. (Indeed in order to acquire territory believed to be beneficial, a society may go to war against another political society or else spend considerable sums of money to purchase that territory. For example, think of U.S. territorial acquisitions made as a result of the Louisiana Purchase, the Gadsen Purchase, and the Mexican-American War.) There is no "natural" moral boundary between states.

Even more fundamental, one lesson of the political experimentation with polities today is that there is not even a "natural" notion of the state, and the present conception and configuration of states need not be permanent features of the political landscape if there are better, more peace-producing vehicles for political order.[39] The peace-securing values of liberalism may best be employed in the service of group identity in political societies that are not traditional nation-states or unicultural states, and in the next century a number of different types of such society may emerge. Hence those who defend either consensual or nonconsensual citizenship policies and the conceptions of the state that undergird them need to consider whether the conception of the state as we know it today is really the best vehicle for the protection of individuals' or groups' rights and well-being or the creation of efficient and productive uses of the world's resources. Particularly for liberals who are ultimately concerned to protect and secure the rights and well-being of individuals, the history of the twentieth century shows that it simply will not do to assume that the modes of political organization relied upon in this century are the only or the best modes possible.

Multiculturalism

The third challenge to the liberal and communitarian defenses of nation-states or unicultural states has to do with a hidden assumption in the argument, namely, that the culture of a nation is best preserved by keeping out anyone who was raised a member of another group. But consider that groups giving us identity can be preserved in a state that is *multicultural* and not merely unicultural; indeed this has been one of the animating principles of Canada.[40] Defenders of consent-based states such as the United States and Canada would insist not only that the various groups defining the cultural identities of the members of these states should enjoy considerable protection but also that members of these groups are enriched by the presence of people with different cultural backgrounds. Nor do I see any compelling argument that the economic order of the world will be best promoted only if each cultural community has its own state; it is arguable that economic growth is fostered better in a multicultural environment.

Hence supporters of the liberal argument for nation-states may be making a substantial mistake about what kind of society is genuinely good for us. Perhaps the best reason to support a consent-based policy of citizenship grounded upon liberal ideals is that such a policy encourages a multicultural society that is both more interesting, more conducive to peace, more economically productive, and more nourishing to the individuals who live within it than societies that have only a single cultural tradition. And if this is so, both ethnic nation-states and "encompassing society" states can be bad for us: Not only might they foster rather than cure conflict among groups, but they might also inhibit the economic development and the diversity of social practices, ideas, and lifestyles that enable us to flourish as individuals.

Note that the defense of multicultural societies I have just given is based on claims about what is good for the *individual*, not on some concept of group rights. Of course a believer in group rights could also defend multiculturalism on the basis of the moral importance of and our obligation to encompassing groups—even while resisting the idea that the rights of such groups include a state of one's own. Indeed if a believer in group rights goes on to insist on any particular group's right to have a nation-state or unicultural state, he will be unable to defend the concept of a multicultural state. The defense of multiculturalism therefore requires abandoning the defense of the unicultural state or nation-state and implicitly commits one to some kind of consensual, rather than a nonconsensual, foundation for citizenship and state membership—based on the consent of either individual members or the groups that make up the multicultural state.

The linkage between multiculturalism and consent-based conceptions of political association has not, I think, been sufficiently appreciated by communitarian supporters of multiculturalism. A communitarian defense of multiculturalism has to be undertaken assuming a conception of the state that does not serve a particular nation or encompassing group and thus presupposes a highly individualistic conception of state membership of the sort normally associated with liberalism. Perhaps more than anything else, this underlying consent-based foundation for multiculturalism in these societies explains the tension in the communitarian positions of these U.S. and Canadian theorists: It is hard to defend the state as an institution devoted to preserving community when membership in the state being discussed, by virtue of being a function of individual consent, includes people from multiple communities, none of whom wants to see the state act as a partisan for any one community. Liberal principles of toleration and a hands-off, neutral attitude toward groups may therefore seem almost inevitable in an environment in which the consent of disparate individuals rather than a single common ethnic or cultural background is the glue of political association.

Almost inevitable—but not quite, at least not when there are strong advocates for recognizing, preserving, and politically supporting multiple cultures in these societies. Just as feminists have claimed that governments have an active role to play in the ending of social practices that promote the abuse of women, so, too, certain communitarians such as Charles Taylor (who uses the Canadian experience as his model) have argued that governments have an active role to play both in recognizing the value of various cultural traditions within the society and in formulating policies (e.g., language laws, systems of education) that help to preserve and strengthen these cultures.[41] For example, if a government takes a hands-off approach toward the education of children in an environment where a dominant culture is going to control what is taught to all children, excluding literature and ideas from other cultures, then that government will be permitting disrespect for and damage to these nondominant cultures unless it intervenes in education policy to support them. A just society, in the view of many, ought to be concerned to create and enforce policies that allow members of all cultural communities to feel at home in that society.[42] And to make everyone feel at home, the state must recognize that people are culturally different and develop legal policies that insist on the respect for those cultural differences. (Compare liberal feminists' insistence on the recognition of gender differences as a way of securing true gender equality, which we discussed in Chapter 5.)

Fine words, but complicating such an aim is the fact that it is morally problematic for a state committed to supporting *all* cultures within it to actively support some cultures through policies that end up disadvantaging others (in the way that, say, a law mandating the language of one group privileges that group over others who speak a different language).

A state in a multicultural society also faces problems when some of its cultures disapprove of practices carried on by other cultures in that state or when part of the tradition of a culture has involved the denial of freedom or equality to some of its members. In order for a multicultural, consent-based political society to be just, it must require that every citizen commit herself to respecting and tolerating the operation and continued existence of the other groups in the society (who would themselves be under the obligation to respect hers) and of all members within its own group. However, this very liberal idea is itself something that members of certain cultures might find difficult to accept, demonstrating that at least for members of these cultures, entry into a consent-based political culture will involve *changing* either the beliefs or the cultural traditions of their group. Some might argue that such change already constitutes a threat to the integrity of such a culture; liberals (and all consistent defenders of multiculturalism) would argue that such change would be a way of morally improving it.[43] In any case, there is a certain sense in which a consistent defense of multiculturalism involves a partial (and I would argue justified) attack on some components of some cultural traditions—that is, those which are intolerant toward other individuals or groups and those which deny freedom or equality to some of its own members.

Moreover, if the moral defense of multiculturalism is based on the moral importance of respecting each individual, whose identity is deeply tied to her bonds with the culture in which she has been reared and in which she lives, then to respect *her* and the integrity of the group of which she is a part cannot morally involve respecting its intolerance, abusive practices, or discriminatory attitudes. The moral foundations of the multicultural defense constrain which cultural practices a state that accepts this defense can support or permit. How a multicultural society charts a legal course so as to adequately recognize and support the cultures within it, even while prohibiting cultural groups from devaluing or limiting the liberty of individuals either within that group or in other groups, even if such practices (e.g., with regard to women) reflect their history and tradition, is a highly complicated and difficult question and the subject of much debate in pluralist societies today.

Secession in Consent-Based States

One danger inherent in any political society with more than one encompassing group, each occupying a (more or less) distinct portion of territory in that society, is that one of these groups will attempt to secede from the larger entity. The issue of secession generated a civil war in the United

States in the nineteenth century and in our day threatens to tear apart—or has already torn apart—many multicultural societies, including Canada, the former Yugoslavia, and Ethiopia. When is secession justified? When should the larger group fight to keep the seceding group within its polity, and when should it be prepared to let the seceding group go?

It may seem that the answer someone gives to this question depends upon whether she takes membership in her state to be consent-based. After all, if the membership of each individual is a function of her consent (either tacitly or expressly given) and something that she can renounce at will, why can't a group of individuals exit from the state, taking with them the territory in which they live, by collectively renouncing their consent to the state and consensually establishing a new polity?[44]

Allen Buchanan has argued that from a moral point of view secession cannot be regarded as unproblematic.[45] Secession can impose costs, perhaps severe ones, on the group it leaves if the seceding group takes with it territory or resources that are highly valuable and fundamental to the larger group's economic health. This might make their secession morally unjustifiable (although perhaps sufficient economic compensation paid by the seceding group to the larger group would allay this moral concern). Secession can also take place for bad reasons and may promote unjust practices, making it morally unacceptable. For example, the seceding group may not be committed to respecting minority cultures who will be within its borders, so that it may be morally justifiable for the larger group to prevent their exit. Or a group may want to secede so that it can perpetuate certain unjust policies, such as slavery or discrimination (think of the reasons for secession given by the American South in the Civil War), so that those in the larger group may believe they are justified in opposing that exit, even with force.

These moral constraints on secession suggest that there is something importantly different about the exit of a particular individual, who does not take with her any territory when she renounces her membership in a state, and the exit of a group of individuals, who believe that they can take territory with them. Because territory is relevant to the well-being of a group in all sorts of ways (involving the economy, political defense, and history of the society), exiting with territory raises a host of issues that exiting without it does not. Moreover, whereas the private reasons individuals may have for their exit do not strike us as by and large politically relevant to the group they are leaving, the reasons a group of individuals gives for exiting a polity may have profound significance, not only symbolically but in actuality, since they may play a role in legislation and thus affect the lives and prospects of many people. Hence those reasons become important in assessing the justifiability of group exit, even if we think that the value of liberty constrains us from inquiring into or subsequently limiting an individual's exit on the basis of her reasons for withdrawing her consent from the polity.

There is another interesting reason secession in a consent-based society is problematic: If that society is democratic, the threat of secession can undercut that form of polity. This was a point that Abraham Lincoln was keen to make in 1860 in order to try to stop the impending secession of the South.[46] In a democracy, Lincoln insists, there is rule by the majority, and if a minority, as a result of losing, decides to secede, it is in effect undercutting and renouncing the democratic form of decisionmaking:

> If the minority will not acquiesce, the majority must, or the government must cease. There is no other alternative; for continuing the government, is acquiescence on one side or the other. If a minority, in such case, will secede rather than acquiesce, they make a precedent which, in turn, will divide and ruin them; for a minority of their own will secede from them, whenever a majority refuses to be controlled by such minority. For instance, why may not any portion of a new confederacy, a year or two hence, arbitrarily secede again, precisely as portions of the present Union now claim to secede from it. All who cherish disunion sentiments, are now being educated to the exact temper of doing this.[47]

In other words, for a democracy to survive, people must be prepared to *lose*, and if groups adopt the attitude that whenever they lose they can quit the game, the game cannot continue. Again, this shows that group exit and individual exit raise different issues: Exiting by individuals does not threaten the democratic form of government, whereas exiting by groups is a way of evading and undercutting rule by majority.

However, undercutting the rule of the majority may have moral legitimacy if the majority policies are threatening the liberty or equality of the minority wishing to exit. So another consideration relevant to the moral legitimacy of secession is the extent to which the seceding group is attempting to evade unjust policies directed toward it by the majority in the polity from which it wants to secede. Moreover, even if the majority is not behaving unjustly, if the reason this minority group became part of the polity has to do more with conquest than consent, that fact may precipitate secessionist activity as a way of restoring lost autonomy and redressing past injustice. (Think of reasons given by Quebec secessionists for quitting Canada.) However, even this point requires qualification, for the moral acceptability of secession in this case still depends upon the moral legitimacy of the culture of the minority; a Nazi culture, for example, is not worth saving, and we would not regard a majority's policies attacking such a culture as unjust or a reason legitimating the secession of the Nazi culture. This illustrates the point, made at the end of the foregoing section, that justice does not and cannot treat all cultures alike.

Hence whether or not it makes "moral sense" for a group to secede from a multicultural polity is a complicated issue, and it is not as tightly connected as one might have thought to that polity's conception of membership as consent-based or not. Yet these moral complexities *are* closely connected to the fact that (as we discussed in Chapter 3) any polity is created and sustained by a convention of people in a territory committed to it. Whether or not it is morally legitimate, a polity may emerge as a result of secession or rebellion if enough people work together collectively (using force if necessary) to establish a leadership convention. Any minorities in the population opposed to that convention (e.g., Tory supporters in America after its independence) are in a vulnerable position, and regardless of the moral legitimacy of their concerns, they may believe that as individuals they must exit from a society in which they have given *no* form of consent—neither convention consent nor endorsement consent nor membership consent. Political theory cannot change the fact that important and morally legitimate political causes usually produce casualties.

Further Reading

For a collection of papers that explores the issues of citizenship and immigration, see Warren Schwartz, ed., *Justice in Immigration*. A sustained discussion of the problems of the contemporary notion of the state can be found in Christopher Morris, *An Essay on the Modern State*. A work critical of nationalism is Russell Hardin's *One for All: The Logic of Group Conflict*. An essay that defends nationalism is Avishai Margalit and Joseph Raz, "National Self-Determination," *Journal of Philosophy* 87, 9 (September 1990). For exploration of the way in which issues of justice should be discussed among nations, see Charles Beitz, *Political Theory and International Relations*, and Thomas Pogge, *Realizing Rawls*.

For a discussion of citizenship that relates it to multiculturalism, see Will Kymlicka's *Multicultural Citizenship: A Liberal Theory of Minority Rights*. Essays on multiculturalism with many points of view can be found in Amy Gutmann, ed., *Multiculturalism*.

For arguments about the legitimacy of secession, see Allen Buchanan, *Secession*, and Harry Beran, *The Consent Theory of Political Obligation*.

Notes

1. Horace Kallen, "Democracy Versus the Melting Pot," in Kallen, *Culture and Democracy in the United States* (New York: Boni and Liveright, 1924); article reprinted from the *Nation*, February 18 and 25, 1915.

2. In this chapter I have relied on information about citizenship policies in various countries supplied by Sarah Harding. I owe Harding a great deal of thanks for her work on my behalf.

250 *Citizenship, Nationalism, and Culture*

3. This particular British notion was partly responsible for the War of 1812, when British ships would seize American sailors on U.S. ships to fight in the Napoleonic wars, arguing that these Americans were really British citizens and thus obliged to fight for "their country."

4. See sec. 12 of the 1981 immigration act. For more on the 1981 law, see Nicholas Blake and Ian MacDonald, *Immigration Law and Practice in the United Kingdom*, 3d ed. (London: Butterworth, 1991).

5. German federal constitution of 1949 (Basic Law), art. 16 (2).

6. William Pfaff, "Neo-Nazi Backlash: Immigration Difficulties Cause Germany to Turn Rightward," *Arizona Daily Star*, April 10, 1992, p. A19.

7. From Jules Coleman and Sarah Harding, "Citizenship, the Demands of Justice, and the Moral Relevance of Political Borders," in Warren Schwartz, ed., *Justice in Immigration* (Cambridge: Cambridge University Press, 1995), pp. 18–62.

8. To state the rules precisely, all people born outside of Germany to German parents or grandparents must accept only German citizenship if they apply for it (and thus renounce any other citizenship they might have at the time of application). Moreover, although such people will be considered "naturalized citizens," they are in the category of citizens "naturalized by right," as opposed to citizens (born of non-German parents) who are "naturalized by discretion" of the German government. For further discussion, see Kay Hailbronner, "Citizenship and Nationhood in Germany," in William R. Brubaker, ed., *Immigration and the Politics of Citizenship in Europe and North America* (New York: University Press of America, 1989), pp. 67–68, 73–74. Cited by Coleman and Harding, "Citizenship."

9. Moreover, oftentimes these immigrants perceive the assimilation requirement as involving changes in their way of life that are disrespectful of their heritage and thus refuse to make them. A very large percentage of German residents of Turkish descent do not wish to apply for citizenship because of the perception that doing so will mean losing all of their Turkish identity. In 1985 only 7.5 percent of Turks in Germany expressed interest in getting German citizenship (see Hailbronner, "Citizenship and Nationhood," p. 75, cited by Coleman and Harding, "Citizenship," n. 122, p. 60).

10. Pfaff, "Neo-Nazi Backlash," p. 19.

11. To be a nation-state, the state need not include all members of the nation. Hungary is a nation-state but does not include Hungarians living in Romania or Croatia. But the members it does include must almost exclusively be members of the nation.

12. This list of characteristics is based on those defined by Avishai Margalit and Joseph Raz in "National Self-Determination," *Journal of Philosophy* 87, 9 (September 1990): 443–447. My fifth characteristic is not, however, one that they recognize, even though it is the animating principle of nations such as Germany, Japan, and Serbia. I include it because of its importance in understanding the citizenship policies of such nations.

13. See Margalit and Raz, ibid. This phrase is also used by Coleman and Harding, "Citizenship," 41.

14. See ibid.

15. These requirements are set out in the 1946 Japanese constitution.

16. See Japan's permanent resident act of 1951.

17. The parents must, however, request this within three months of the child's birth.

18. For example, see John Locke's *Two Treatises of Government,* ed. Peter Laslett (Cambridge: Cambridge University Press, 1988); Jean-Jacques Rousseau's *Social Contract,* trans. G.D.H. Cole (London: J. M. Dent and Sons, 1968), and Immanuel Kant's *Metaphysical Elements of Justice,* trans. John Ladd (New York: Bobbs-Merrill, 1965).

19. For example, in Hume's "Of the Original Contract," in *Hume's Ethical Writings,* ed. Alasdair MacIntyre (New York: Collier, 1965).

20. In a way, Hume's criticisms work better against theories that rely on tacit or explicit consent to *legitimate* governmental authority over its citizens. In "Of the Original Contract," Hume asks, "Should it be said, that, by living under the dominion of a prince, which one might leave, every individual has given a *tacit* consent to his authority, and promised him obedience; it may be answered that such an implied consent can only have place, where a man imagines, that the matter depends upon his choice. . . . We may as well assert, that a man, by remaining in a vessel, freely consents to the dominion of the master; though he was carried on board while asleep, and must leap into the ocean and perish, the moment he leaves her"; ibid., p. 263. But while tacit consent, as I have defined it, may not justify the legitimacy of an individual's domination by a government, in countries such as the United States and Canada it explains why the political society takes people to be members of it.

21. In *Citizenship Without Consent: Illegal Aliens in American Polity* (New Haven: Yale University Press, 1985), Peter Schuck and Rogers Smith argue that citizenship in America is based on "mutual consent."

22. Still, it is unlikely, as I observed in note 20 above, that this consent is *sufficient* to legitimate a government's authority over its citizens in these sorts of countries.

23. Great Britain also allows joint British and Israeli citizenship.

24. See Charles Beitz, *Political Theory and International Relations* (Princeton: Princeton University Press, 1979), and Thomas Pogge, *Realizing Rawls* (Ithaca: Cornell University Press, 1989), for a discussion of how Rawls's theory of justice might be applied internationally.

25. In Schwartz, *Justice in Immigration.*

26. See Margalit and Raz, "National Self-Determination," on conditions necessary for the exercise of a national right to self-determination, esp. pp. 459–461.

27. See ibid., p. 449.

28. Will Kymlicka, *Liberalism, Community and Culture* (Oxford: Clarendon Press, 1991), pp. 162–181.

29. See the discussion of this point by Coleman and Harding, "Citizenship," pp. 42–44.

30. Coleman and Harding, who are sympathetic to nonconsensual citizenship policies, still maintain that there is a right to be a member of a political community, so that if a person is born into a state with an ethnic requirement for citizenship and her ethnicity would normally preclude her receiving citizenship in that state, then she should be granted citizenship anyway if she would otherwise be stateless. See ibid.

31. This last point is relevant to a moral evaluation of Proposition 187, passed in California in 1994, which refuses to illegal immigrants certain public services such as education, health care, and welfare support. Opponents of 187 argue that the "illegal" status of these immigrants, most of whom are relied upon as workers in the California economy and whose poverty attracted them to that economy, is morally irrelevant, given the requirements of due process and equal treatment under the law for all residents. Opponents might also maintain that considerations of distributive justice raise moral quesions about immigration laws that make so many of these people "illegal."

32. I believe that this is the argument Coleman and Harding are implicitly putting forward in their essay; see ibid.

33. It is, however, challenged by Stephen Perry, in his article "Immigration, Justice and Culture," in Schwartz, *Justice in Immigration*.

34. See Stephen Jay Gould, *Ever Since Darwin* (New York: Norton, 1977).

35. How might one argue otherwise? Might one maintain that ethnic groups deserve preservation in the same way that breeds of dog or horse (e.g., golden retrievers, thoroughbreds) deserve preservation, an argument that presupposes that ethnicities are like human breeds? The idea is hard to take seriously, although at times the rhetoric of defenders of ethnicity suggests it.

36. But the citizenship policies of Israel would seem to survive this argument. Not only can non-Jews receive citizenship in Israel, but citizenship for Jews can be defined along lines of religious affiliation regardless of ethnicity. Yet the nature of citizenship for Jewish Israelis differs from the nature of citizenship defined for non-Jewish Israelis (such as Arabs or Druze), Palestinian residents of the West Bank live in legal limbo despite limited self-rule, and the question "Who is a Jew?" is a highly charged political issue. The importance of this last question is obvious: The answer determines the definition of the nation that Israel was created to protect.

37. I am indebted to Paul Weithman for encouraging me to think about this issue.

38. I take this idea to be implicit in the way Hume discusses political association in *A Treatise of Human Nature*, ed. L. A. Selby-Bigge, rev. P. H. Nidditch (Oxford: Clarendon Press, 1978), book III, part ii, sec. vii, pp. 534–539.

39. For a sustained discussion of this point, see Christopher Morris, *An Essay on the Modern State* (Cambridge: Cambridge University Press, 1996).

40. See Coleman and Harding, "Citizenship," and Kymlicka, *Liberalism, Community and Culture*. Note that in countries such as the United States and Canada there are some groups (e.g., French Canadians and native populations) whose history is that of having been conquered by members of another culture and eventually included in the country as a result of that conquest. It is not surprising that the participation of members of these groups in the polities reflects a history of mastery rather than consent. The special claims they have made to group preservation and autonomy in their political societies are surely connected to the fact that the origin of their association with those societies is not properly consent-based.

41. See the essays in Amy Gutmann, ed., *Multiculturalism* (Princeton: Princeton University Press, 1994).

42. See Susan Wolf's comment on Charles Taylor's essay in ibid.

43. Note Taylor's recognition of this point and his insistence that liberalism is a "fighting creed"; see Taylor, "The Politics of Recognition," in Gutmann, *Multiculturalism.*

44. See Harry Beran, "A Liberal Theory of Secession," *Political Studies* 32 (1984): 21–31, which argues along these lines. And see Beran's *Consent Theory of Political Obligation* (London: Croom Helm, 1987).

45. See Allen Buchanan, *Secession* (Boulder: Westview Press, 1991).

46. Abraham Lincoln's first inaugural address can be found in *Abraham Lincoln: Speeches and Writings, 1859–1865* (New York: Library of America, 1989).

47. Ibid., p. 220. I am indebted to Allen Buchanan for pointing out this passage to me.

Epilogue

This book began with the anarchist's challenge to the legitimacy of any government. In order to answer the anarchist, we have pursued two fundamental issues: the nature of political authority and the extent of political authority in a just state. Understanding the former is necessary for understanding what a political society *is;* understanding the latter is necessary for understanding how a political society can be a morally legitimate institution. Achieving either understanding is not easy, and there are any number of controversies surrounding the nature of justice and the state. This book has aimed to air many of these controversies and to show how possible ways of resolving them have implications for a variety of concrete political policies that affect all of us, from property laws and immigration policies to civil rights and affirmative action legislation.

So have we succeeded in answering the anarchist? In a sense, you the reader will have to judge. We have attempted to define systems of political authority in a way that shows them to be necessary for as long as the "circumstances of justice" (which include the limited benevolence of human beings) persist, and we have argued that states are importantly different in structure from systems of mastery, precisely because they involve not merely power but also authority and because they presuppose the equality of ruler and ruled. We have also discussed various theories of justice, which would have to be appended to any system of political authority in order to make it morally legitimate. The controversy surrounding the nature of justice means that any political system will be perceived as just only if the theory of justice animating it is accepted by the person evaluating that system.

While different theories of justice agree about many things (e.g., that murder and theft are wrong and merit punishment or that the society requires laws of contract or tort), they disagree in a wide variety of areas—especially in the areas of property and distributive justice. So part of the anarchist's uneasiness about the state may stem not only from her failure to appreciate the way in which states are different from systems of mastery but also from the uncertainty about what the moral guideposts of a just state should be, such that she is unsure that any state she knows actually respects the right guideposts. Moreover, the ease with which a political system can degenerate into a system of mastery makes it in many respects a very dangerous institution, one that any lover of liberty or justice has reason to worry about.

Such uneasiness has been shared, I believe, by virtually everyone who has reflected on the state. One reason I have pursued the nature and extent of political authority using a variety of historical materials going back to the ancient Greeks is to show how the state has always been viewed with ambivalence—perceived as both a powerful force for good and also a dangerous tool of evil. While theorists from Plato to Catharine MacKinnon have called for the state to use its power to make the community better, other theorists—particularly those with misanthropic tendencies—have feared handing state officials considerable power to do good, lest they use that power in ways that bring about damage, injustice, and oppression. The political scandals of our time remind us that optimism about the goodwill of political officials is often not rewarded. Yet many contemporary societies have become heavily dependent upon the state and its officials for social programs everyone values, including social security, health care, job training, subsidies to the arts, education, and so forth.

Thus we are in many ways still working out what we take to be the correct role of the just state and the extent to which we can design political institutions so as to be able to trust those who govern to pursue the good and spurn (what they correctly recognize as) injustice. Those among us who wish to be part of the debate about how a just state should understand itself, its citizens, its role toward communities, its responsibilities with respect to wealth and opportunities, and its relationship to outsiders need to understand the philosophical ideas that have or could be used to explain the nature of political authority, the nature of justice, and our sense of our own political identities as members of the state. The aim of this book is to help you, the reader, to achieve that understanding, so you may be a more powerful and effective participant in that debate.

Bibliography

Annas, Julia. *The Morality of Happiness.* Oxford: Oxford University Press, 1993.

Anscombe, G.E.M. *Ethics, Religion and Politics: Collected Philosophical Papers,* vol. 3. Minneapolis: University of Minnesota Press, 1981.

Aristotle. *The Politics.* Trans. T. A. Sinclair, rev. Trevor J. Saunders. Harmondsworth: Penguin, 1992.

Arneson, Richard. "Equality and Equal Opportunity for Welfare." *Philosophical Studies* 56 (1989): 77–93.

Arrow, Kenneth. *Social Choice and Individual Values.* New York: John Wiley and Sons, 1951.

Austin, J. *The Province of Jurisprudence Determined.* Ed. Wilfrid E. Rumble. Cambridge: Cambridge University Press, 1995.

Avrich, Paul. *Anarchist Portraits.* Princeton: Princeton University Press, 1988.

Axelrod, Robert. *The Evolution of Cooperation.* New York: Basic Books, 1984.

Barnett, Randy. "Unenumerated Constitutional Rights and the Rule of Law." *Harvard Journal of Law and Public Policy* 14, 3 (Summer 1991): 615–644.

Bedau, Hugo, ed. *Civil Disobedience: Theory and Practice.* New York: Pegasus, 1969.

Beitz, Charles. *Political Theory and International Relations.* Princeton: Princeton University Press, 1979.

Benn, Stanley, and Gerald Gaus. *Public and Private in Social Life.* London: Croom Helm, 1983.

Bentham, Jeremy. *Collected Works of Jeremy Bentham.* Eds. James H. Burns, John R. Dinwiddy, and Frederick Rosen. Oxford: Oxford University Press and London: Athlone Press, 1983.

———. *An Introduction to the Principles of Morals and Legislation.* Eds. J. H. Burns and H.L.A. Hart. London: Athlone Press, 1970.

Beran, Harry. *The Consent Theory of Political Obligation.* London: Croom Helm, 1987.

———. "A Liberal Theory of Secession." *Political Studies* 32 (1984): 21–31.

Blackstone, William. *Commentaries on the Law of England.* Ed. William Draper Lewis. Philadelphia: Rees Welsh and Company, 1897.

Blake, Nicholas, and Ian MacDonald. *Immigration Law and Practice in the United Kingdom.* 3d ed. London: Butterworth, 1991.

Bloom, Allan. *The Closing of the American Mind.* New York: Simon and Schuster, 1987.

Bramhall, John. "The Catching of Leviathan or the Great Whale." Appendix to *Castigations of Mr. Hobbes . . . Concerning Liberty and Universal Necessity.* Printed by E.T. for John Crooke, at the sign of the ship in Paul's churchyard, 1658.

Brotz, Howard, ed. *Negro Social and Political Thought, 1850–1920.* New York: Basic Books, 1966.

Buchanan, Allen. *Secession.* Boulder: Westview Press, 1991.

Buchanan, James. *The Limits of Liberty.* Chicago: University of Chicago Press, 1975.

Burke, Edmund. *Reflections on the Revolution in France*. Harmondsworth: Penguin, 1969.

Card, Claudia. "Rape as a Terrorist Institution." In R. G. Frey and Christopher Morris, eds., *Violence, Terrorism and Justice*. Cambridge: Cambridge University Press, 1991.

Christiano, Thomas. *The Rule of the Many*. Boulder: Westview Press, 1996.

Cohen, Gerald A. *Karl Marx's Theory of History: A Defence*. Oxford: Oxford University Press, 1978.

———. "Robert Nozick and Wilt Chamberlain: How Patterns Preserve Liberty." In John Arthur and William H. Shaw, eds., *Justice and Economic Distribution*. Englewood Cliffs, N.J.: Prentice-Hall, 1981.

———. *Self-Ownership, Freedom, and Equality*. Cambridge: Cambridge University Press, 1995.

Coleman, Jules, and Sarah Harding. "Citizenship, the Demands of Justice, and the Moral Relevance of Political Borders." In Warren Schwartz, ed., *Justice in Immigration*. Cambridge: Cambridge University Press, 1995.

Cooke, J. E., ed. *The Federalist Papers*. Middletown, Conn.: Wesleyan University Press, 1961.

Copp, David, Jean Hampton, and John Roemer, eds. *The Idea of Democracy*. Cambridge: Cambridge University Press, 1992.

Cranston, Maurice. "Liberalism." In Paul Edwards, ed., *Encyclopedia of Philosophy*. New York: Macmillan and London: Collier, 1967.

Daniels, Norman, ed. *Reading Rawls*. New York: Basic Books, 1974.

Davidson, Terry. *Conjugal Crime*. New York: Hawthorn Books, 1978.

de Jouvenal, Bertrand. *Power: The Natural History of Its Growth*. Trans. J. F. Huntington. London: Hutchison, 1948.

Dunn, John. *The Political Thought of John Locke*. Cambridge: Cambridge University Press, 1969.

Dworkin, Andrea. *Right-wing Women: The Politics of Domesticated Females*. New York: Putnam, 1983.

Dworkin, Ronald. "Do We Have a Right to Pornography?" In *A Matter of Principle*. Cambridge: Harvard University Press, 1985.

———. *Taking Rights Seriously*. Cambridge: Harvard University Press, 1977.

———. "What Is Equality? Part I: Equality of Welfare." *Philosophy and Public Affairs* 10, 3 (1981): 185–246.

———. "What Is Equality? Part II: Equality of Resources." *Philosophy and Public Affairs* 10, 4 (1981): 283–345.

Eickelman, Dale F. *Moroccan Islam*. Austin: University of Texas Press, 1976.

Elshtain, Jean Bethke. "Family, Feminism and Community." *Dissent* 29 (Fall 1982): 442.

———. *Public Man, Private Woman*. Princeton: Princeton University Press, 1981.

Elster, Jon. *Making Sense of Marx*. Cambridge: Cambridge University Press, 1985.

Elster, Jon, and John Roemer, eds. *Interpersonal Comparisons of Wellbeing*. New York: Cambridge University Press, 1991.

Feinberg, Joel. *Harm to Others*. Vol. 1 of *The Moral Limits of the Criminal Law*. New York: Oxford University Press, 1984.

———. *Harm to Self*. Vol. 3 of *The Moral Limits of the Criminal Law*. New York: Oxford University Press, 1986.

———. *Harmless Wrongdoing*. Vol. 4 of *The Moral Limits of the Criminal Law*. New York: Oxford University Press, 1988.

———. *Offense to Others*. Vol. 2 of *The Moral Limits of the Criminal Law*. New York: Oxford University Press, 1985.

———. *Rights, Justice and the Bounds of Liberty*. Princeton: Princeton University Press, 1980.

———. "Some Unswept Debris from the Hart-Devlin Debate." *Synthese* 72 (1987): 249–275.

Figgis, John. *Divine Right of Kings*. Cambridge: Cambridge University Press, 1904.

Filmer, Robert. *Patriarcha and Other Writings*. Ed. Johann Sommerville. Cambridge: Cambridge University Press, 1991.

Flood, Merrill. "Some Experimental Games." *Management Science* 5 (October 1958): 5–26.

Fortenbaugh, William W. "Aristotle on Slaves and Women." Jonathan Barnes, Malcolm Schofield, and Richard Sorabji, eds., *Articles on Aristotle*, vol. 2. London: Duckworth, 1977.

Freeman, Kathleen. *Ancilla to the Pre-Socratic Philosophers*. Cambridge: Harvard University Press, 1948.

Gadd, C. J. *The Ideas of Divine Rule in the Ancient East*. London: Oxford University Press, 1945.

Galston, William. *Liberal Purposes: Goods, Virtues and Diversity in the Liberal State*. Cambridge: Cambridge University Press, 1991.

Gauthier, David. *The Logic of Leviathan*. Oxford: Oxford University Press, 1969.

———. *Morals by Agreement*. Oxford: Oxford University Press, 1986.

———. "The Social Contract as Ideology." *Philosophy and Public Affairs* 6, 2 (1977): 130–164.

Glover, Jonathan, ed. *Utilitarianism and Its Critics*. New York: Macmillan, 1990.

Goldberg, Steven. *The Inevitability of Patriarchy*. New York: William Morrow, 1973.

Gould, Stephen Jay. *Ever Since Darwin*. New York: Norton, 1977.

Gray, John. *Post-liberalism: Studies in Political Thought*. London: Routledge, 1993.

Green, Leslie. *The Authority of the State*. Oxford: Clarendon Press, 1984.

Gutmann, Amy. "Communitarian Critics of Liberalism." *Philosophy and Public Affairs* 14, 3 (Summer 1985): 308–322.

———. ed. *Multiculturalism*. Princeton: Princeton University Press, 1994.

Hailbronner, Kay. "Citizenship and Nationhood in Germany." In William R. Brubaker, ed., *Immigration and the Politics of Citizenship in Europe and North America*. New York: University Press of America, 1989.

Hampton, Jean. "The Common Faith of Liberalism." *Pacific Philosophical Quarterly* 75, 3 and 4 (1995): 186–216.

———. "The Contractarian Explanation of the State." In Theodore Uehling, ed., *The Philosophy of the Human Sciences, Midwest Studies in Philosophy*, vol. 15. Minneapolis: University of Minnesota Press, 1990.

———. "Contracts and Choices: Does Rawls Have a Social Contract Theory?" *Journal of Philosophy* 77, 6 (June 1980): 315–338.

———. "Correcting Harms Versus Righting Wrongs." *UCLA Law Review* 39, 6 (1992): 1659–1702.

———. "The Failure of Expected Utility Theory as a Theory of Reason." *Economics and Philosophy* 10, 2 (October 1994): 195–242.

———. "Feminist Contractarianism." In Louise Anthony and Charlotte Witt, eds., *A Mind of One's Own*. Boulder: Westview Press, 1993.

———. *Hobbes and the Social Contract Tradition*. Cambridge: Cambridge University Press, 1986.

————. "Liberalism, Retribution and Criminality." In Jules Coleman and Allen Buchanan, eds., *Harm's Way: Essays in Honor of Joel Feinberg.* Cambridge: Cambridge University Press, 1994.

————. "Should Political Philosophy Be Done Without Metaphysics?" *Ethics* 99 (1989): 791–814.

————. "Two Faces of Contractarian Thought." In Peter Vallentyne, ed., *Contractarianism and Rational Choice: Essays on Gauthier.* Cambridge: Cambridge University Press, 1990.

Hardin, Russell. *Collective Action.* Baltimore: Johns Hopkins University Press, 1982.

————. *One for All: The Logic of Group Conflict.* Princeton: Princeton University Press, 1995.

Harsanyi, John. "Can the Maximin Principle Serve as a Basis for Morality? A Critique of Rawls's Theory." *American Political Science Review* 69 (1975): 594–606.

————. *Essays on Ethics, Social Behavior and Scientific Explanation.* Dordrecht: D. Reidel, 1976.

Hart, H.L.A. *The Concept of Law.* Oxford: Clarendon Press, 1961.

Hegel, G.W.F. *The Philosophy of Right.* Trans. T. M. Knox. London: Oxford University Press, 1976.

Hirschman, Linda. "Making Safety a Civil Right." *Ms. Magazine,* September-October 1994, pp. 44–47.

Hobbes, Thomas. *The Elements of Law: Natural and Politic.* Ed. Ferdinand Tönnies. Cambridge: Cambridge University Press, 1928.

————. *Leviathan.* Ed. Richard Tuck. Cambridge: Cambridge University Press, 1991.

————. *Man and Citizen.* Ed. Bernard Gert. Atlantic Highlands, N.J.: Humanities Press, 1968.

Hume, David. *Hume's Ethical Writings.* Ed. Alasdair MacIntyre. New York: Collier, 1965.

————. "Of the Original Contract." In Eugene E. Miller, ed., *David Hume: Essays; Moral, Political and Literary.* Indianapolis: Liberty Press, 1985.

————. *A Treatise of Human Nature.* Ed. L. A. Selby-Bigge, rev. P. H. Nidditch. Oxford: Clarendon Press, 1978.

Irwin, Terence. *Plato's Ethics.* Oxford: Oxford University Press, 1981.

Jagger, Alison. *Feminist Politics and Human Nature.* Totowa, N.J.: Rowman and Allanheld, 1983.

Jefferson, Thomas. "Query XVII: Religion." In *Notes on the State of Virginia.* Chapel Hill: University of North Carolina Press, 1955.

Kahn, Charles. "The Origins of Social Contract Theory." In G. B. Kerferd, ed., *The Sophists and Their Legacy.* Wiesbaden, Germany: Franz Steiner Verlag, 1981.

Kallen, Horace. *Culture and Democracy in the United States.* New York: Boni and Liveright, 1924.

Kant, Immanuel. *Groundwork of the Metaphysics of Morals.* Trans. H. J. Paton. London: Harper Torchbooks, 1964.

————. *Kant's Political Writings.* Ed. Hans Reiss. Cambridge: Cambridge University Press, 1970.

————. *Metaphysical Elements of Justice.* Trans. John Ladd. New York: Bobbs-Merrill, 1965.

Kavka, Gregory. *Hobbesian Moral and Political Theory.* Princeton: Princeton University Press, 1986.

Keyt, David, and Fred D. Miller, eds. *A Companion to Aristotle's Politics*. Oxford: Oxford University Press, 1995.

Knox, John. *The Works of John Knox*. Ed. David Laing. Edinburgh: AMS Press, 1966.

Kymlicka, Will. *Contemporary Political Philosophy: An Introduction*. Oxford: Clarendon Press, 1990.

―――. *Liberalism, Community and Culture*. Oxford: Clarendon Press, 1991.

―――. *Multicultural Citizenship: A Liberal Theory of Minority Rights*. New York: Oxford University Press, 1995.

Levin, Michael. *Feminism and Freedom*. New Brunswick, N.J.: Transaction Books, 1987.

Lewis, David. *Convention*. Cambridge: Harvard University Press, 1969.

Lincoln, Abraham. "First Inaugural Address." In *Abraham Lincoln: Speeches and Writings, 1859–1865*. New York: Library of America, 1989.

Locke, John. *Two Treatises of Government*. Ed. Peter Laslett. Cambridge: Cambridge University Press, 1988.

Lomasky, Loren. *Persons, Rights and the Moral Community*. New York: Oxford University Press, 1987.

Luce, R. Duncan, and Howard Raiffa. *Games and Decisions*. New York: John Wiley and Sons, 1957.

MacIntyre, Alasdair. *After Virtue*. Notre Dame: Notre Dame University Press, 1981.

MacKinnon, Catharine. "Crimes of War, Crimes of Peace." In Kate Mehuron and Gary Percesepe, eds., *Free Spirits: Feminist Philosophers on Culture*. Englewood Cliffs, N.J.: Prentice-Hall, 1995.

―――. *Feminism Unmodified*. Cambridge: Harvard University Press, 1987.

―――. *Only Words*. Cambridge: Harvard University Press, 1993.

Manly, H. *The South Vindicated from the Treason and Fanaticism of the Northern Abolitionists*. New York: Negro Universities Press, 1969.

Margalit, Avishai, and Joseph Raz. "National Self-Determination." *Journal of Philosophy* 87, 9 (September 1990): 443–447.

Marx, Karl. *Selected Writings*. Ed. David McLellan. Oxford: Oxford University Press, 1977.

Matthews, Richard K. *The Radical Politics of Thomas Jefferson: A Revisionist View*. Lawrence: University of Kansas Press, 1984.

Miedzian, Myrian. *Boys Will Be Boys*. New York: Anchor Books, 1991.

Mill, John Stuart. "Chapters on Socialism." In *Collected Works*, vol. 5. Toronto: University of Toronto Press, 1967.

―――. *The Subjection of Women*. In *Essays in Sex Equality by John Stuart Mill and Harriet Taylor Mill*. ed. Alice Rossi. Chicago: University of Chicago Press, 1970.

―――. *Utilitarianism*. In *Utilitarianism, Liberty and Representative Government*. Ed. H. B. Acton. New York: E. P. Dutton, 1972.

Miller, Fred D. *Nature, Justice and Rights in Aristotle's Politics*. Oxford: Oxford University Press, 1995.

Moen, Phyllis. *Women's Two Roles*. New York: Auburn House, 1992.

Morall, John B. *Political Thought in Medieval Times*. London: Hutchinson, 1971.

Morgenstern, Oskar, and John von Neumann. *Theory of Games and Economic Behavior*. Princeton: Princeton University Press, 1953.

Morris, Christopher. *An Essay on the Modern State*. Cambridge: Cambridge University Press, 1996.

Nagel, Thomas. "Libertarianism Without Foundations." In Jeffrey Paul, ed., *Reading Nozick*. Totowa, N.J.: Rowman and Littlefield, 1981.

Nozick, Robert. *Anarchy, State and Utopia.* New York: Basic Books, 1974.

Okin, Susan Moller. "Justice and Gender." *Philosophy and Public Affairs* 16, 1 (1987): 42–72.

———. *Justice, Gender and the Family.* New York: Basic Books, 1989.

Parfit, Derek. "Overpopulation and the Quality of Life." In Jonathan Glover, ed., *Utilitarianism and Its Critics.* New York: Macmillan, 1990.

———. *Reasons and Persons.* Oxford: Oxford University Press, 1984.

Pfaff, William. "Neo-Nazi Backlash: Immigration Difficulties Cause Germany to Turn Rightward." *Arizona Daily Star,* April 10, 1992, p. A19.

Pitkin, Hannah. *The Concept of Representation.* Berkeley: University of California Press, 1967.

Plato. *The Laws.* Trans. Alfred E. Taylor. London: Dent, 1960.

———. *Protagoras.* Trans. W.R.M. Lamb. Cambridge: Harvard University Press, 1967.

———. *Republic.* Trans. G.M.A. Grube, rev. C.D.C. Reeve. Indianapolis: Hackett, 1992.

———. *The Statesman.* Trans. Robin Waterfield, with an introduction by Julia Annas. Cambridge: Cambridge University Press, 1995.

Pogge, Thomas. *Realizing Rawls.* Ithaca: Cornell University Press, 1989.

Przeworski, Adam, and John Sprague. *Paper Stones.* Chicago: University of Chicago Press, 1986.

Rawls, John. *Political Liberalism.* New York: Columbia University Press, 1993.

———. *A Theory of Justice.* Cambridge: Harvard University Press, 1971.

Raz, Joseph. *The Authority of Law.* Oxford: Clarendon Press, 1979.

———. *The Morality of Freedom.* Oxford: Clarendon Press, 1986.

Regan, Tom. *The Case for Animal Rights.* Berkeley: University of California Press, 1983.

Richards, Janet Radcliffe. *The Sceptical Feminist: A Philosophical Enquiry.* London: Routledge and Kegan Paul, 1980.

Riley, Patrick. *Will and Political Legitimacy.* Cambridge: Harvard University Press, 1982.

Roemer, John. *Free to Lose: An Introduction to Marxist Economic Philosophy.* Cambridge: Harvard University Press, 1988.

Rorty, Richard. "The Priority of Democracy to Philosophy." In Merrill Peterson and Robert Vaughan, eds., *The Virginia Statute for Religious Freedom.* New York: Cambridge University Press, 1988.

Rousseau, Jean-Jacques. *Emile.* Ed. Allan Bloom. New York: Basic Books, 1979.

———. *The Social Contract.* Trans. G.D.H. Cole. London: Dent, 1968.

Sandel, Michael J. *Liberalism and the Limits of Justice.* Cambridge: Cambridge University Press, 1982.

———. "Morality and the Liberal Ideal." *New Republic,* May 7, 1984, 15–17.

Savage, Leonard. *The Foundations of Statistics.* New York: Dover, 1972.

Scanlon, Thomas. "Contractualism and Utilitarianism." In Amartya Sen and Bernard Williams, eds., *Utilitarianism and Beyond.* Cambridge: Cambridge University Press, 1982.

Schauer, Frederick. *Free Speech: A Philosophical Inquiry.* Cambridge: Cambridge University Press, 1982.

Schelling, Thomas. *The Strategy of Conflict.* Cambridge: Harvard University Press, 1960.

Schmittroth, Linda, comp. *Statistical Record of Women Worldwide.* Detroit: Gale Research, 1991.

Schuck, Peter, and Rogers Smith. *Citizenship Without Consent: Illegal Aliens in American Polity.* New Haven: Yale University Press, 1985.

Schwartz, Warren, ed. *Justice in Immigration.* Cambridge: Cambridge University Press, 1995.

Sen, Amartya. "Equality of What?" In Sterling McMurrin, ed., *The Tanner Lectures on Human Values.* Salt Lake City: University of Utah Press, 1980.

Shklar, Judith. *Ordinary Vices.* Cambridge: Harvard University Press, 1984.

Simmons, A. John. *On the Edge of Anarchy: Locke, Consent, and the Limits of Society.* Princeton: Princeton University Press, 1993.

Singer, Peter, ed. *In Defence of Animals.* Oxford: Blackwell, 1985.

Singer, Peter, and Tom Regan, eds. *Animal Rights and Human Obligations.* Englewood Cliffs, N.J.: Prentice-Hall, 1989.

Skinner, Quentin. *The Foundations of Modern Political Thought.* 2 vols. Cambridge: Cambridge University Press, 1978.

Stalley, R. F. *An Introduction to Plato's Laws.* Indianapolis: Hackett, 1983.

Steffen, Lloyd. "In Defense of Dominion." *Environmental Ethics* 13 (1992): 63–80.

Sterba, James. *Contemporary Social and Political Philosophy.* Belmont, Calif.: Wadsworth, 1995.

Stiehm, Judith Hicks. "The Unit of Political Analysis: Our Aristotelian Hangover." In Sandra Harding and Merrill Hintikka, eds., *Discovering Reality.* Dordrecht: D. Reidel, 1983.

Straus, Murray, Richard J. Gelles, and Suzanne K. Steinmetz. *Behind Closed Doors: Violence in the American Family.* New York: Anchor Books, 1980.

Sugden, Robert. "Thinking as a Team: Towards an Explanation of Nonselfish Behavior." In Ellen Paul, Jeffrey Paul, and Fred Miller, eds., *Altruism.* Cambridge: Cambridge University Press, 1993.

Taylor, Charles. "Alternative Futures: Legitimacy, Identity and Alienation in Late Twentieth Century Canada." In A. Cairns and C. Williams, eds., *Constitutionalism, Citizenship and Society in Canada.* Toronto: University of Toronto Press, 1986.

———. *The Malaise of Modernity.* Toronto: Anansi, 1991.

———. *Philosophical Papers.* Cambridge: Cambridge University Press, 1985.

Taylor, Michael. *Community, Anarchy and Liberty.* Cambridge: Cambridge University Press, 1982.

———. *The Possibility of Cooperation.* Cambridge: Cambridge University Press, 1987.

Tong, Rosemarie. *Feminist Thought.* Boulder: Westview Press, 1989.

Tuck, Richard. *Hobbes.* Oxford: Oxford University Press, 1989.

———. *Natural Rights Theories: Their Origin and Development.* Cambridge: Cambridge University Press, 1979.

Tully, James. *An Approach to Political Philosophy: Locke in Contexts.* Cambridge: Cambridge University Press, 1993.

Valcke, Catherine. "Civil Disobedience and the Rule of Law—A Lockean Insight." In Ian Shapiro, ed., *The Rule of Law.* New York: New York University Press, 1994.

Vlastos, Gregory. "Justice and Happiness in the *Republic.*" In Gregory Vlastos, ed., *Plato: A Collection of Critical Essays,* vol. 2. Garden City, N.J.: Anchor Books, 1971.

———. "The Theory of Social Justice in the Polis in Plato's *Republic.*" In Gregory Vlastos, *Studies in Greek Philosophy,* vol. 2. Princeton: Princeton University Press, 1994.

Waldron, Jeremy. "Theoretical Foundations of Liberalism." *Philosophical Quarterly* 37, 147 (1987): 127–150.

———, ed. *Theories of Rights*. Oxford: Clarendon Press, 1984.

Washington, James Melvin, ed. *A Testament of Hope*. New York: Harper and Row, 1986.

Waterbury, John. *The Commander of the Faithful: The Moroccan Political Elite—A Study in Segmented Politics*. New York: Columbia University Press, 1970.

West, Cornel. *Race Matters*. New York: Vintage Books, 1994.

White, Lynn. "The Historical Roots of Our Ecological Crisis." *Science* 211–212 (1967): 1203–1207.

White, Morton. *Philosophy, the Federalist and the Constitution*. Oxford: Oxford University Press, 1987.

Williams, Bernard. *Shame and Necessity*. Berkeley: University of California Press, 1993.

Williams, Joan. "Deconstructing Gender." In Patricia Smith, ed., *Feminist Jurisprudence*. New York: Oxford University Press, 1993.

Wolff, Robert Paul. *In Defense of Anarchism*. New York: Harper and Row, 1970.

Wollstonecraft, Mary. *A Vindication of the Rights of Woman*. Harmondsworth: Penguin, 1978.

Wootton, David, ed. *Divine Right and Democracy: An Anthology of Political Writing in Stuart England*. Harmondsworth: Penguin, 1986.

Young, Iris. "Impartiality and the Civic Public." In Seyla Benhabib and Drucilla Cornell, eds., *Feminism as Critique*. Minneapolis: University of Minnesota Press, 1987.

———. *Justice and the Politics of Difference*. Princeton: Princeton University Press, 1990.

About the Book and Author

Political philosophy, perhaps even more than other branches of philosophy, calls for constant renewal to reflect not just re-readings of the tradition but also the demands of current events. In this lively and readable survey, Jean Hampton has created a text for our time that does justice both to the great traditions of the field and to the newest developments. In a marvelous feat of synthesis, she links the classical tradition, the giants of the modern period, the dominant topics of the twentieth century, and the new questions and concerns that are just beginning to rewrite contemporary political philosophy.

Hampton presents these traditions in an engaging and accessible manner, adding to them her own views and encouraging readers to critically examine a range of ideas and to reach their own conclusions. Of particular interest are the discussions of the contemporary liberalism-communitarianism debates, the revival of interest in issues of citizenship and nationality, and the way in which feminist concerns are integrated into all these discussions.

Political Philosophy is the most modern text on the topic now available, the ideal guide to what is going on in the field. It will be welcomed by scholars and students in philosophy and political science, and it will serve as an introduction for readers from outside these fields.

Until her recent, tragic death Jean Hampton was professor of philosophy at the University of Arizona. She is the author of *Hobbes and the Social Contract Tradition* and many articles on moral and political theory.

Index